Westminster College
Through Time

Robert Zorn

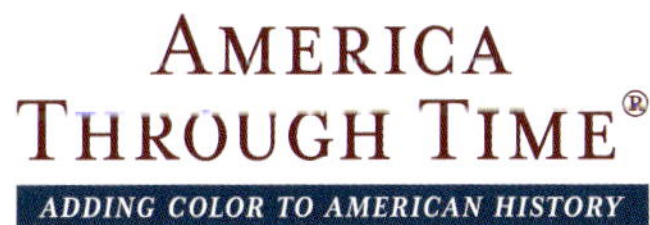

This book is dedicated to all the people: past, present, and future, associated with Westminster College including students, faculty, parents, staff, administration, and alumni.

AMERICA THROUGH TIME is an imprint of Fonthill Media LLC

First published 2015

ISBN 978-1-63500-003-0

Typeset in Mrs Eaves XL Serif Narrow
Printed in the United States of America

Published by Arcadia Publishing by arrangement with Fonthill Media LLC

For all general information, please contact Arcadia Publishing:
Telephone 843-853-2070
Fax 843-853-0044
E-mail sales@arcadiapublishing.com
For customer service and orders:
Toll-Free 1-888-313-2665

Visit us on the internet at www.arcadiapublishing.com

Introduction

There is a saying that a picture is worth a thousand words, and another saying that every picture tells a story. The pictures in this book show the ongoing, evolving story of Westminster College, one of America's leading small private liberal arts colleges. From Westminster's obscure beginnings in 1852 as a literary institution, to its liberal arts prominence in 2014, Westminster College has developed a rich heritage of tradition, excellence, and Christian character.

Located on a beautiful campus of over three hundred acres in the rolling hills of Western Pennsylvania, the college provides an idealistic setting for scholarship and college life for students and faculty. The college is proud of its Christian character, which continues to this day.

Westminster made higher educational history in 1852, at its very founding, when it opened doors equally to men and women at a time when that was unheard of. Westminster was truly a pioneer in coeducational higher education.

In 2014, Westminster ranks first in the nation as "Best College for Women in Science, Technology, Engineering and Math" according to *Forbes.com*. As well, Westminster is a top-tier liberal arts college and a national leader in graduation rate performance according to *US News Best Colleges* guide for 2014. Westminster is also honored as one of "The Best 378 Colleges" in the nation for 2014 by *The Princeton Review* and is also named to the *President's Honor Roll* for excellence in service learning.

In its 163rd year, Westminster College has come a long way from its humble start in April 1852 when two professors met with only twenty students to begin academic studies in higher education. The years of progress, success, achievement and a tradition of excellence have been made possible by many people, and Westminster's future, like its past, lies with people who care about this college.

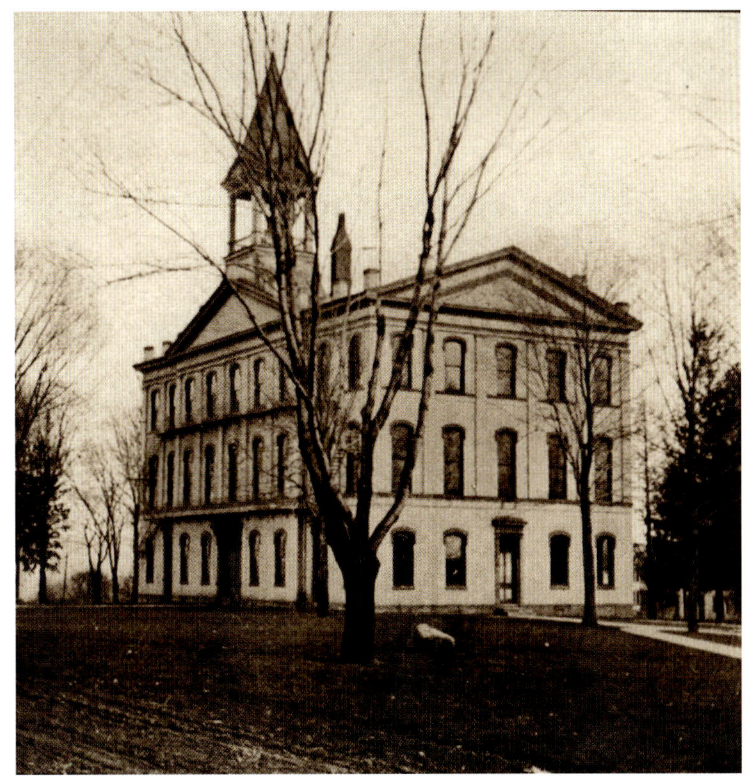

OLD MAIN: Westminster College's main building, built in 1861, and in its later years dubbed by students as Old Main was destroyed by fire in 1927. A new structure built on the same site opened in 1929 and was named Old Main Memorial. This structure is still called Old Main in the 2010s and is the keystone to the college's quadrangle in the center of the campus.

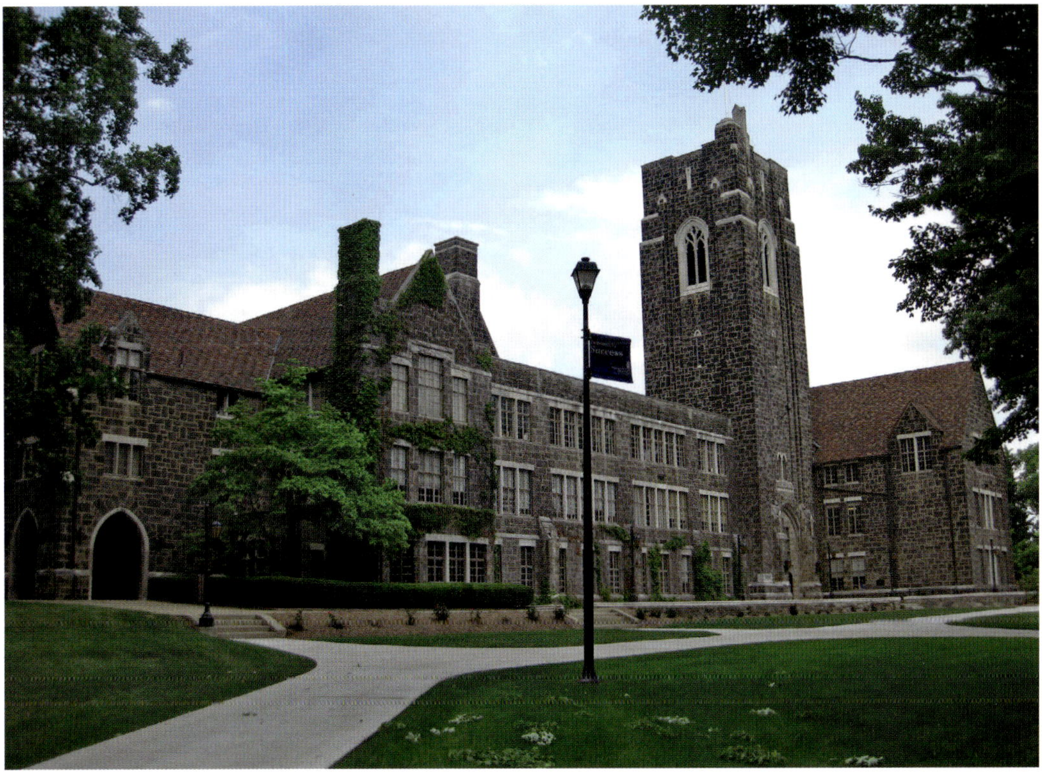

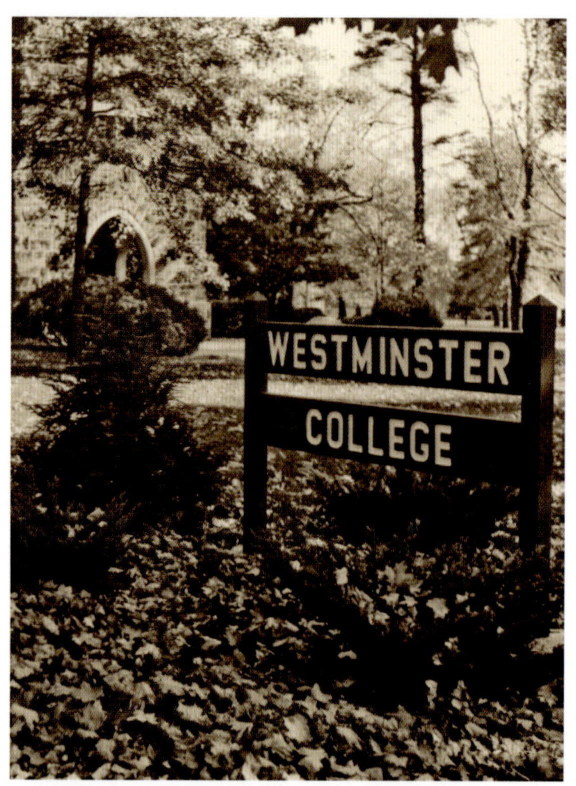

THE COLLEGE SIGN: The traditional old wooden sign "Westminster College," as seen in 1967, at the corner of South Market Street and Maple Street, long viewed by many as the entrance to the campus, was replaced in the 1980s by a substantial new stone marker. The students' tradition of posing for a graduation picture at this site continues to this day.

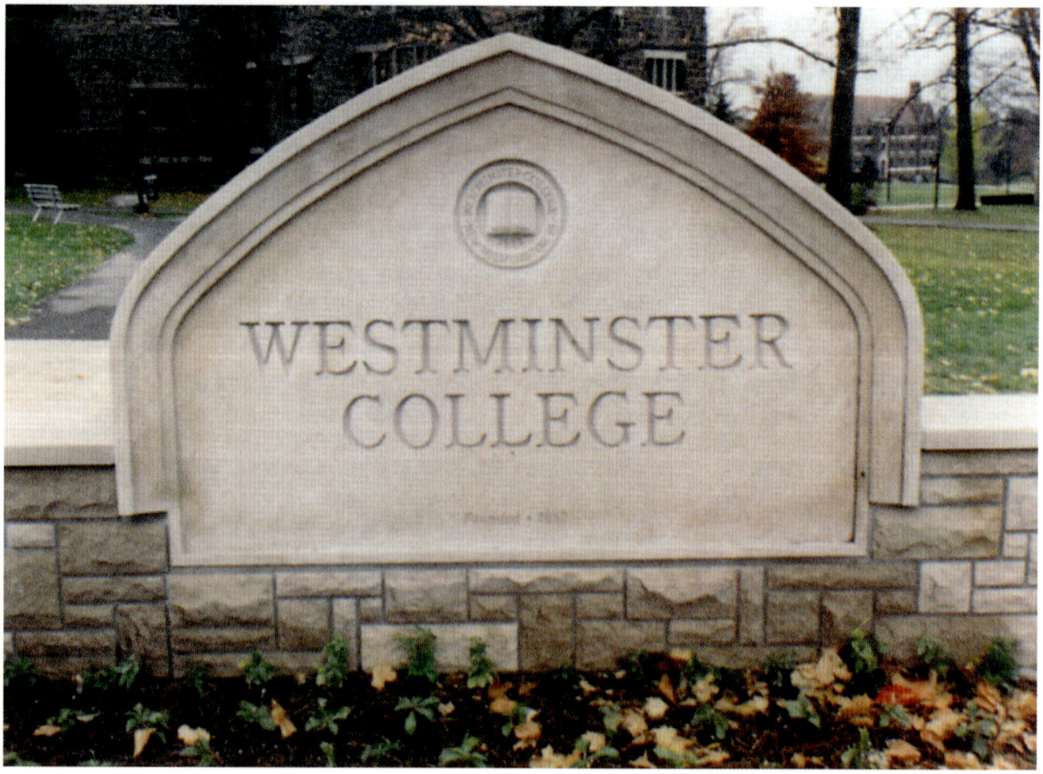

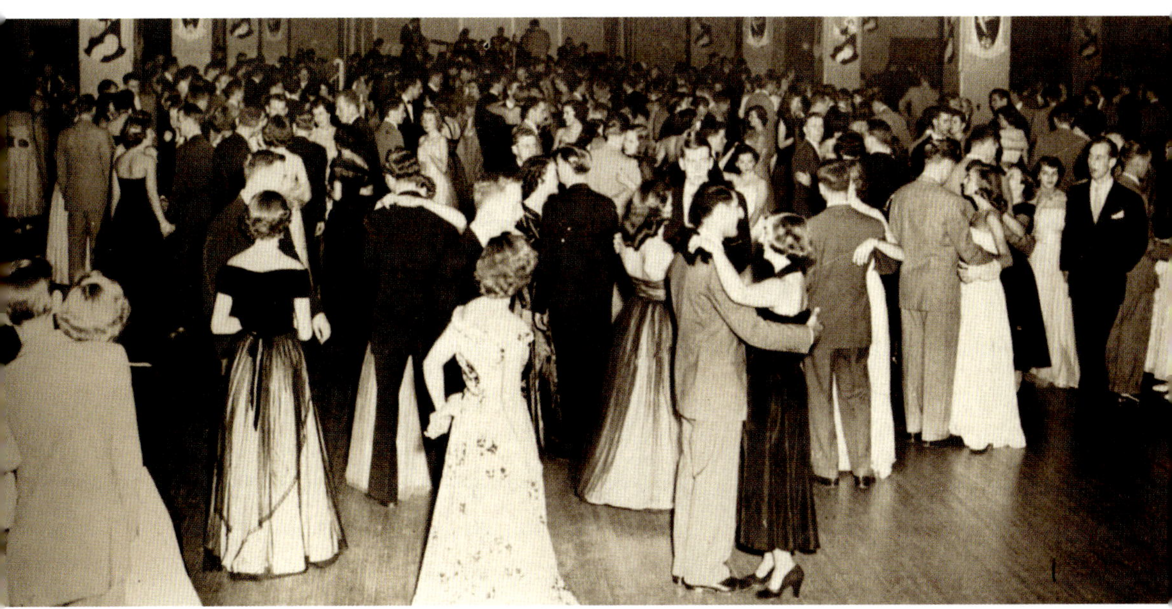

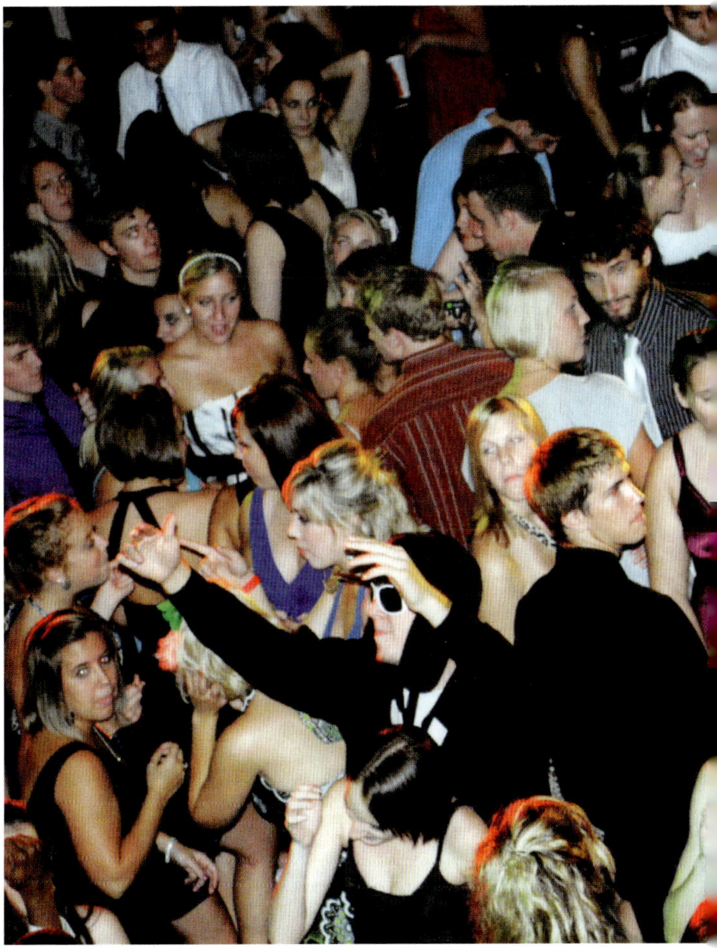

AUTUMN DANCE: The college tradition of an autumn dance continues. The 1953 autumn dance, above, shows more formal attire than that seen in 2010. The event came to be called the Gateway Clipper Dinner Dance Cruise in Pittsburgh, and is held each fall.

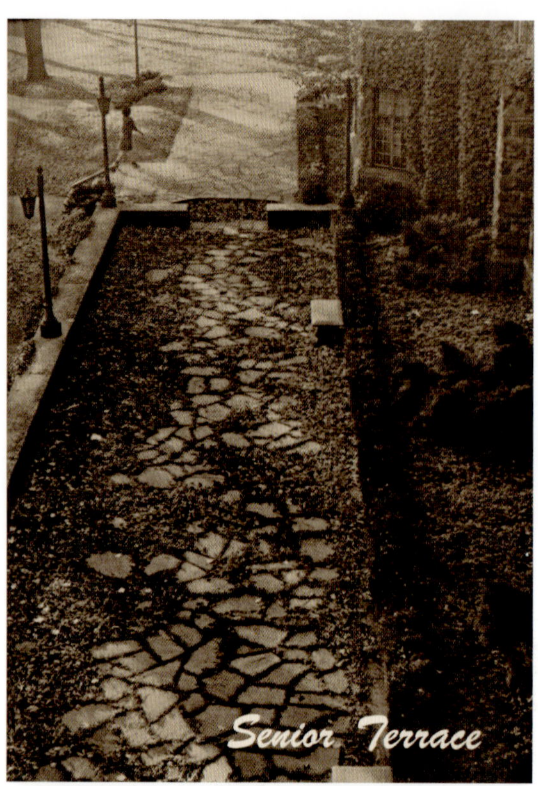

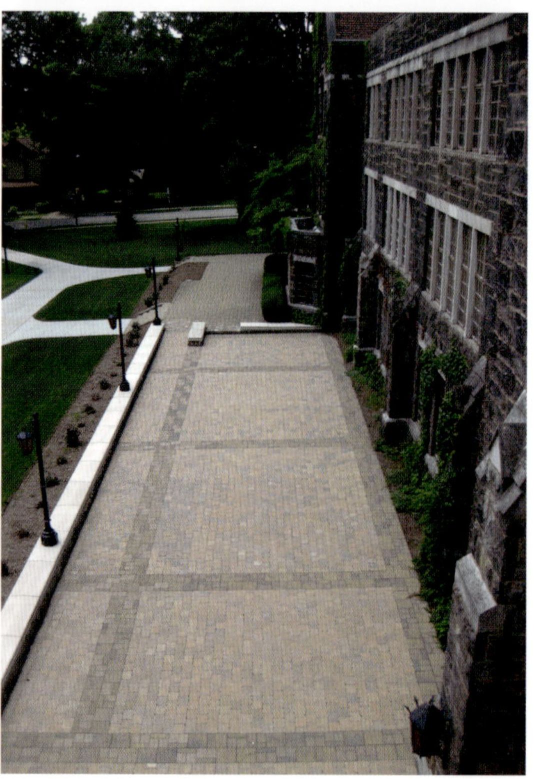

SENIOR TERRACE AT OLD MAIN: The patio attached to the south side of Old Main is known as Senior Terrace. Tradition limits access to graduating seniors and alumni. The 1947 terrace shown here was renovated in 2012 by donations from the Weisel family. New pavers replaced the old flagstone and the Terrace was made handicapped accessible. Senior Terrace still serves as the site for the college's graduation ceremonies each May. Tradition says if you are an underclassman and walk on the terrace, you will endanger your graduating.

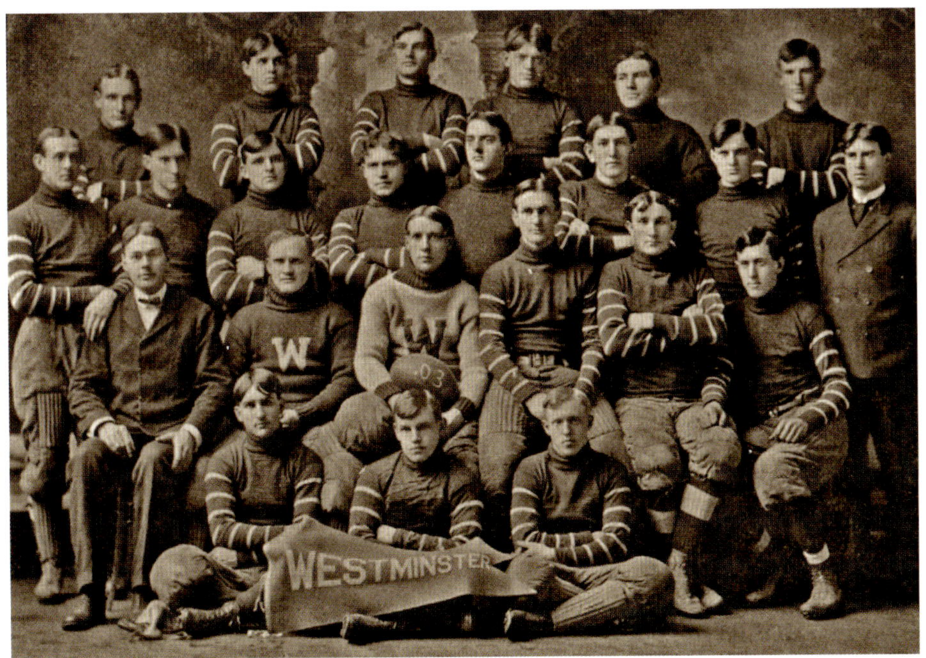

FOOTBALL: This gridiron sport started at Westminster in 1891 and is in its 124th season with six national championships and a string of victories that tie the Westminster Titans for the ninth all-time winningest record in NCAA division III history. Westminster, in the early years of football, played teams like Penn State and Pitt. The 1904 uniforms, above, can be compared to those in 2006 when some of the team members posed in Burry Stadium shortly after renovations that included new artificial turf- playing surface, lights for evening games, and a new all-weather track that can be seen in the background.

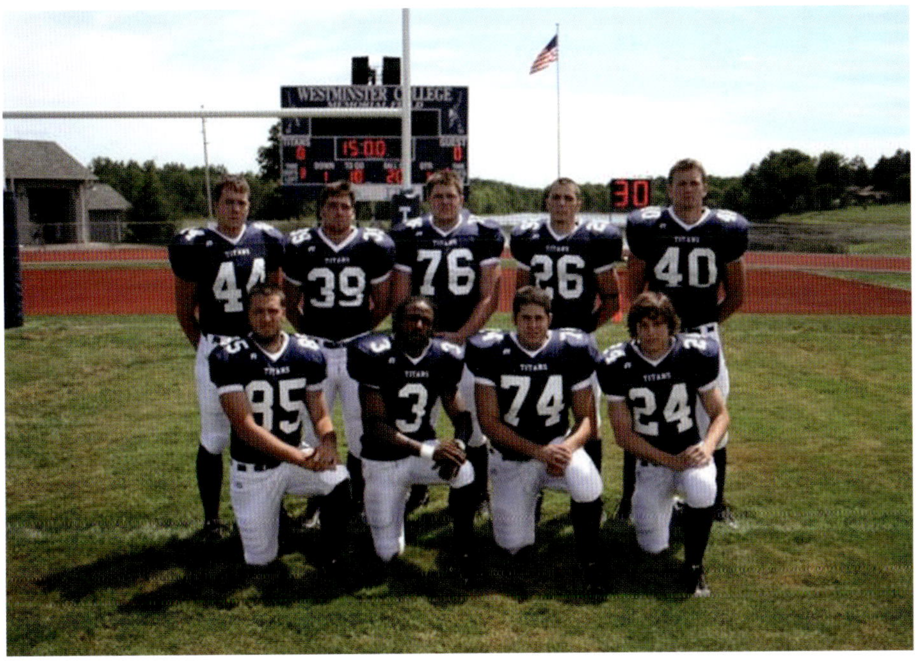

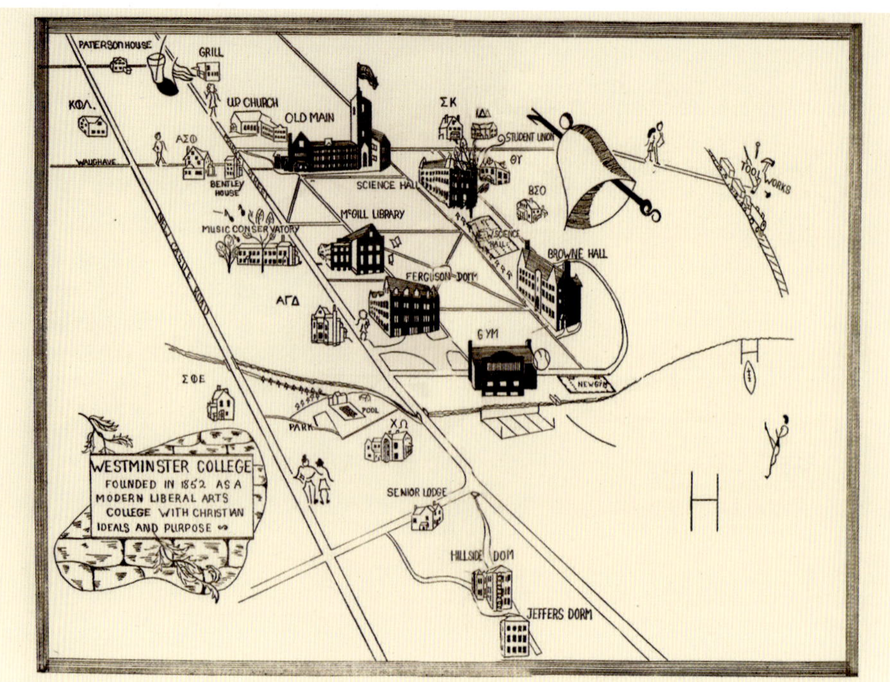

CAMPUS AERIAL VIEW: From a single building in the 1850s to multiple buildings on the quadrangle, as shown in the 1947 map above, the College has evolved, with numerous facilities in the early twenty-first century, such as Shaw Hall, Patterson Hall, Hoyt Science Resources Center, Orr Auditorium, Memorial Field House, Brittain Lake, Amphitheater, Natatorium, Russell Hall, Beeghly Theater, Eichenauer Hall, Faculty Housing, McKelvey Campus Center, Remick Admissions House, Burry Stadium, Galbreath Hall, Freeman's Science Hall, the President's manse and students' Townhouses in Berlin Village.

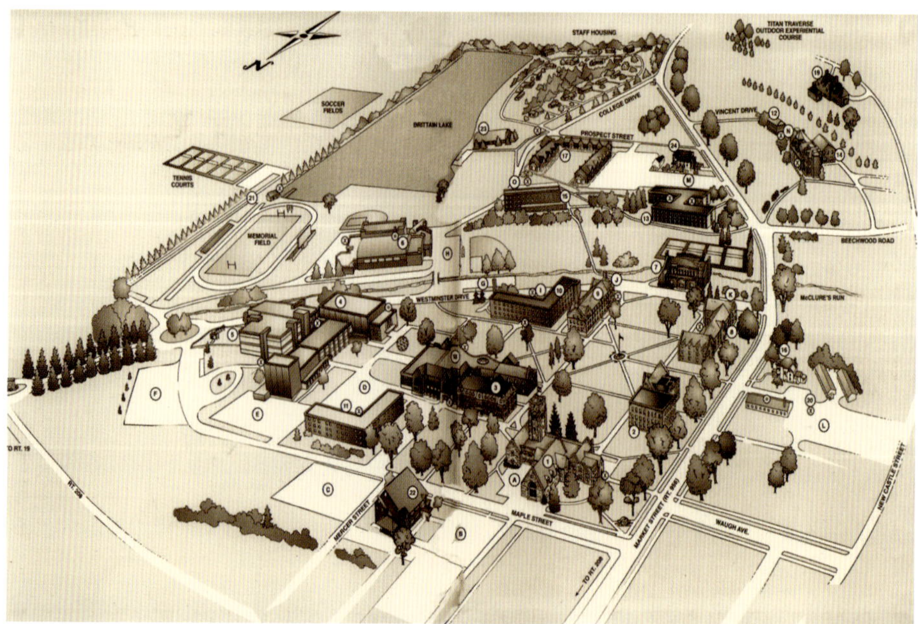

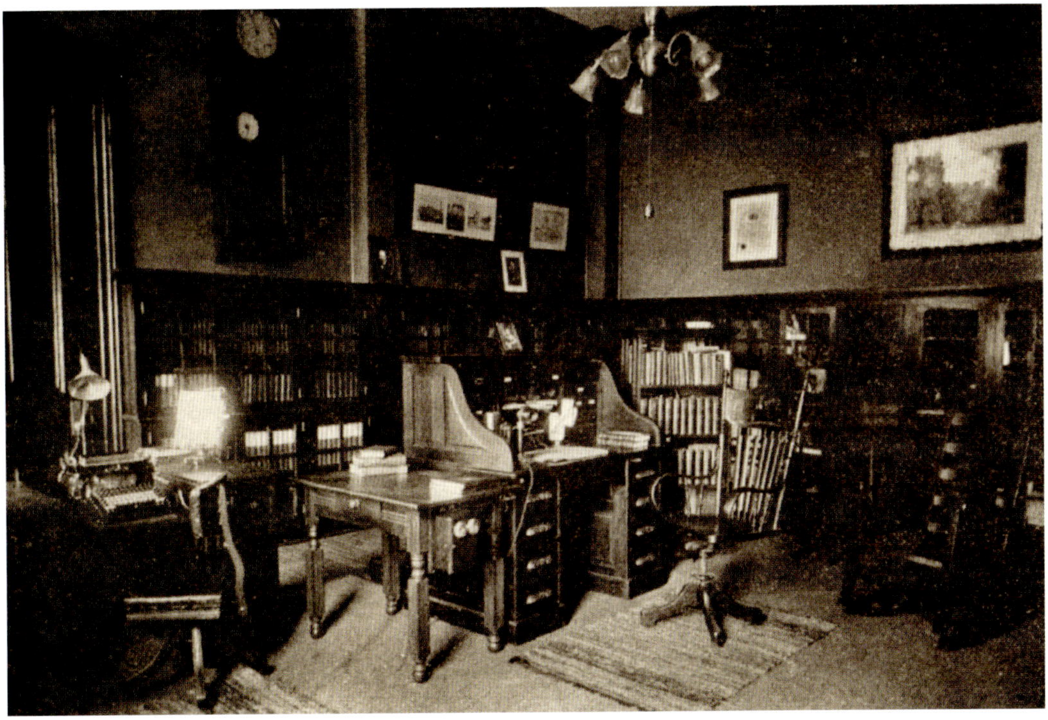

President's Office: The college president's office, while still located on the first floor in Old Main, has come a long way from the 1920s, when technology consisted of one telephone, and now includes more modern technology: computers, email, Skype, I-phones and world-wide access of information via the Internet. Notice the significant change in office decorum.

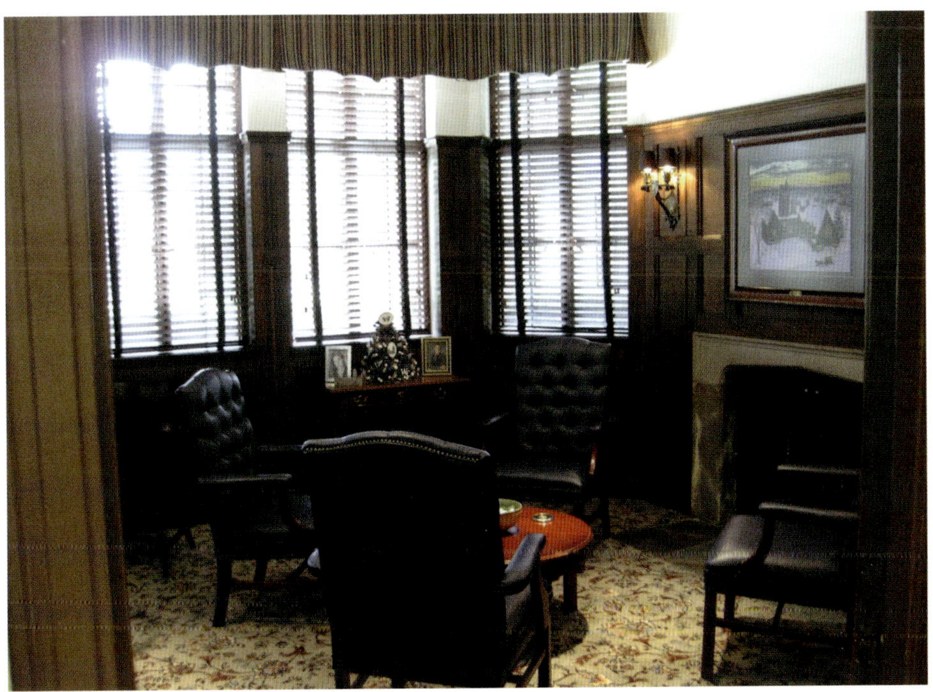

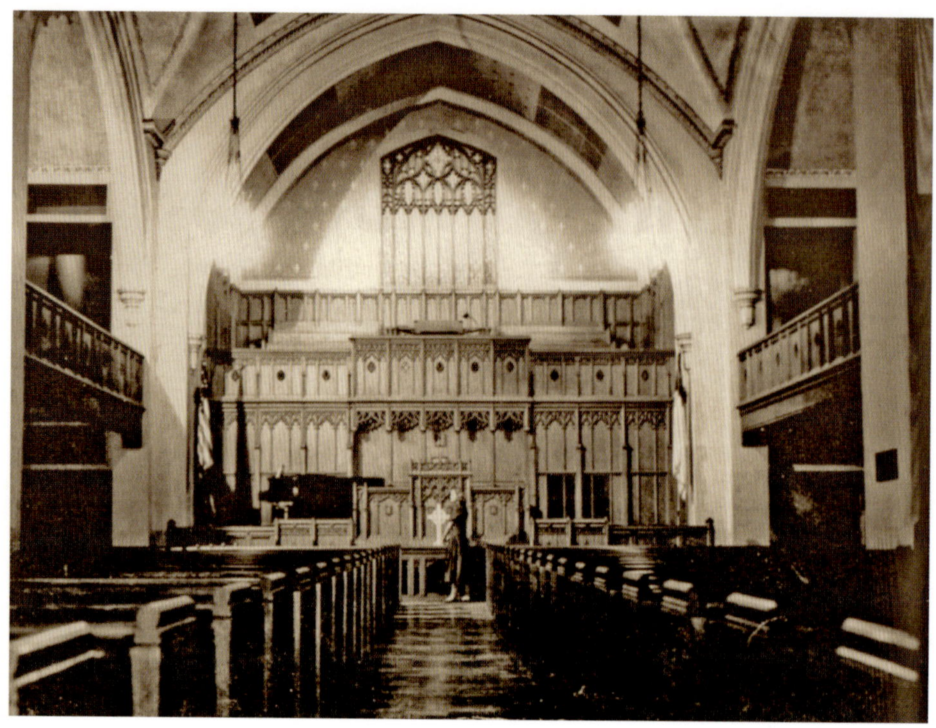

WALLACE CHAPEL: Shown here when new in 1929, it was named after Westminster's sixth president, W. Charles Wallace, because building a chapel was one of his goals for the college when the Old Main Memorial was built in 1928-1929, seating approximately 750. In 2014, the Chapel is still an integral part of college life at Westminster.

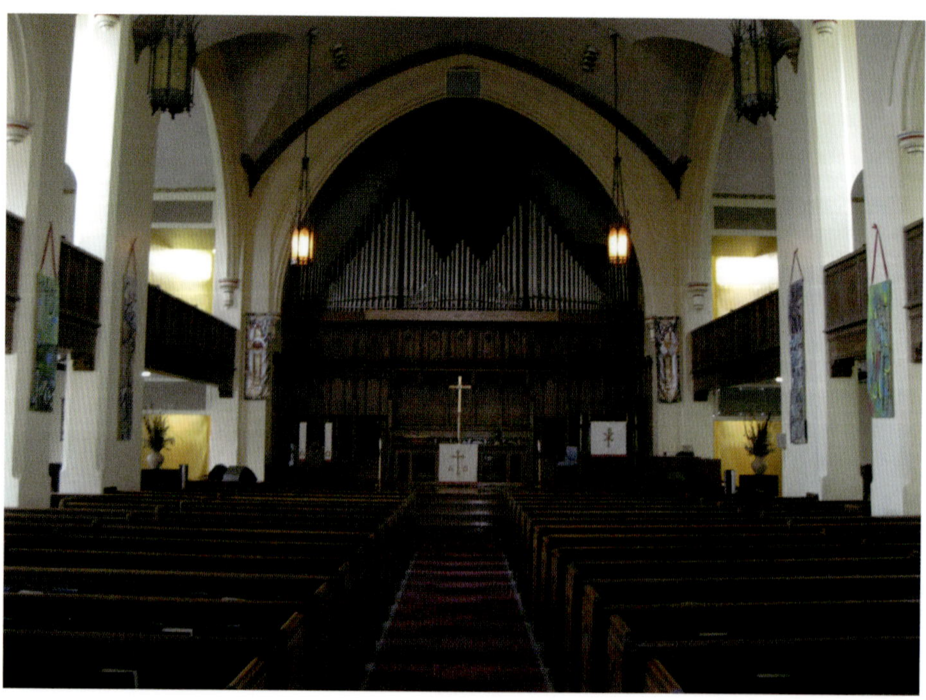

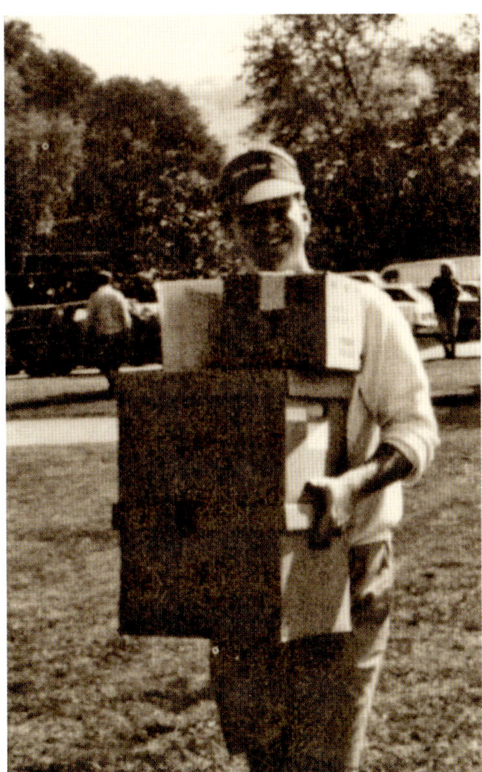

MOVE-IN DAY: This is still a tradition at Westminster, when football players and the college's "Fresh Start Staff," consisting of volunteer sophomore, junior, and senior students, help freshmen move in to their dorms – their new home away from home. This event is under the direction of the Student Services Office and is a good ice-breaker for the students helping them to get to know each other and to know the college campus.

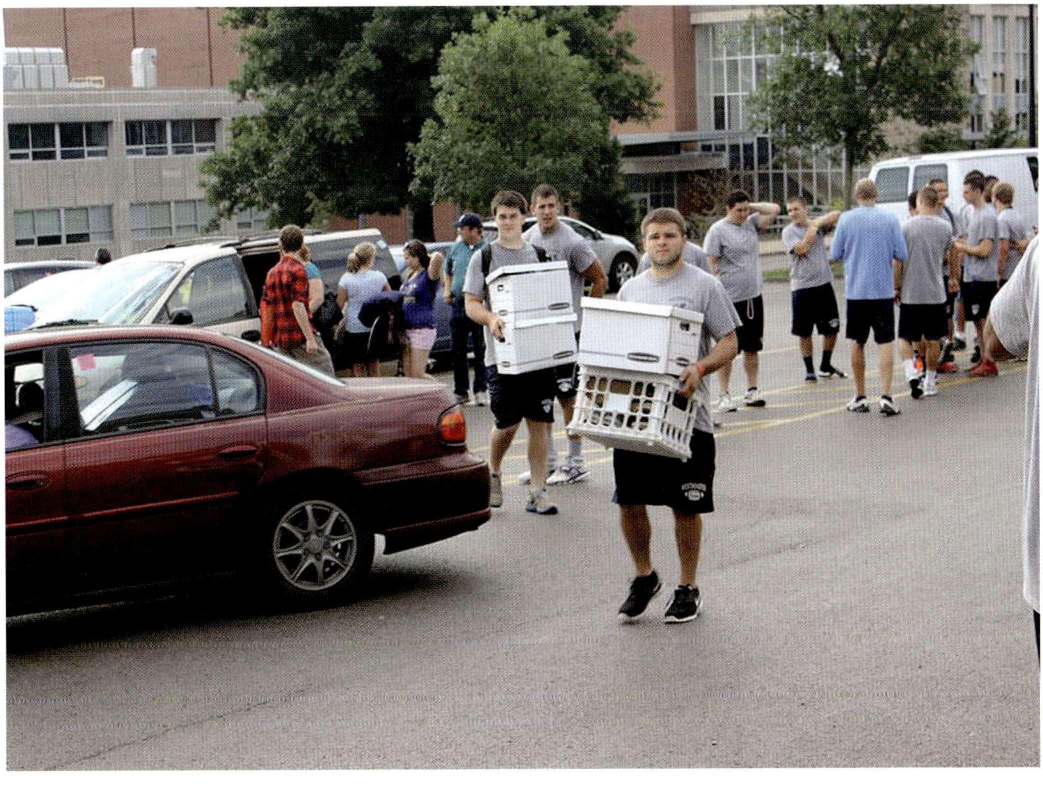

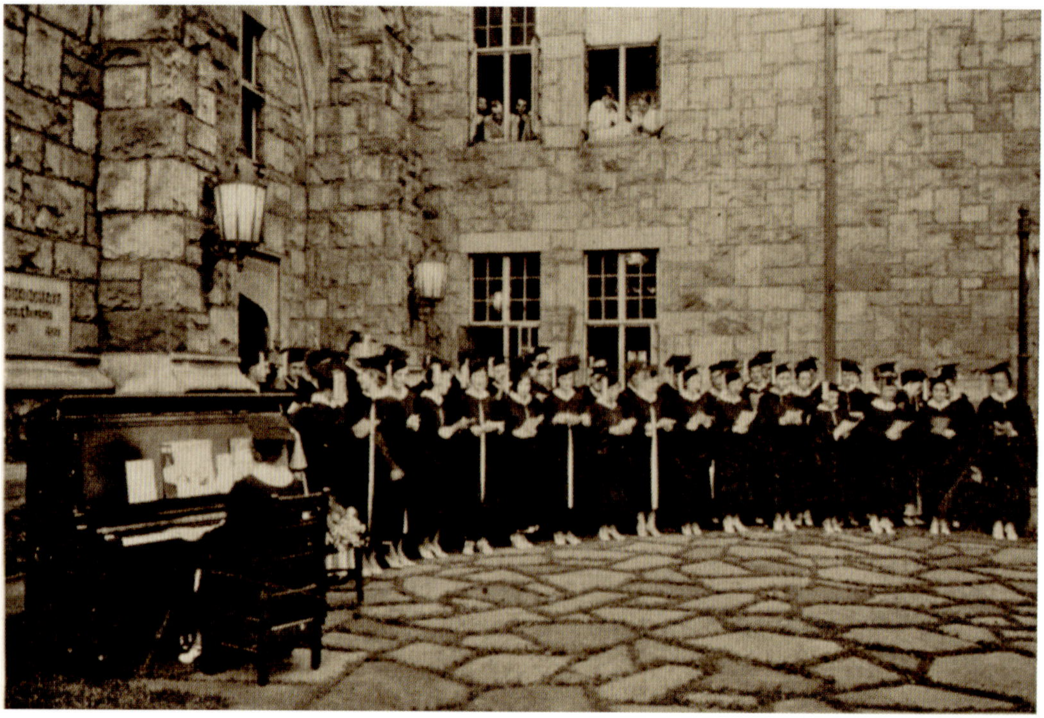

GRADUATION: The class of 1932, in cap and gown is shown above on Senior Terrace, adjacent to Old Main. Below, the class of 2012 continues the tradition of graduation on Senior Terrace as they receive their college diplomas.

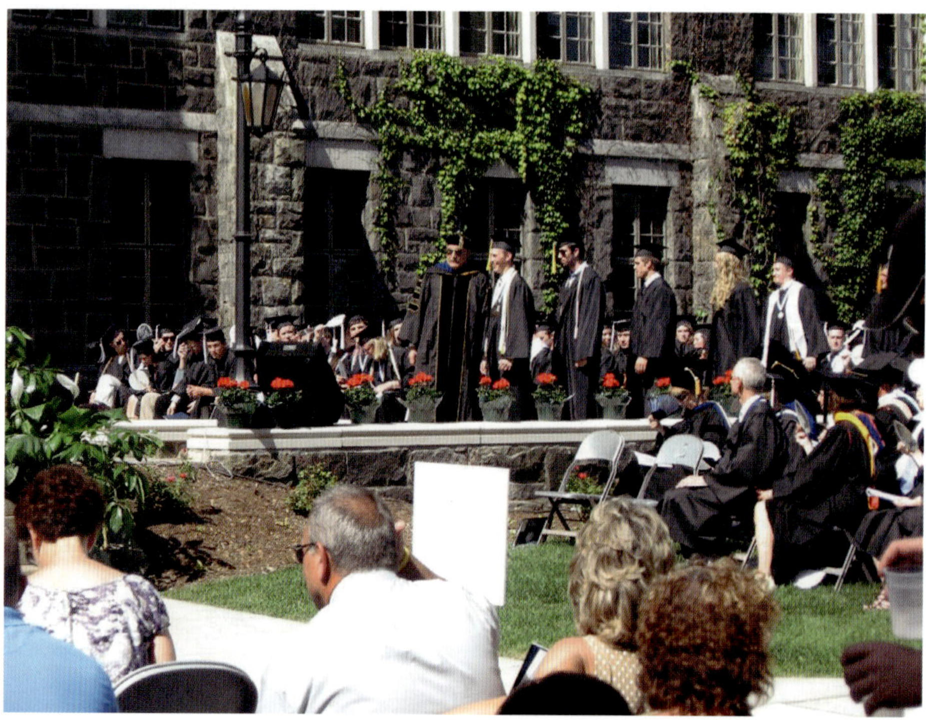

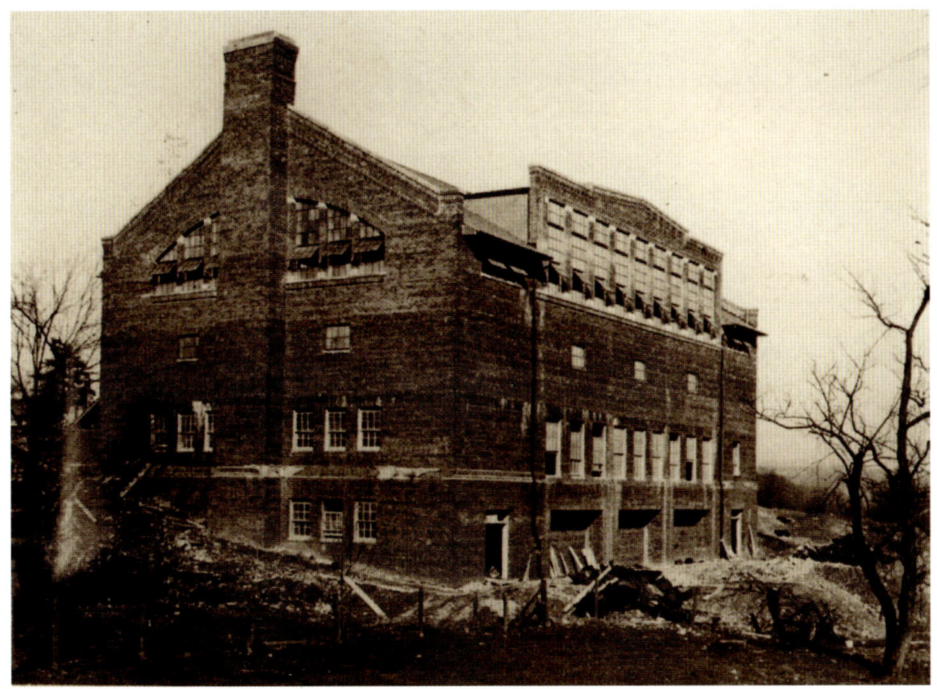

OLD 77: The gymnasium building is shown here under construction in 1921. It was home to Westminster's basketball teams and had an indoor track balcony, locker rooms and offices. It was the second gym for the college, replacing the first gym built in 1878. The building was named "Old 77" in honor of the string of 77 consecutive wins on the Titan's home court at the time. The team discontinued its home games there in 1951. In 2014, "Old 77" serves as a recreational and physical fitness center.

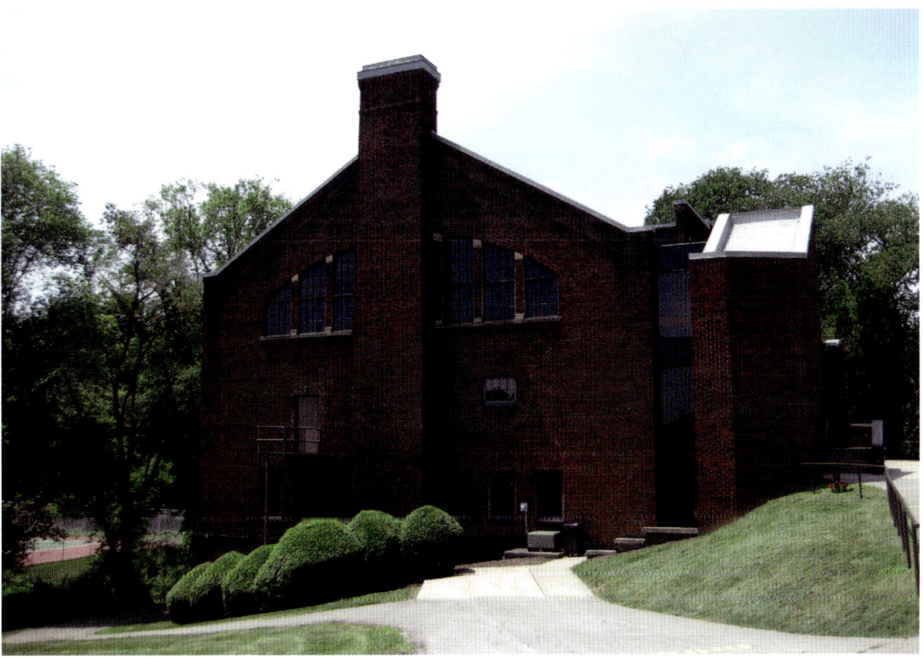

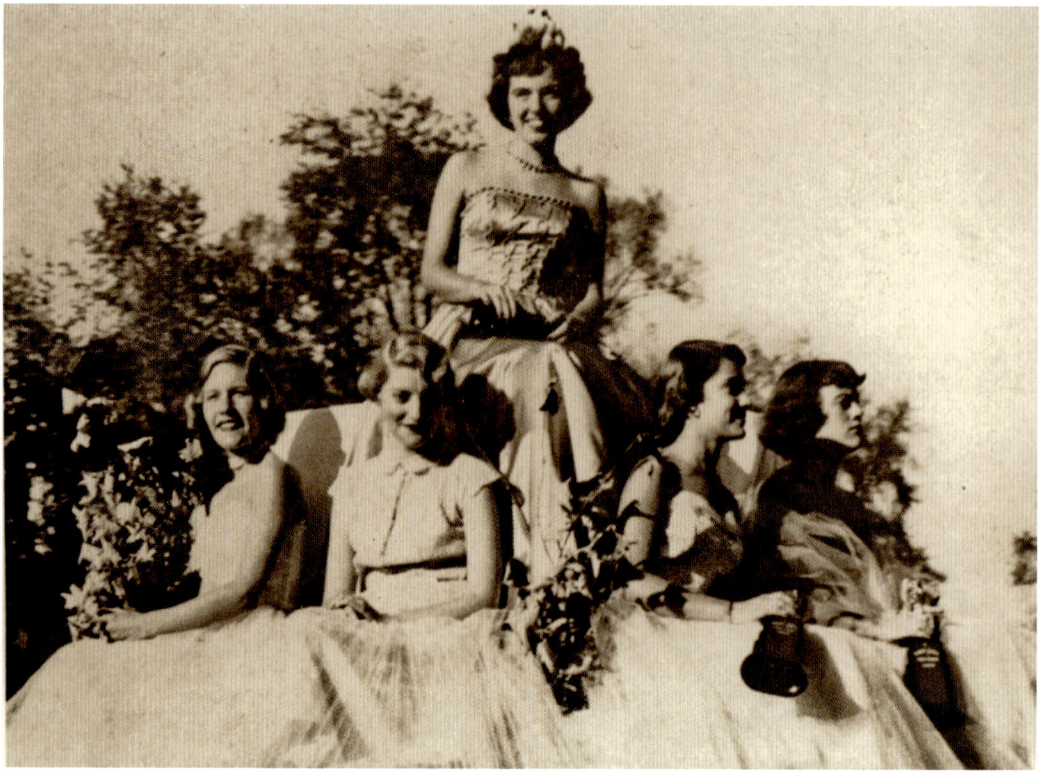

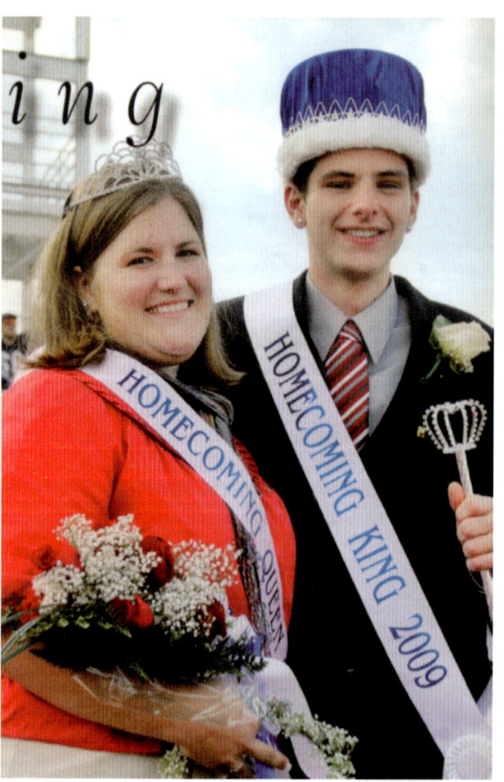

HOMECOMING: The process of crowning a homecoming queen and selecting a royalty court has continued over the years, as evidenced by the 1952 homecoming queen, shown above, and the Titans' queen in 2009. Homecoming queen and her court are still an annual tradition at the Titans' homecoming football game.

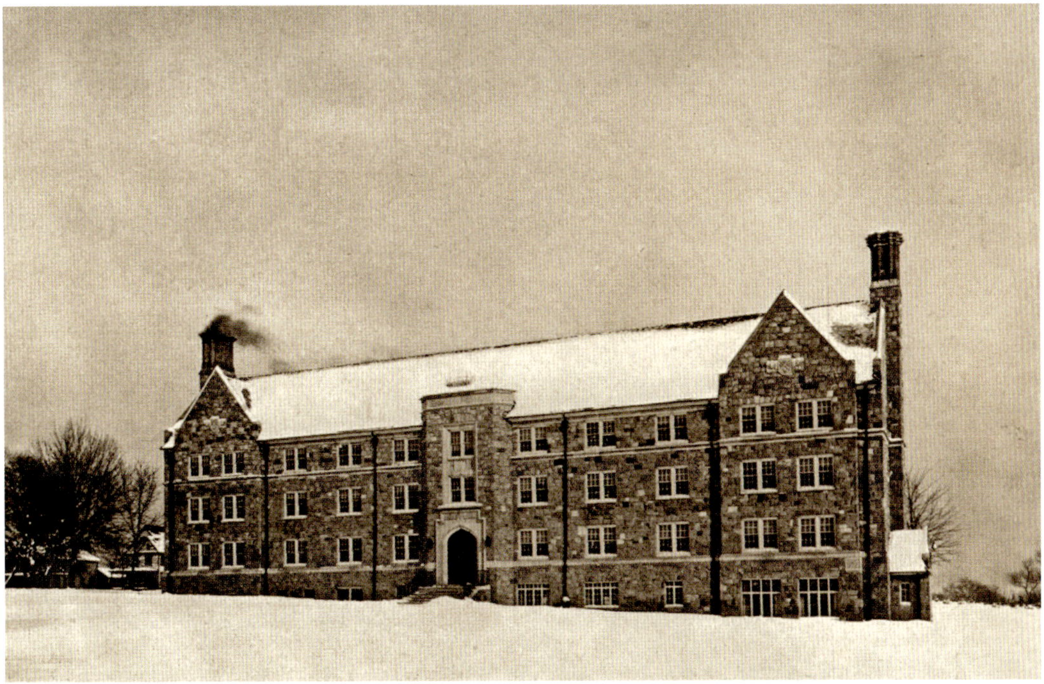

BROWNE HALL: Here's how it looked facing the quadrangle shortly after it opened in 1928. This girls' dormitory was built to memorialize Westminster's second president, Dr. Robert A. Browne. The dormitory was a gift to the college by the citizens of New Castle in recognition of the community service rendered by Dr. Browne. The dorm in the early twenty-first century is even more impressive surrounded by massive trees on the quad.

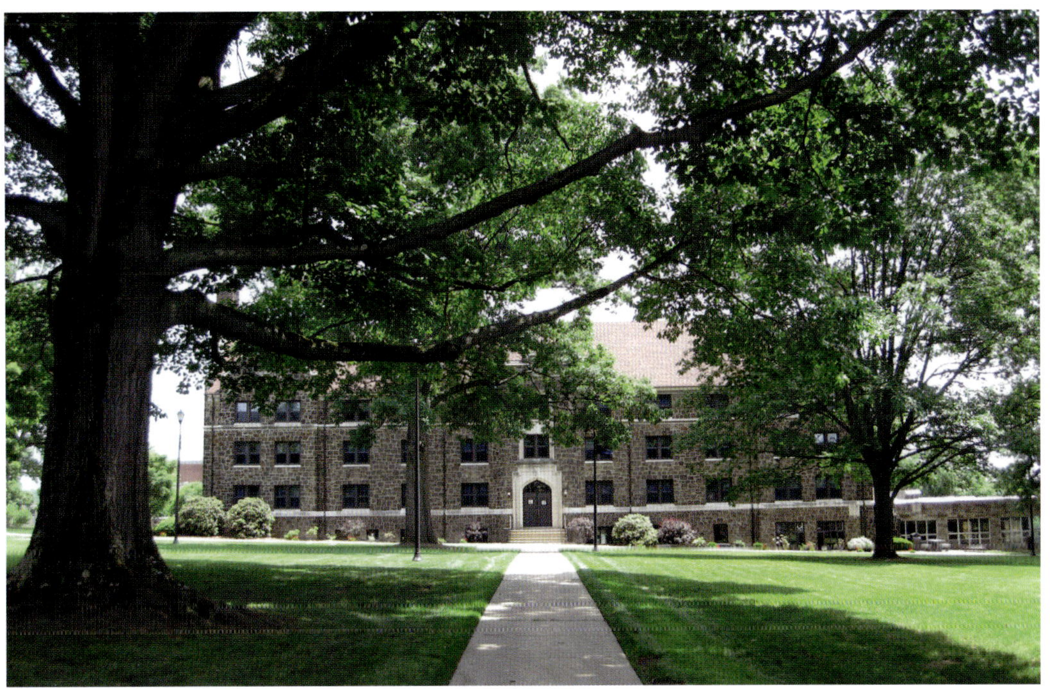

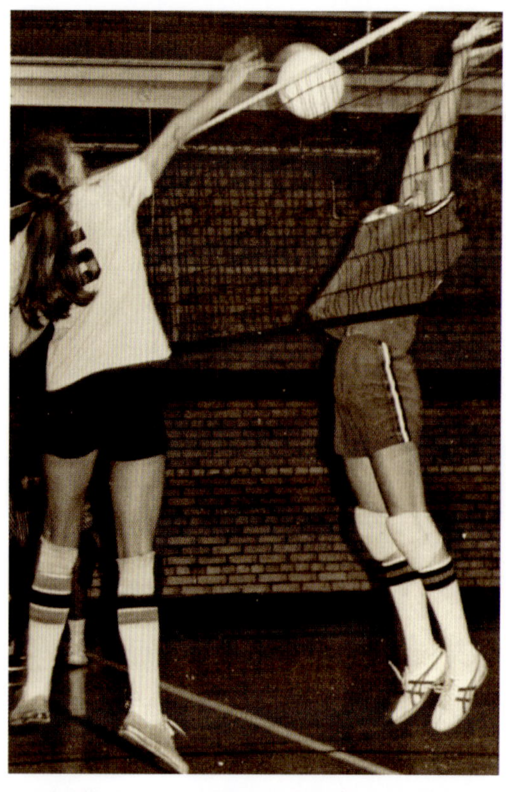

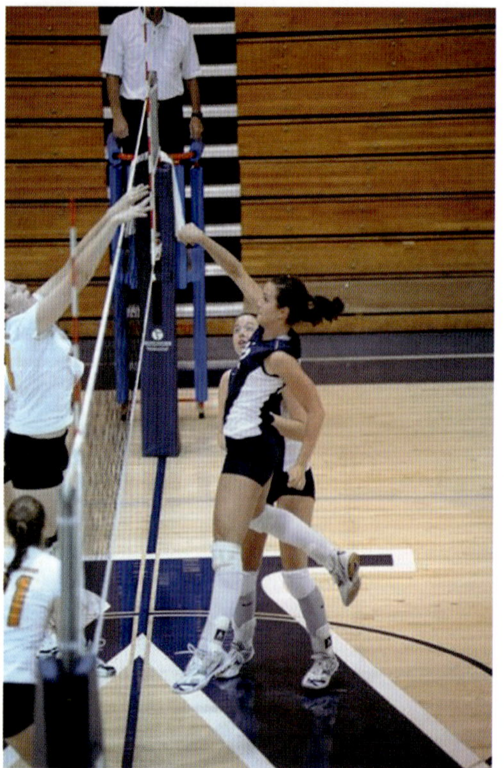

Volleyball: The first varsity team was in 1976 and concluded with an 11-7 record. The 1997 team qualified for the NAIA national tournament and did so again in NCAA in 2007 and 2008. PAC championships were won in 2002, 2007 and 2008. The Titan volleyball teams have an all-time winning percentage of 61% since 1976. The volleyball apparel from 1976 to 2009, as shown in these photos, hasn't changed much.

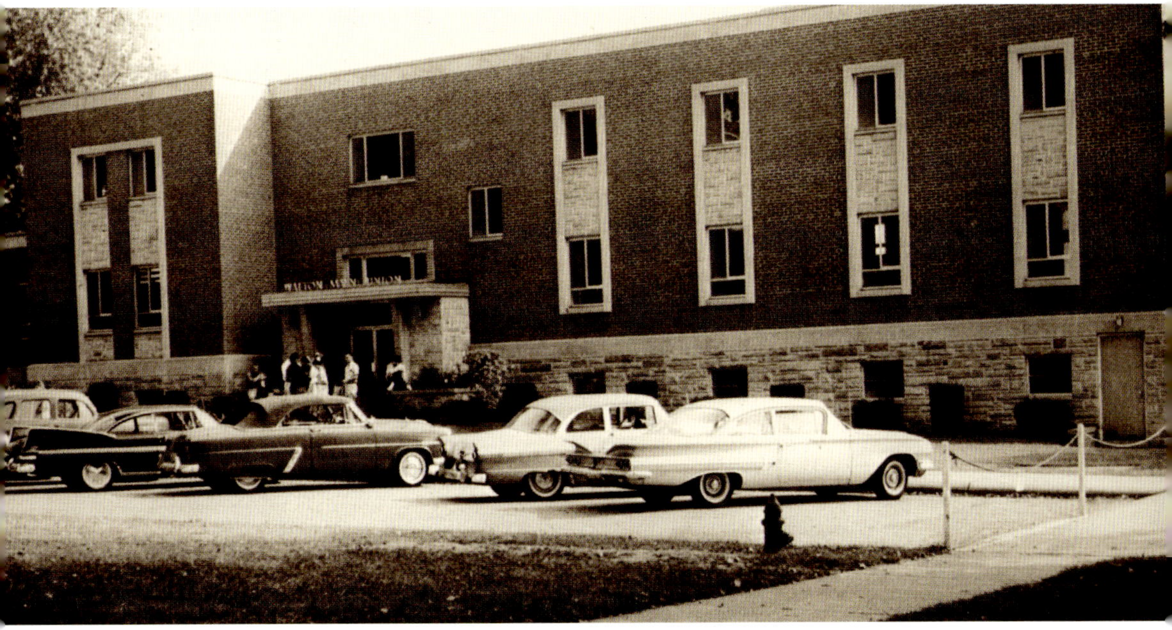

STUDENTS CAMPUS CENTER: The Walton-Mayne Student Union building, opened in 1958, was called "The Tub" by students and was the center of student life on campus for almost fifty years, until the new $13 million McKelvey Campus Center was built in 2003. The students continue the tradition of calling the new center the Tub. The new campus center overlooks part of the quadrangle and houses other functions such as the college bookstore, career services for students, College Chaplain's office, a conference center, meeting rooms, a Titan gift shop, public safety office, graduate school office, and Student Services offices.

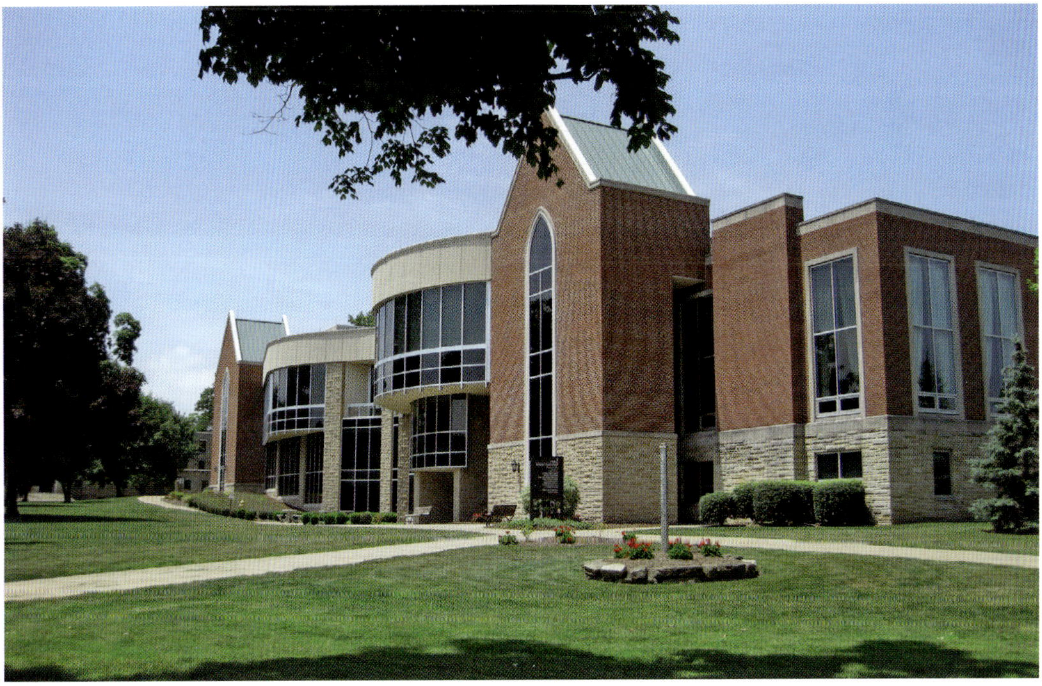

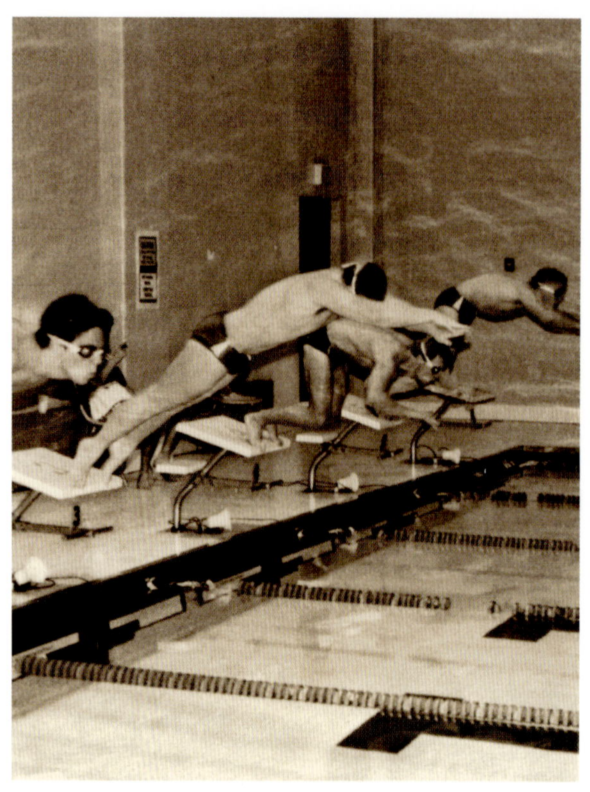

MEN'S SWIM TEAM: Westminster's Natatorium was dedicated in February 1976 and provides excellent facilities for swimming classes, swim teams and recreational swimming. The Natatorium replaced the old pool which had been built in the early 1930s in the basement of Old 77. That pool was in the planning stage even when Old 77 was built in the 1920s. The old pool was covered with a wooden floor in the 1980s, and this floor area is used for physical education and recreational activities in the 2010s.

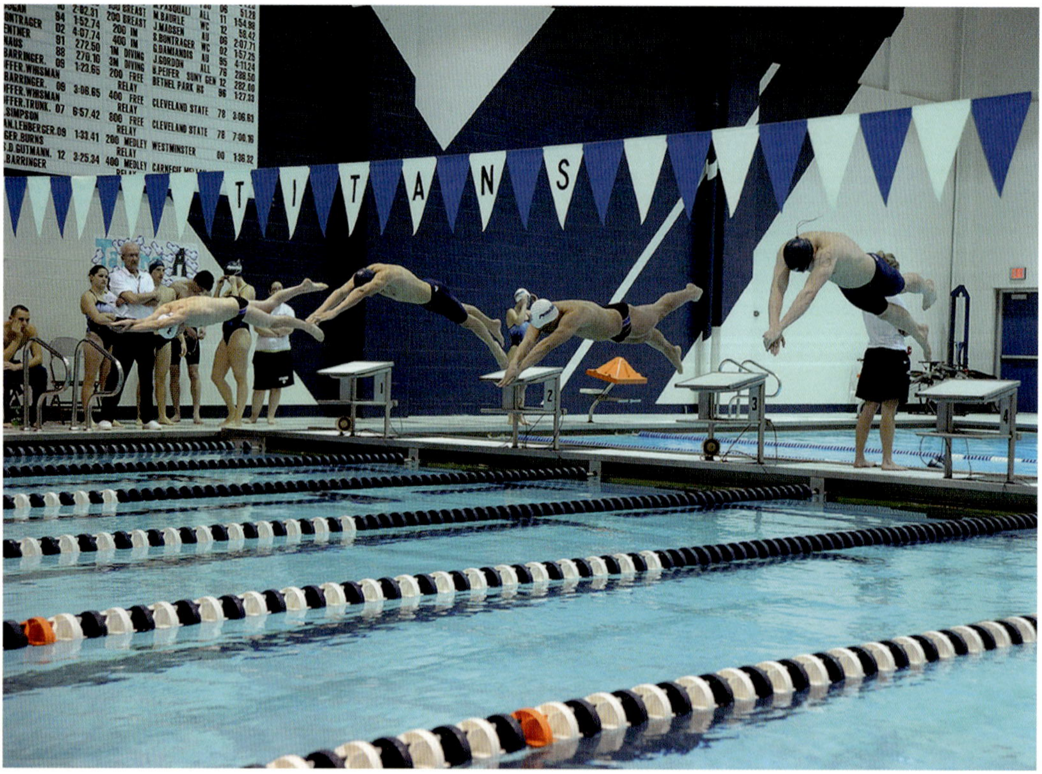

FIRST PRESIDENT: Reverend George Vincent was chosen as the college's first President by his fellow pastors and Elders serving as the college's founding fathers' committee. Numerous colleges were founded by various religious denominations in America during the period 1820-1860 for the purpose of preparing ministers and to provide opportunities for the cultural, religious, social, and educational advantages of a college education.

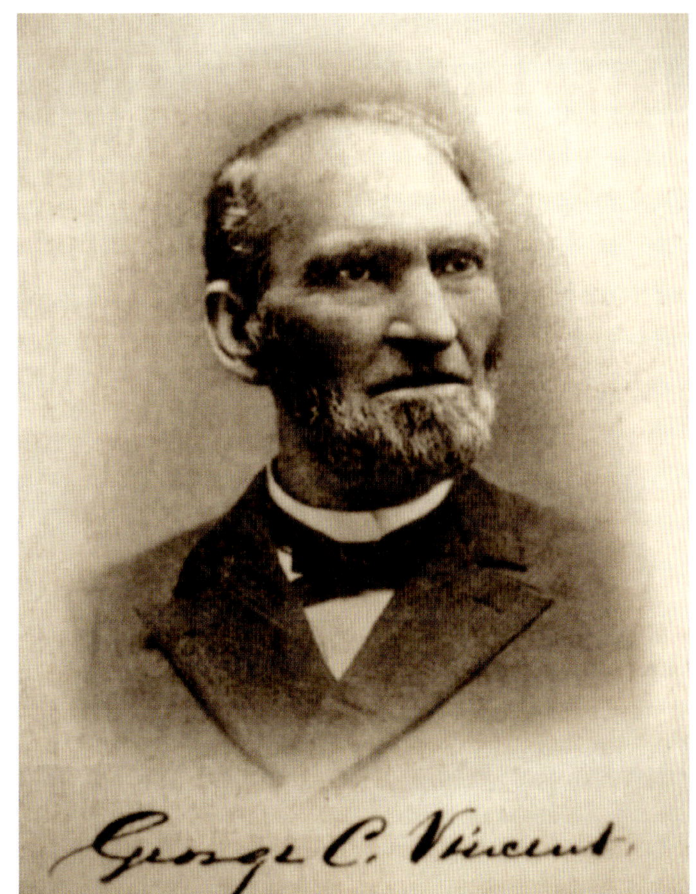

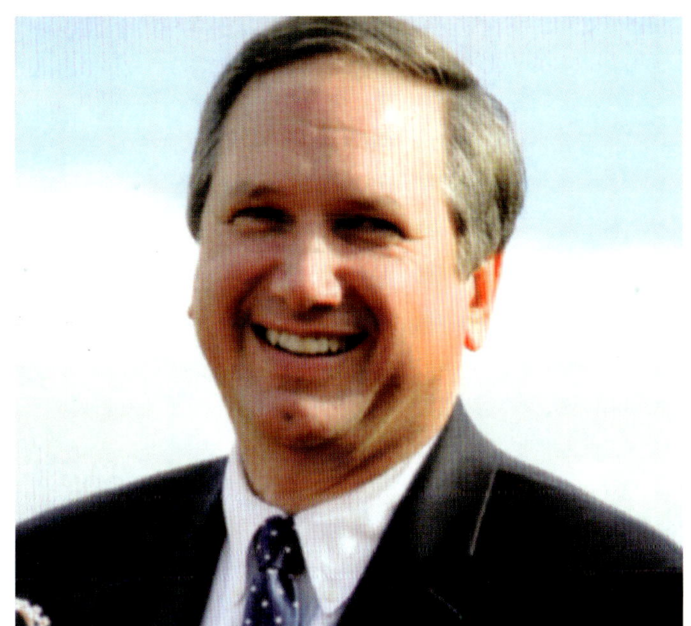

PRESIDENT IN 2014: Dr. Richard Dorman brings a wealth of higher education experience to his post as the President of Westminster College. Dr. Dorman provides a steady hand at the helm of the college, guiding it through the early twenty-first century and leading it into the future, with his vision for planning.

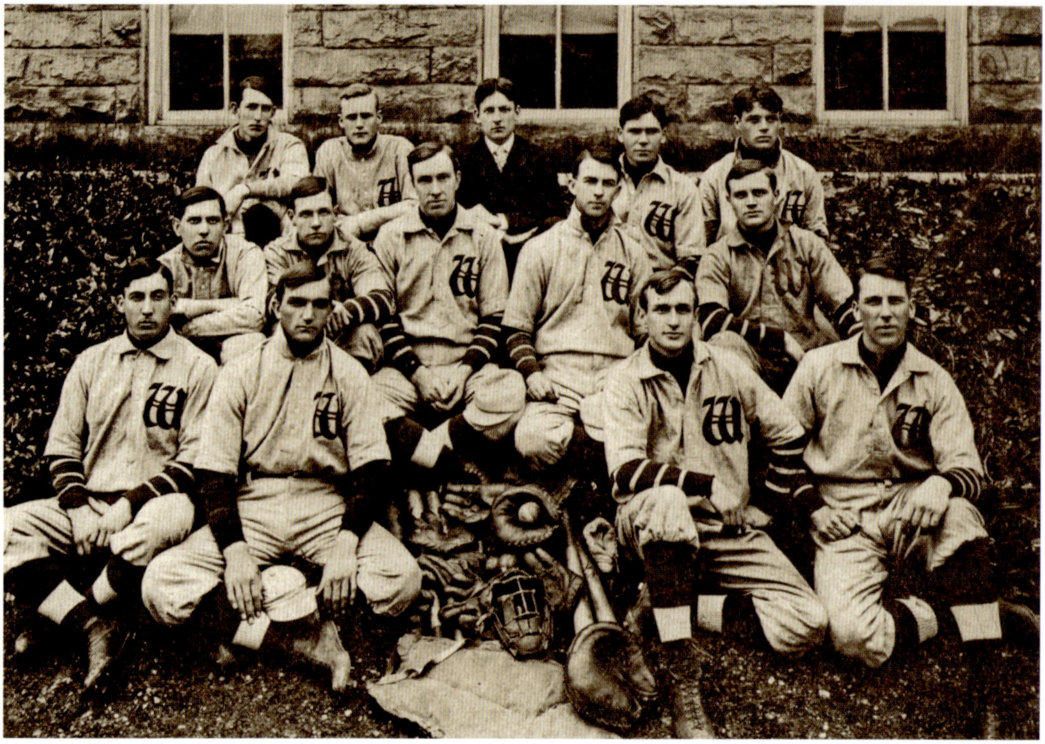

BASEBALL TEAM: The 1909 baseball team and the 2010 baseball team may be over a hundred years apart, but their team spirit is just as intense. Baseball at Westminster began in 1884 as the beginning of organized athletics at the college. Early games were with Geneva College and Grove City College.

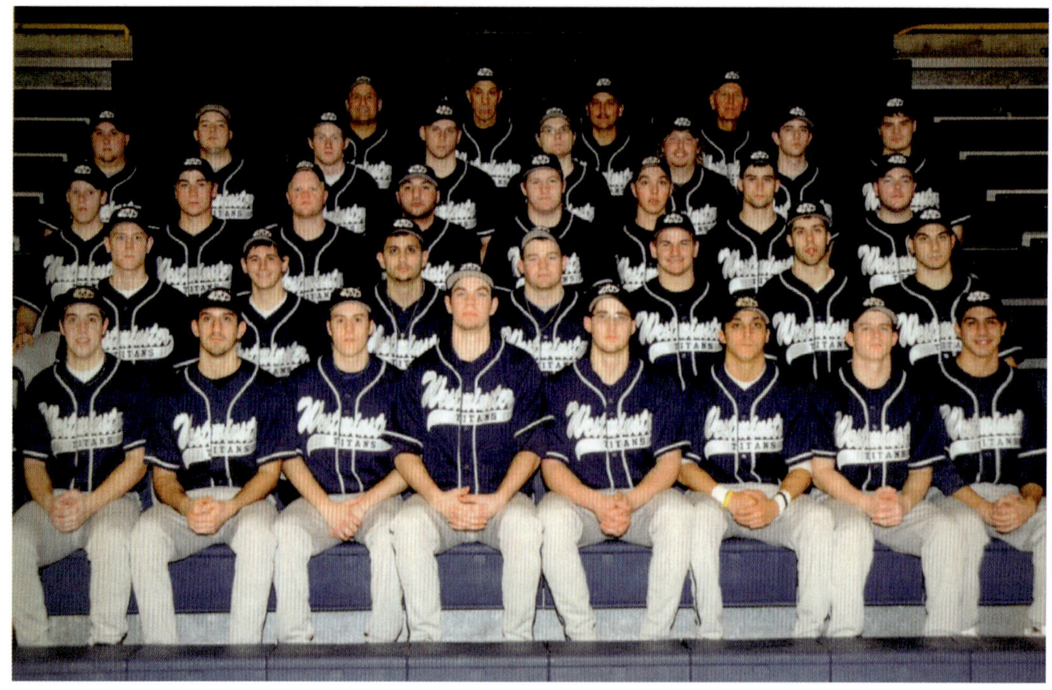

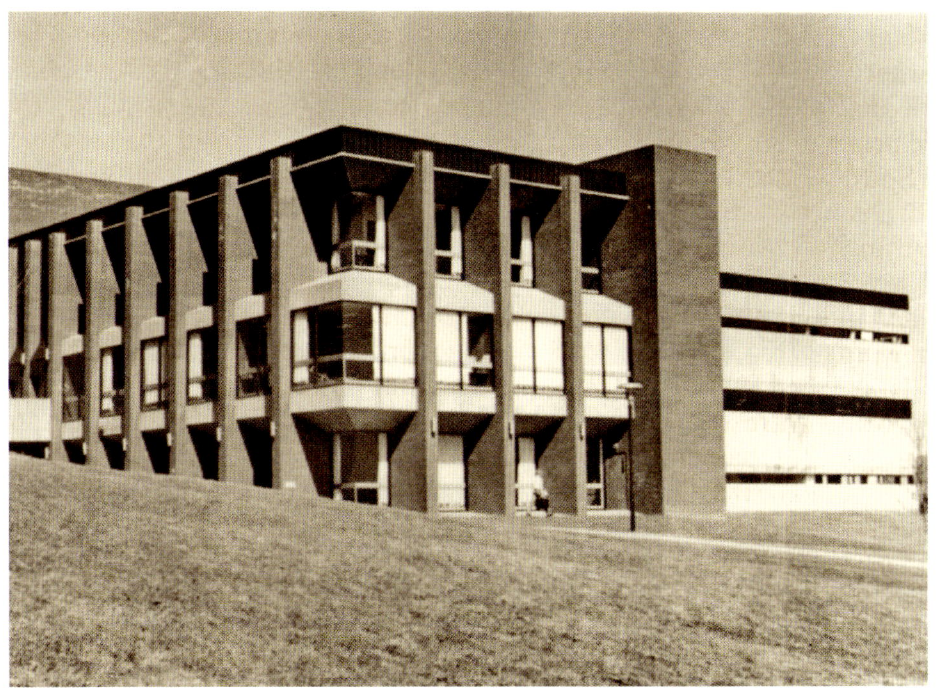

Hoyt Science Center: Completed in 1974, the building was named for Alex Hoyt, a Trustee Emeritus and major donor for the building. The Science Center was one of the key goals of the 1971 capital gifts campaign. The building provides facilities for chemistry, mathematics, a science library, biological sciences, computer labs, and computer center. The $2.7 million science center was dedicated debt-free in 1974, when it opened. Recently remodeled, the building continues to provide state-of-the-art technology in science, mathematics, and computers.

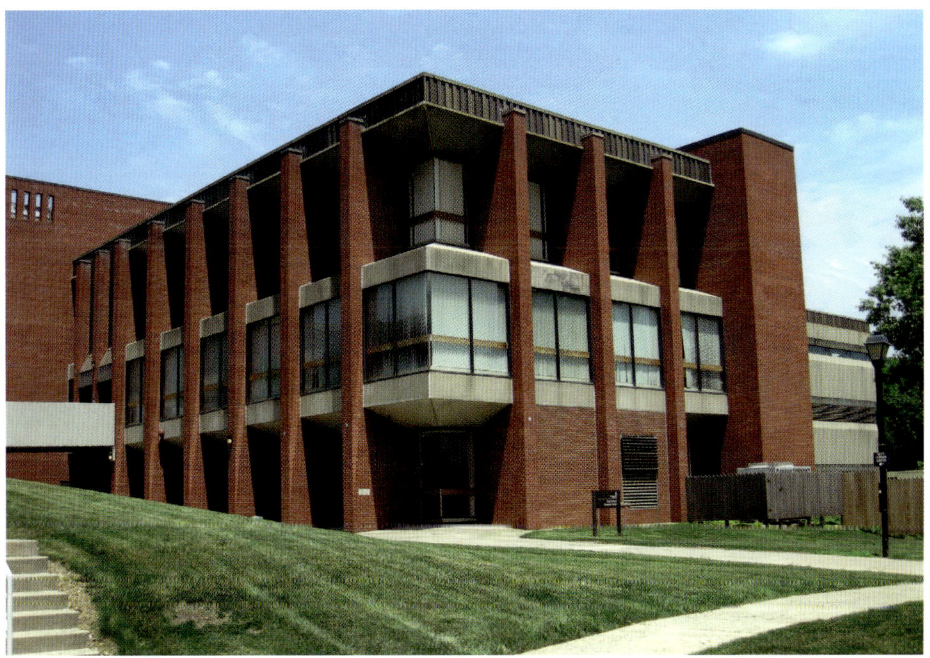

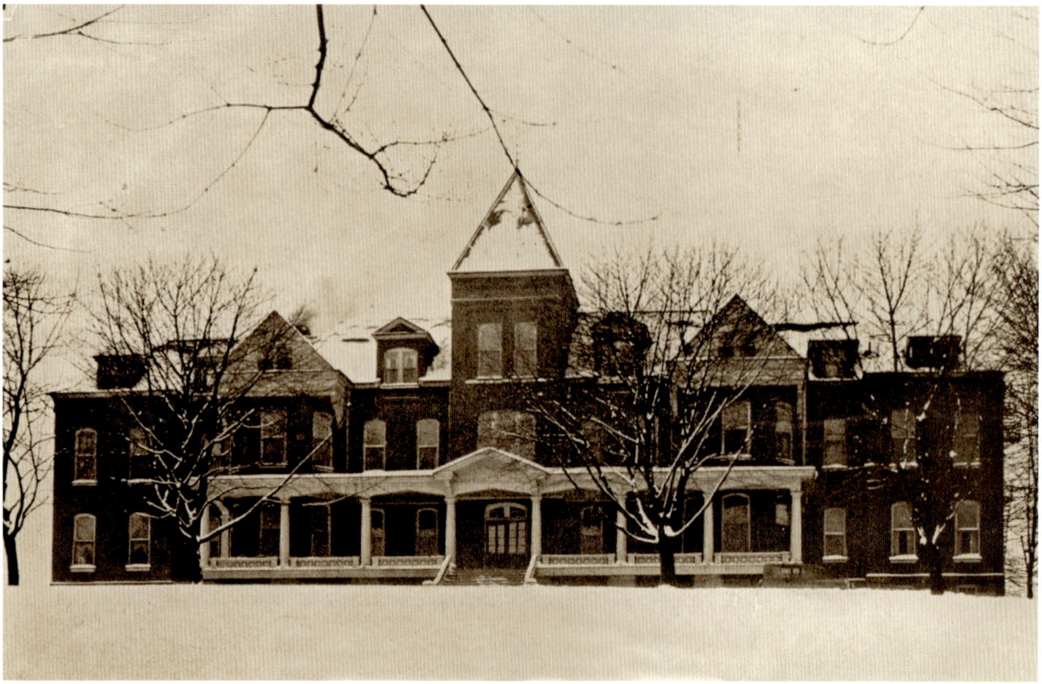

Hillside Dormitory: The oldest building on campus, completed and occupied in 1885. Originally known as "The Ladies Hall," it has been remodeled numerous times. During World War II, the building housed Navy cadets training to be pilots. The cadets liked to say they were stationed at "U.S.S. Hillside," where they lived, ate, and had classes under their own instructors. Following the war, the building again served as a girls' dormitory. At one time, it was a music conservatory and once was even a men's dorm. It is once again a ladies' dorm.

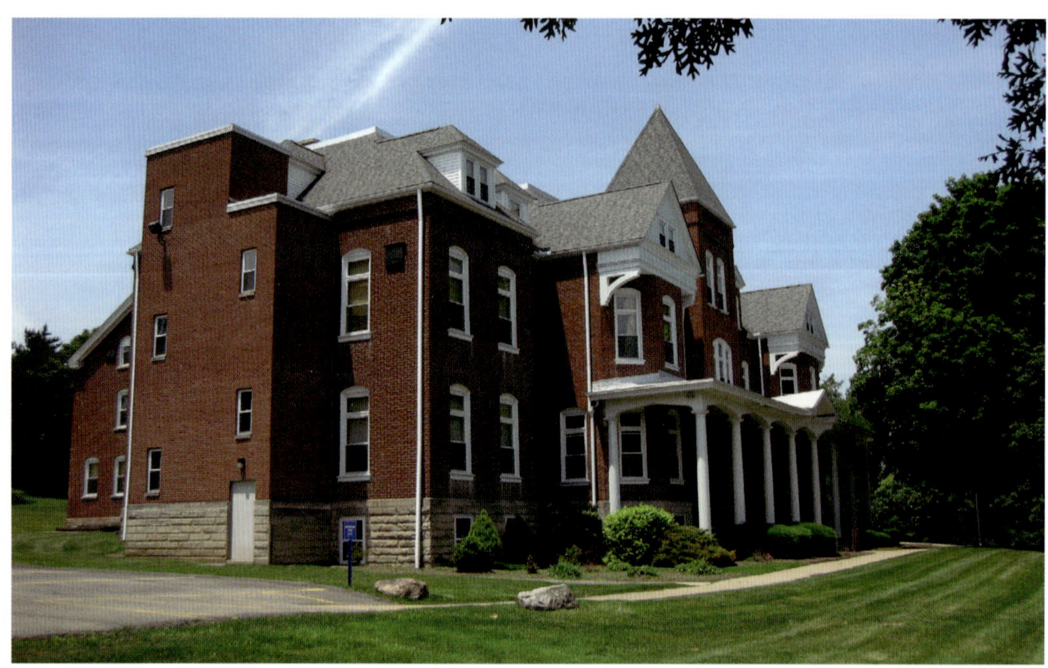

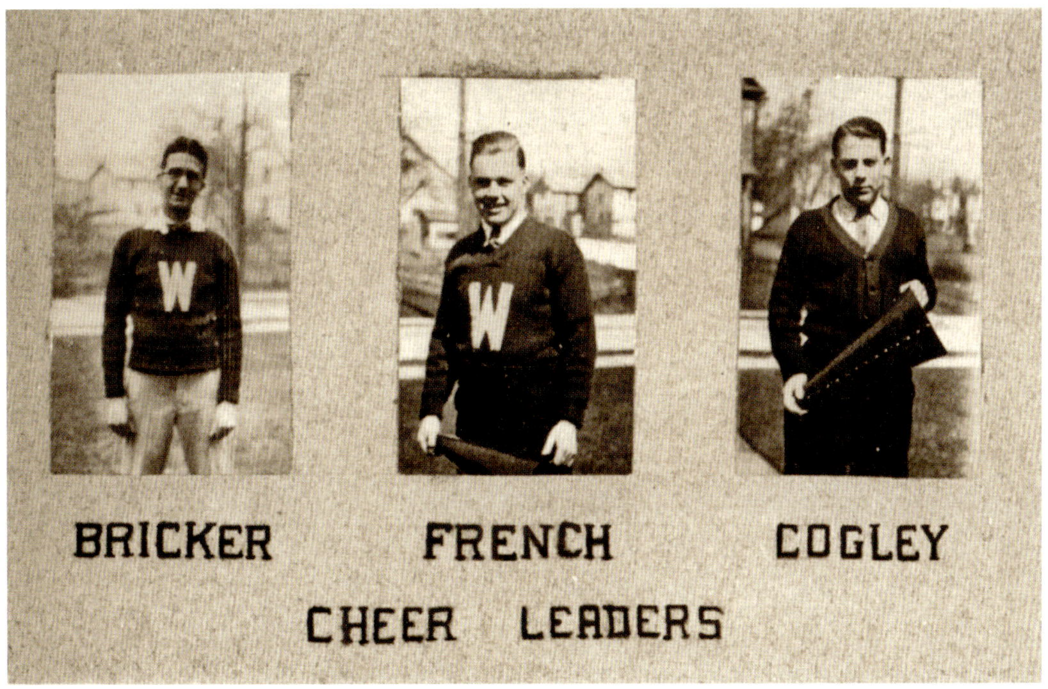

CHEERLEADERS: From the 1927 cheerleaders, shown above, to the cheerleaders of 2011, shown below, to the cheerleaders of 2014, they make up an integral part of the college's support for the athletic teams. They are always enthusiastic, always pleasant and cheerful, and always cheering the Titans on to victory. Cheerleading at Westminster was first adopted in 1911 and is still going strong in the 2010s. A Titan home game in football and basketball just wouldn't be the same without Westminster's cheerleading tradition.

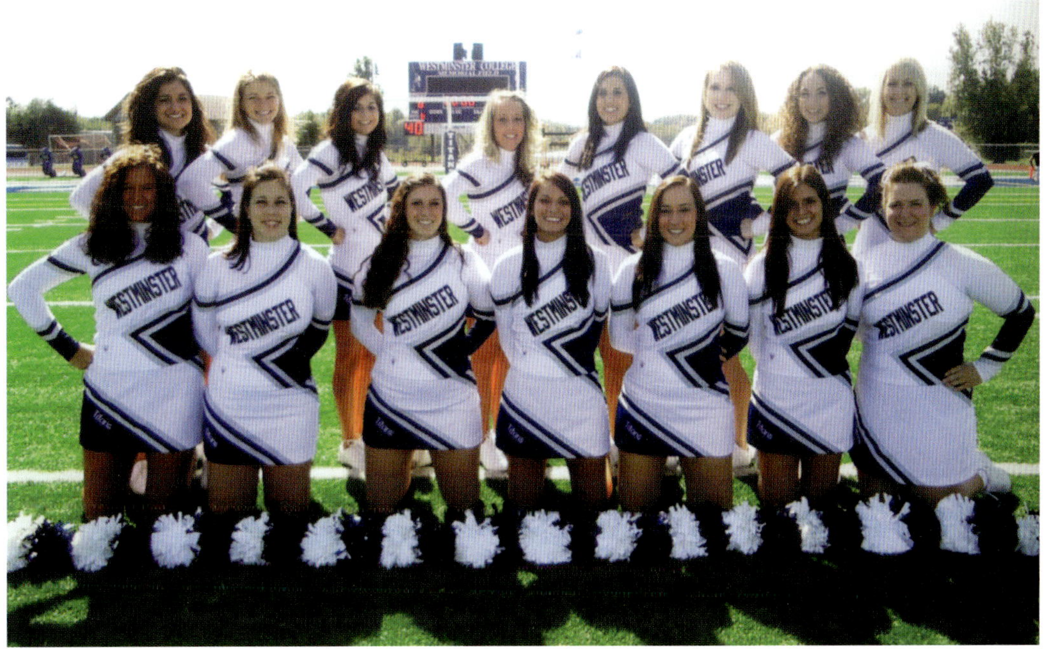

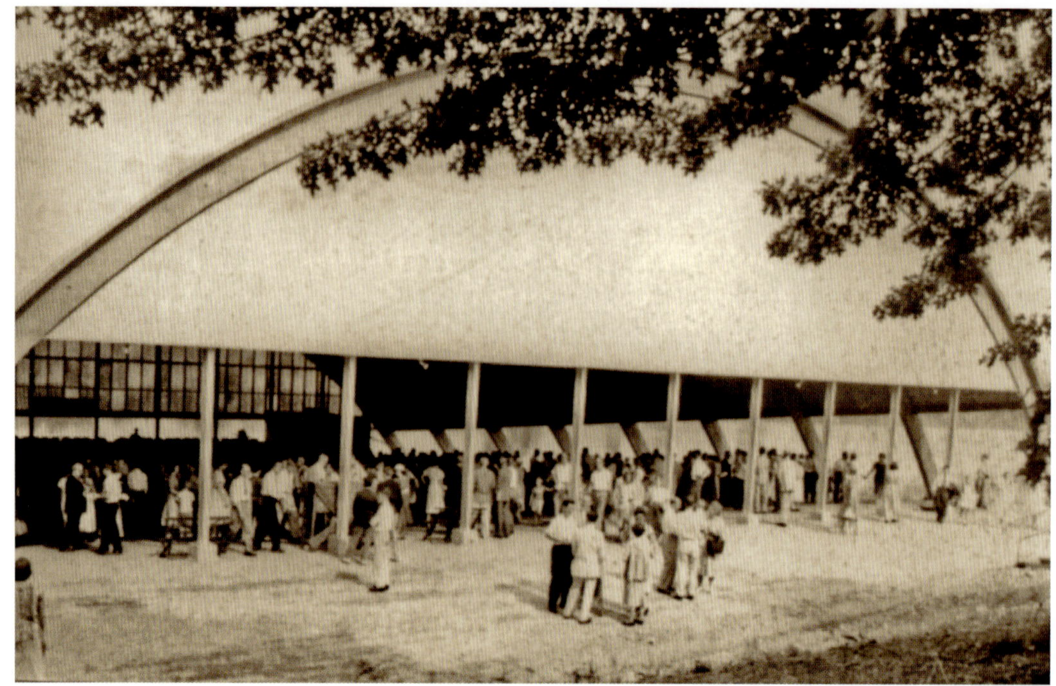

AMPHITHEATRE: Overlooking Brittain Lake, situated pleasantly on the lake's west bank, the Amphitheatre was built in 1958 by the New Wilmington Missionary Conference for its annual assembly. Here's how it looked when the open-sided auditorium was used for its first conference. Brittain Lake had been built in 1951 and enlarged in 1956 just before the construction of the Amphitheatre. In 2014, the structure is used by the college for events such as the annual fall "Welcome Back Dinner" and football's family day as well as the Missionary Conference.

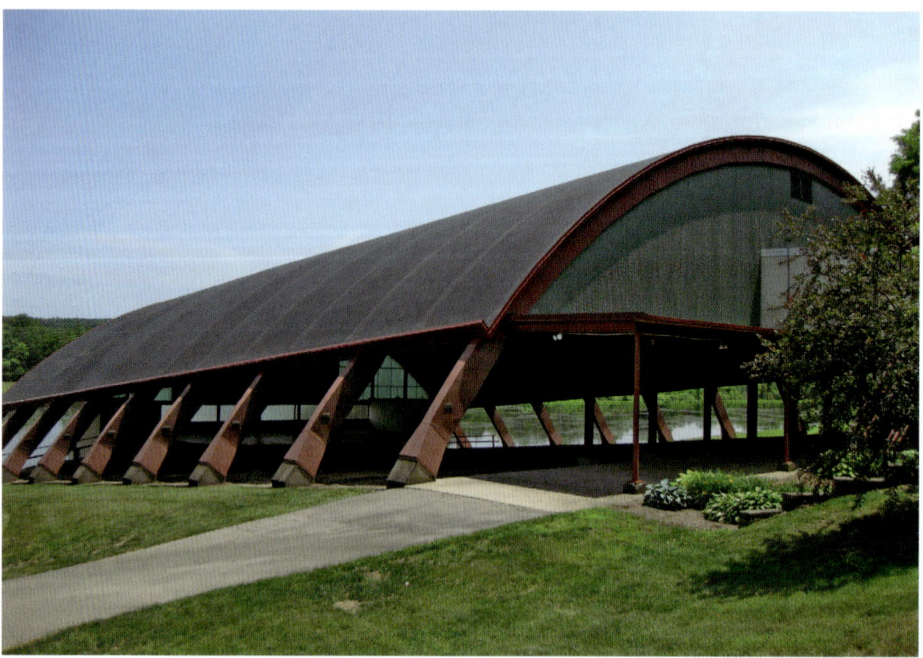

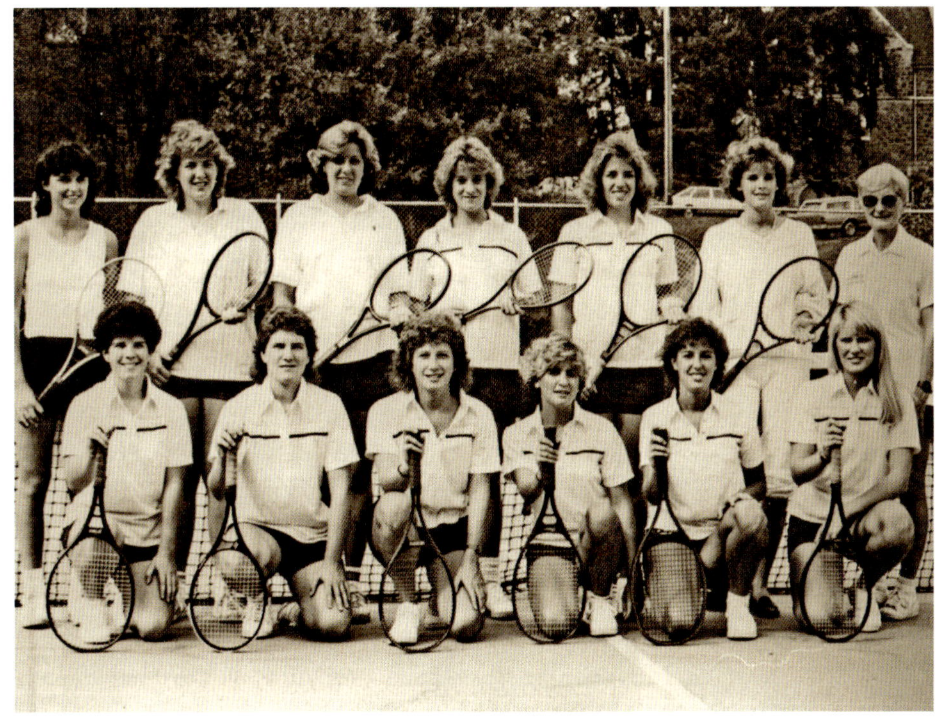

WOMEN'S TENNIS: Started in 1976 with a 7-3-1 record. In the seasons since then, overall, the women's tennis teams have a 59.2% winning record. The 1987 team was 7-4 under long time coach, Irene Walters, and the 2011 team was 18-0 under long time coach Scott Remminger. Since 2002, women's tennis team members won thirteen PAC championships in singles and doubles.

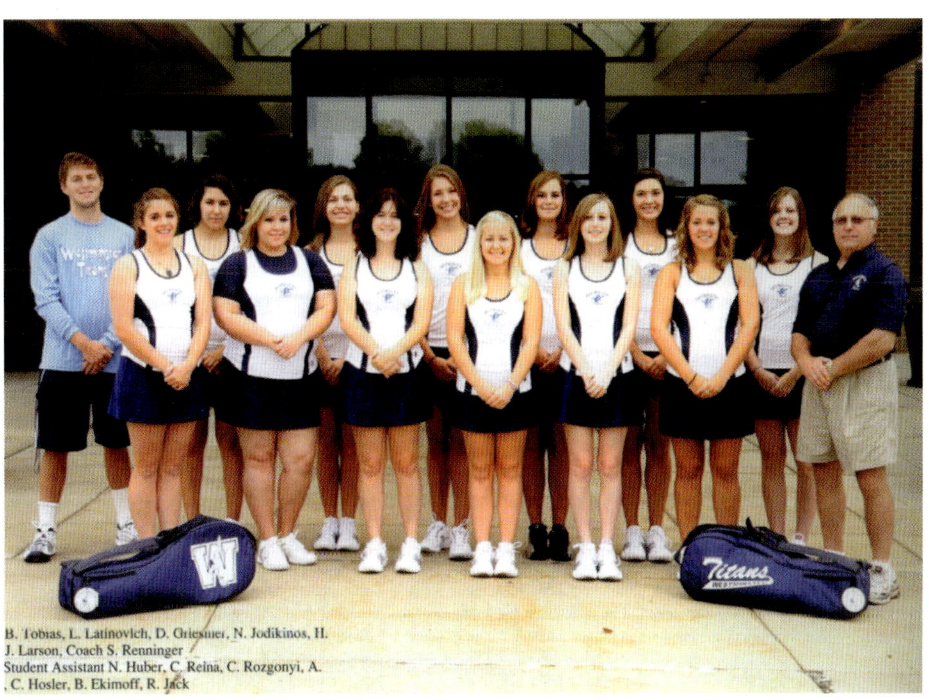

B. Tobias, L. Latinovich, D. Griesmer, N. Jodikinos, H.
J. Larson, Coach S. Renninger
Student Assistant N. Huber, C. Reina, C. Rozgonyi, A.
, C. Hosler, B. Ekimoff, R. Jack

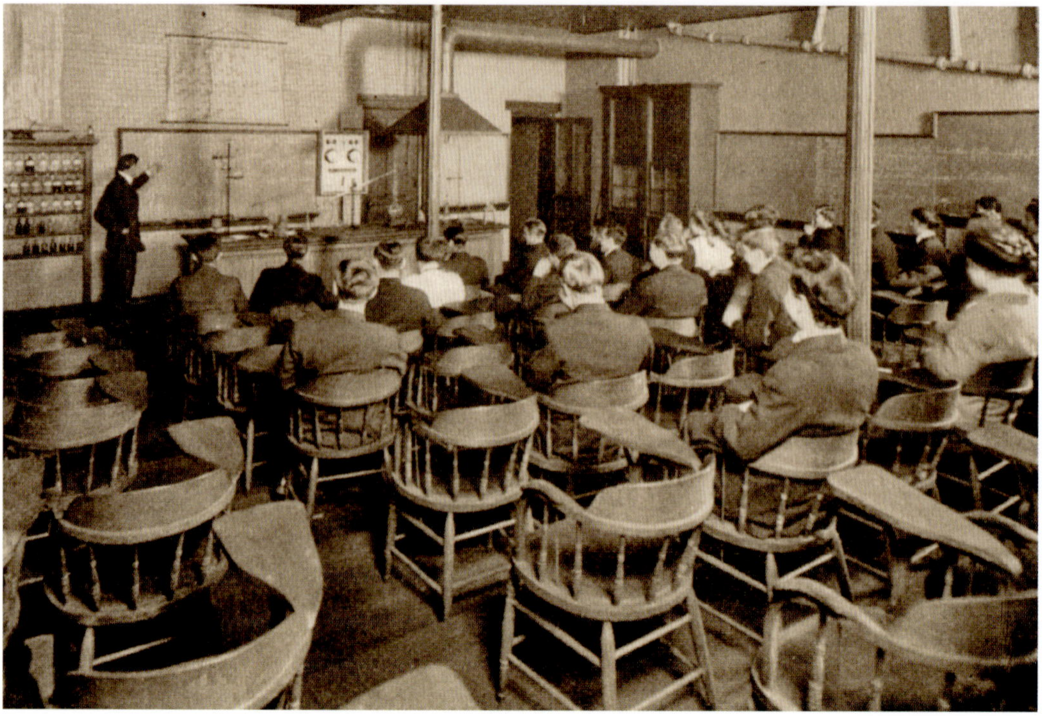

OLD MAIN CLASSROOMS: Compare the typical classrooms in Old Main in 1913 to the early twenty-first century Old Main classrooms with smart boards and computers. The black chalkboards have been replaced with white dry-erase boards and smart boards. Notice too the difference in students' seats.

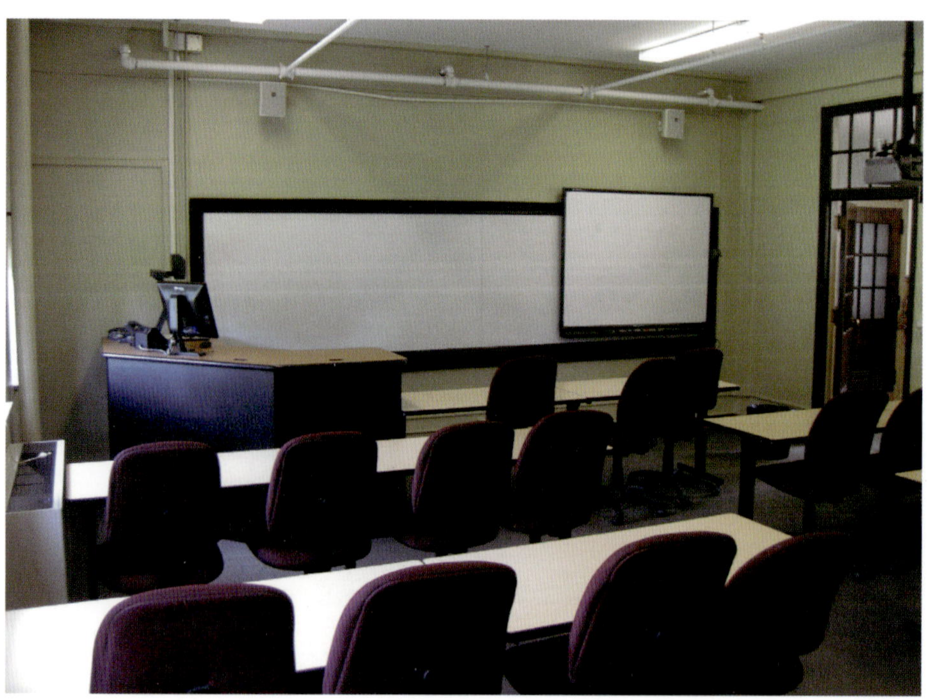

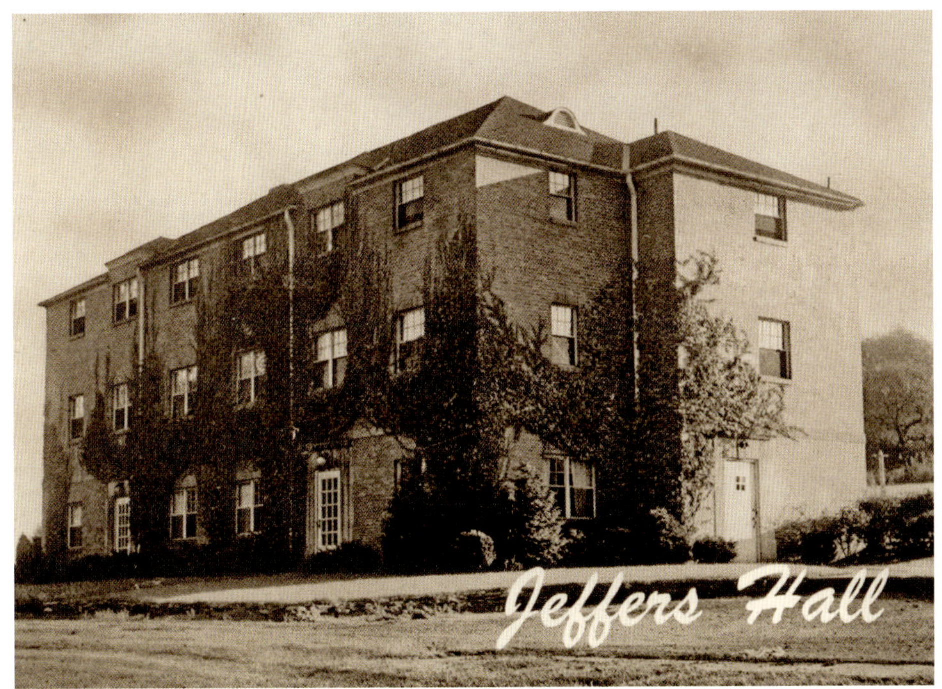

JEFFERS HALL: Built as a college dormitory in 1940, shortly before World War II. In 1943-44, the US Army used the building as a part of the nation's war effort to house cadets in the US Army Student Training Program while they attended regular college classes. This program ended in March 1944 three months before D-Day. The building was suddenly once again a civilian Westminster College dorm. Here's how it looked in 1947. Jeffers Hall, in 2014, is used as a women's dormitory.

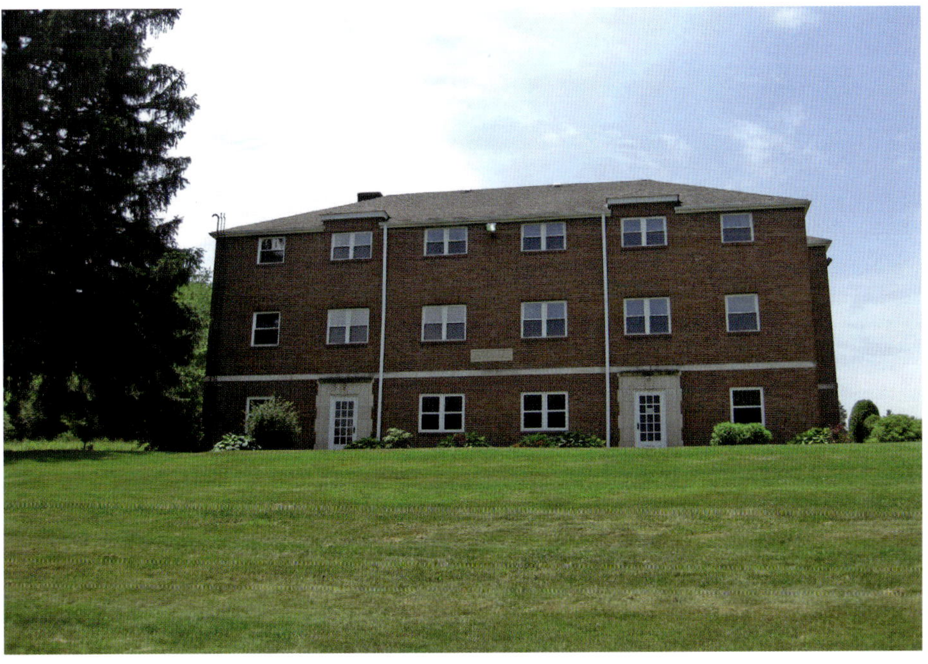

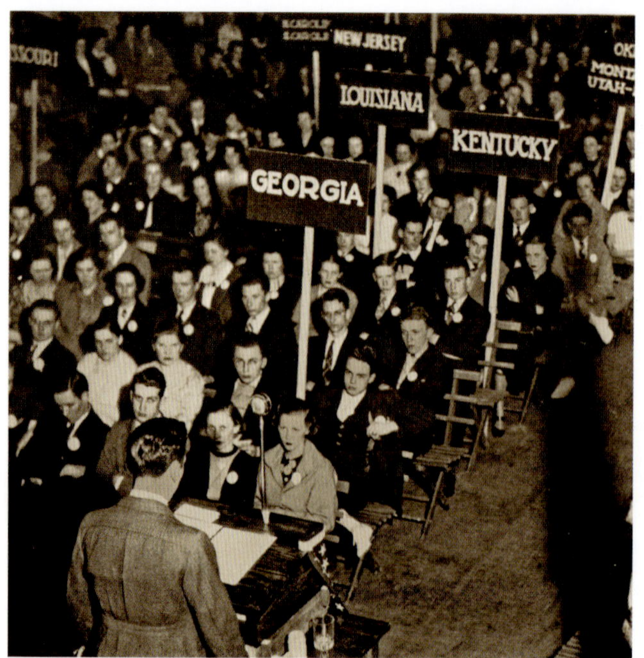

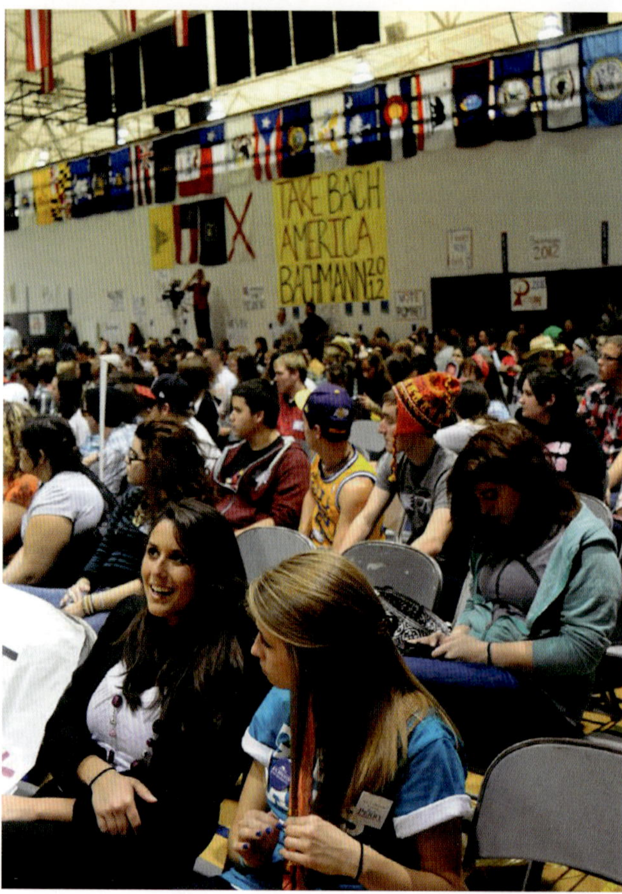

MOCK CONVENTION: Student interest in national politics was keen in 1936 and led to the college's first mock convention as shown here. Westminster continues this tradition in 2014, the third oldest mock convention in the nation, holding a mock presidential election every four years. Over the years, students have nominated candidates such as: Herbert Hoover, Robert Taft, Dwight Eisenhower, Adlai Stevenson, Richard Nixon, Jimmy Carter and George Bush. In modern times, the student dress at the mock convention is less formal, as can be seen in these photos, but the interest and enthusiasm continue as much as ever.

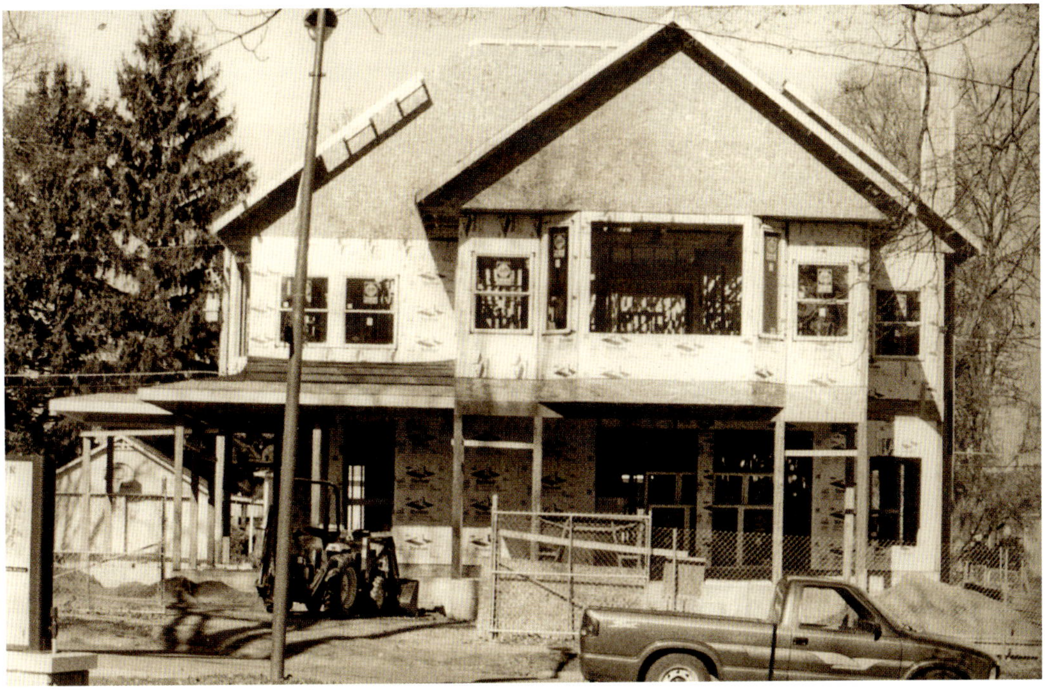

REMICK ADMISSIONS HOUSE: Named after a former president, Oscar Remick, this was completed in 1999 at a cost of $1.4 million. It is shown above during its construction phase. A grant of $500,000 covered a third of the cost. In 2014, the 5,100 square-foot Remick House serves as the center for the college's admissions offices and financial aid department.

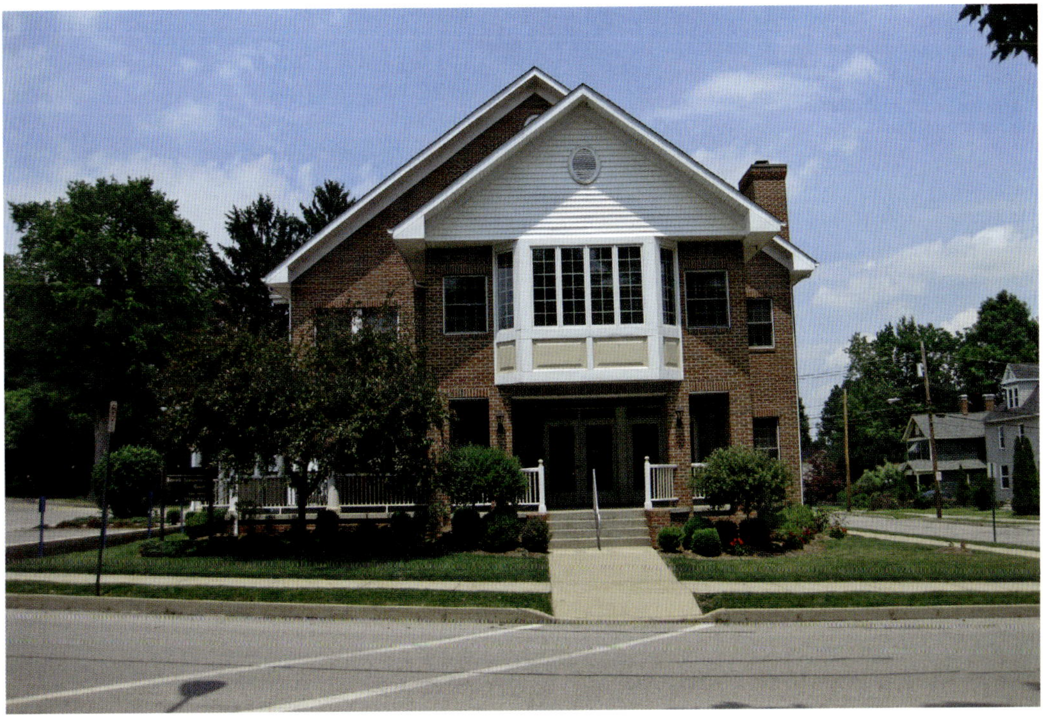

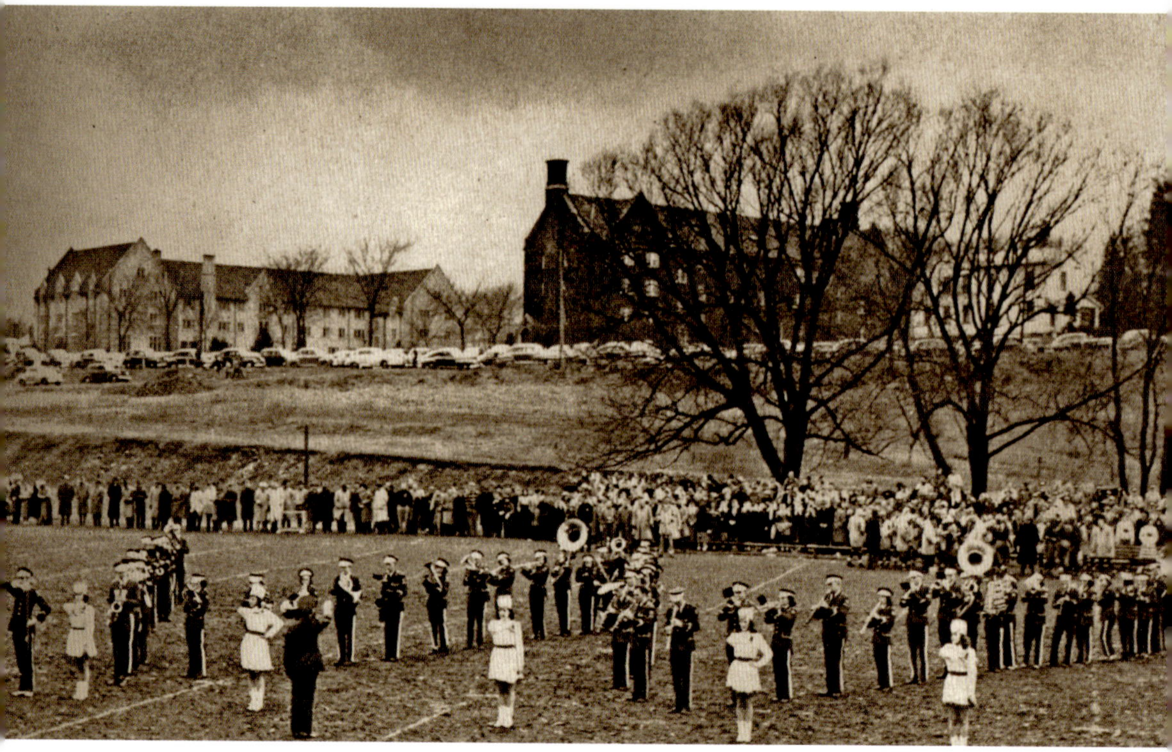

MARCHING BAND: The Titans' Marching Band has come a long way from the 1950s half-time performances, as shown above, to the more elaborate and thrilling presentations of the 2010s. Tradition continues with the band's blue and white uniforms. Homecoming festivities would not be complete without the band's ritual half-time entertainment. Note the new uniforms in the photo taken at the Burry Stadium, shown after its remodeling in 2001, with its new press box and refurbished bleachers.

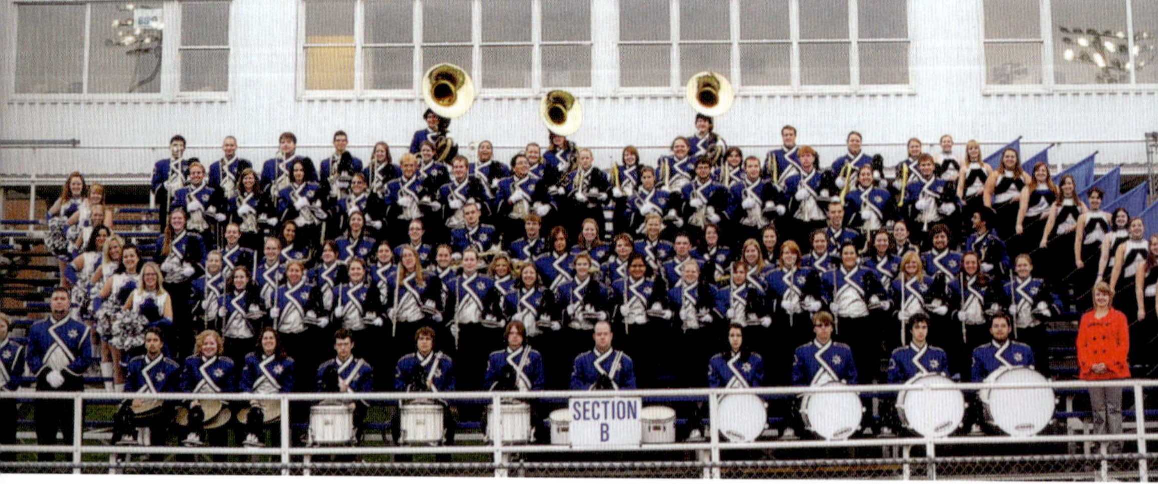

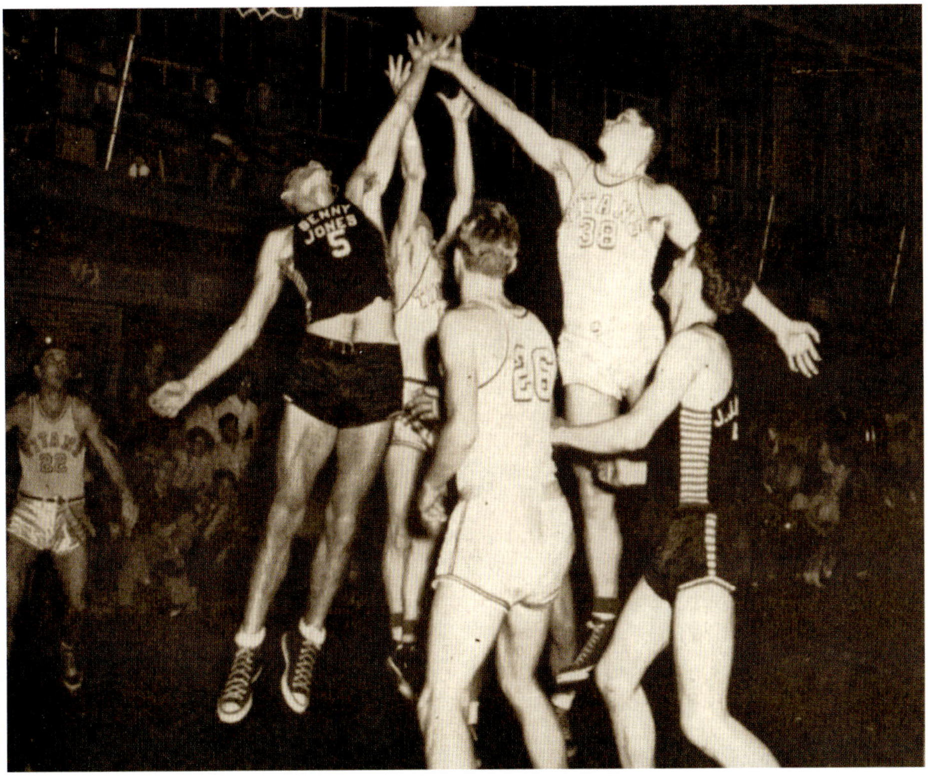

Men's Basketball: Started at Westminster in 1897 and met with much success. December 1934 saw the Titans make national basketball history by playing in the first collegiate double-header at Madison Square Garden when they upset the highly touted St. John's University. In 1961-1962 the Titans were rated the number one small college team in the nation by both wire services. The Titans also hold the honor of the all-time winningest program in NAIA history with 1,299 wins. The uniforms on the teams here are over sixty years apart and still show the high flying leaps of the Titans. Note the change in the length of the shorts.

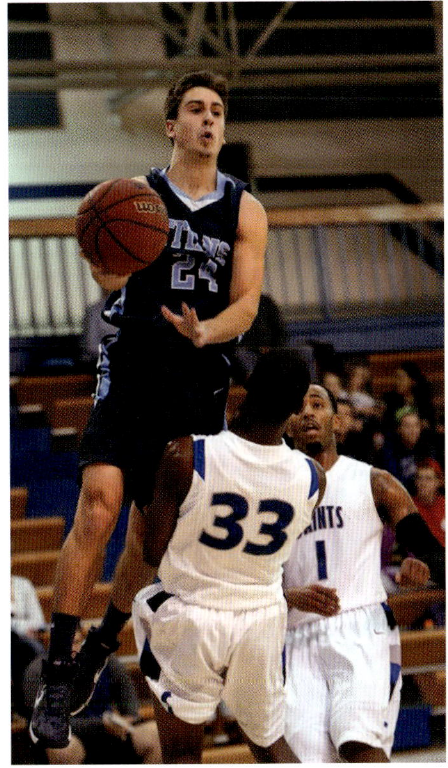

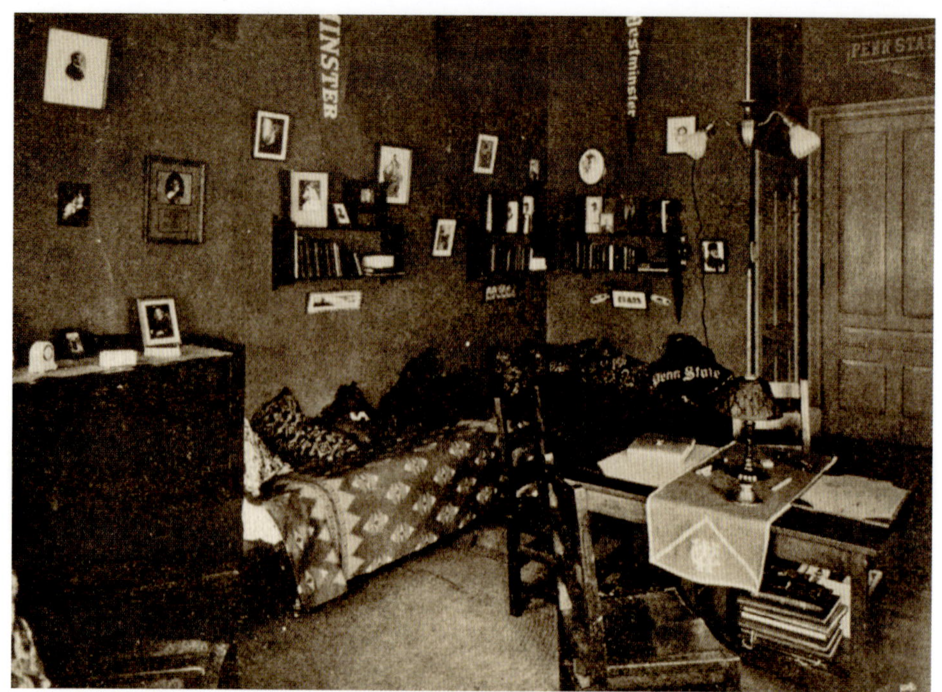

WOMEN'S DORM ROOMS: This 1919 photo of a women's dorm room in Hillside Dormitory can be compared to a women's dorm room in Shaw Hall in 2014. From the oldest dorm to the newest dorm room, the biggest change is the TV prominent in the middle of the room. Students still continue to decorate their rooms with their prized photos, posters, lamps, chairs, and favorite bed spreads.

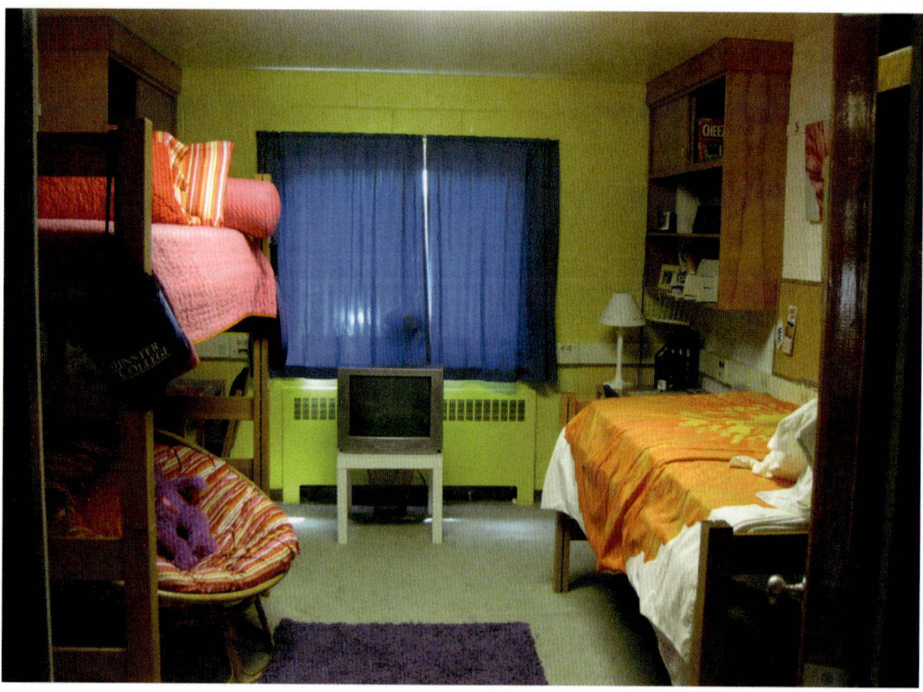

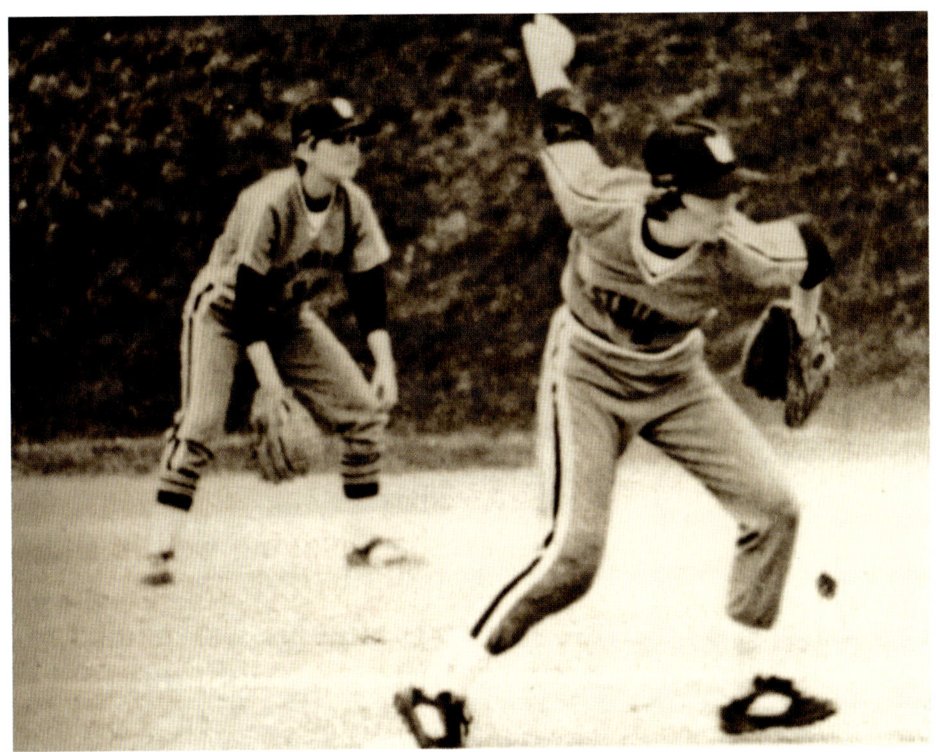

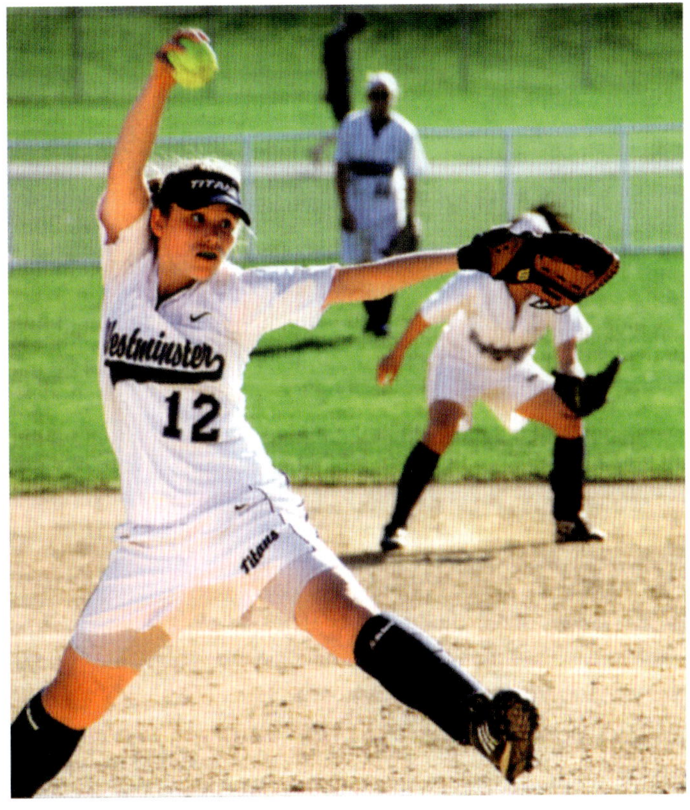

SOFTBALL: The pitcher in 1981 is about to let go a fast one as is the pitcher on the 2010 team. Softball started at Westminster in 1980 and since then has accumulated a 62.0% winning record. Westminster joined the Presidents' Athletic Conference in 2000 and became eligible for the PAC title and all-PAC awards in 2002-03. Since then, the softball team members have won numerous All-PAC, NFCA Division III All-Central Region and ECAC Division III South Region All-Star awards.

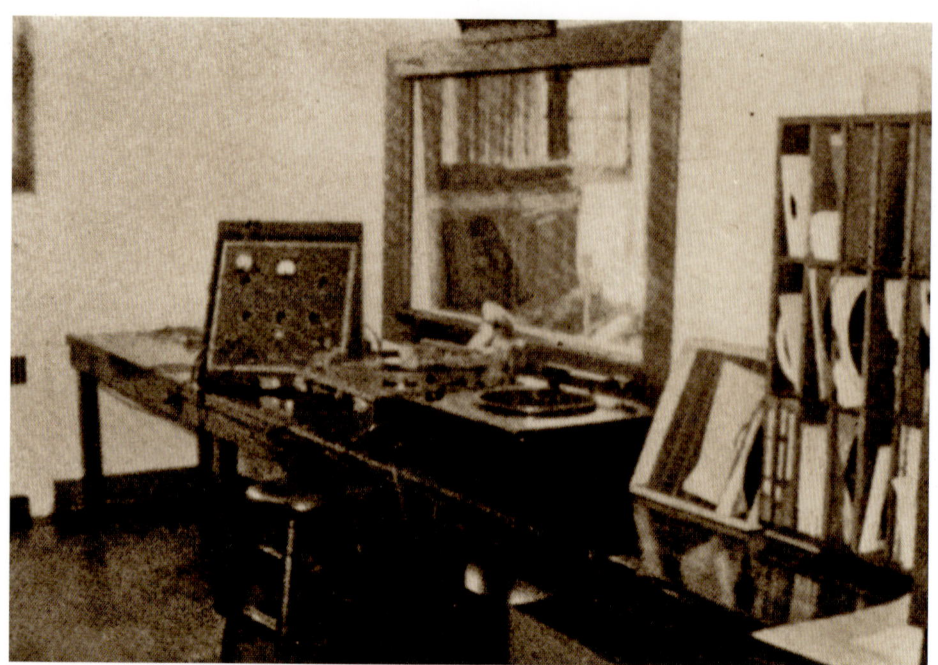

College Radio Station: Westminster College students started broadcasting several times weekly for a few hours from a New Castle radio station in 1938. The radio station, shown above, is the college's broadcasting center in 1947. By 1958, the college broadcasts from a new AM station – WCRW – eight hours a day. In 1968, WKPS-FM became Westminster's first licensed broadcasting station on campus. The college station in 2014, shown below, is WWNW-FM at 88.9 FM and is on 24/7, playing students' favorite music. The station also broadcasts the college's major athletic contests. The radio station is located in Thompson-Clark Hall.

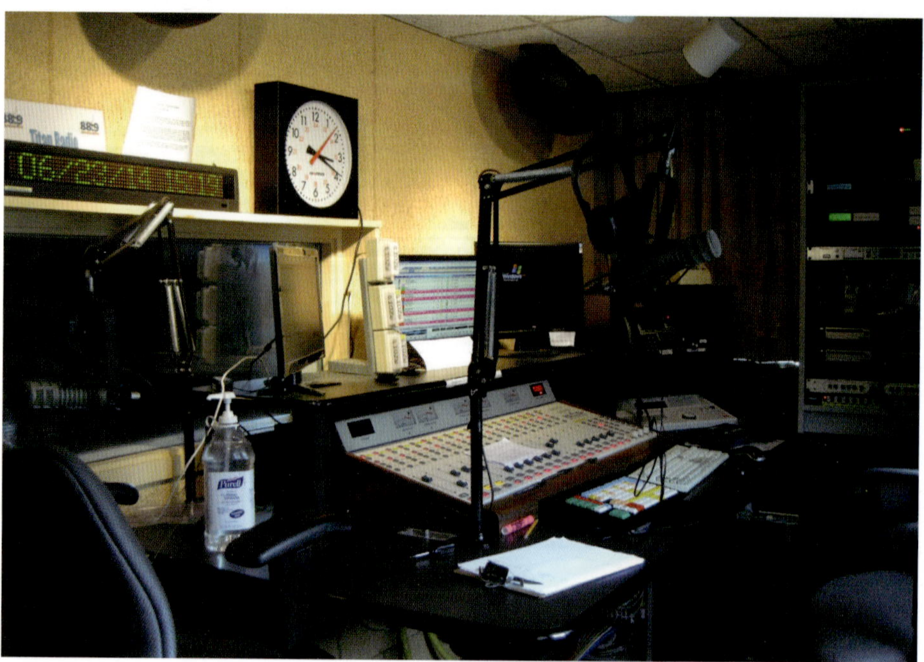

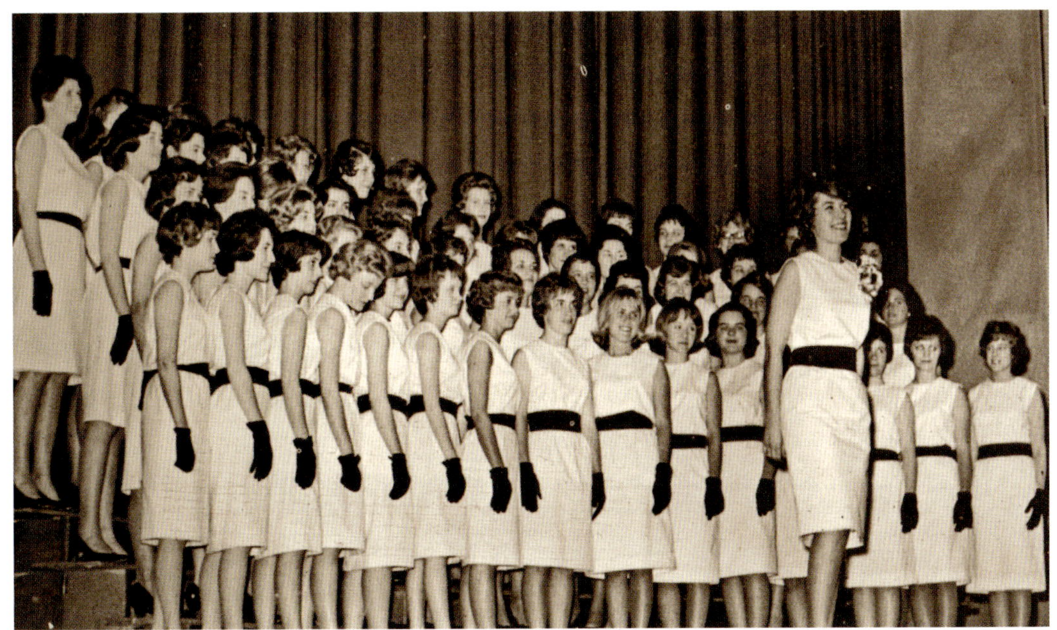

SING AND SWING: An annual tradition for sororities and fraternities at Westminster. Each spring, at the end of Greek Week, the sisters and brothers put on a show of songs and dance. Each fraternity and sorority performs a five-minute dance to a medley of songs. Tickets are sold to the public, and all money received is donated to charity. The event is a crowd pleaser. The 1963 and the 2011 photos here show the sororities performing at Sing 'N Swing. The 2014 Sing and Swing event raised $11,600 for charity.

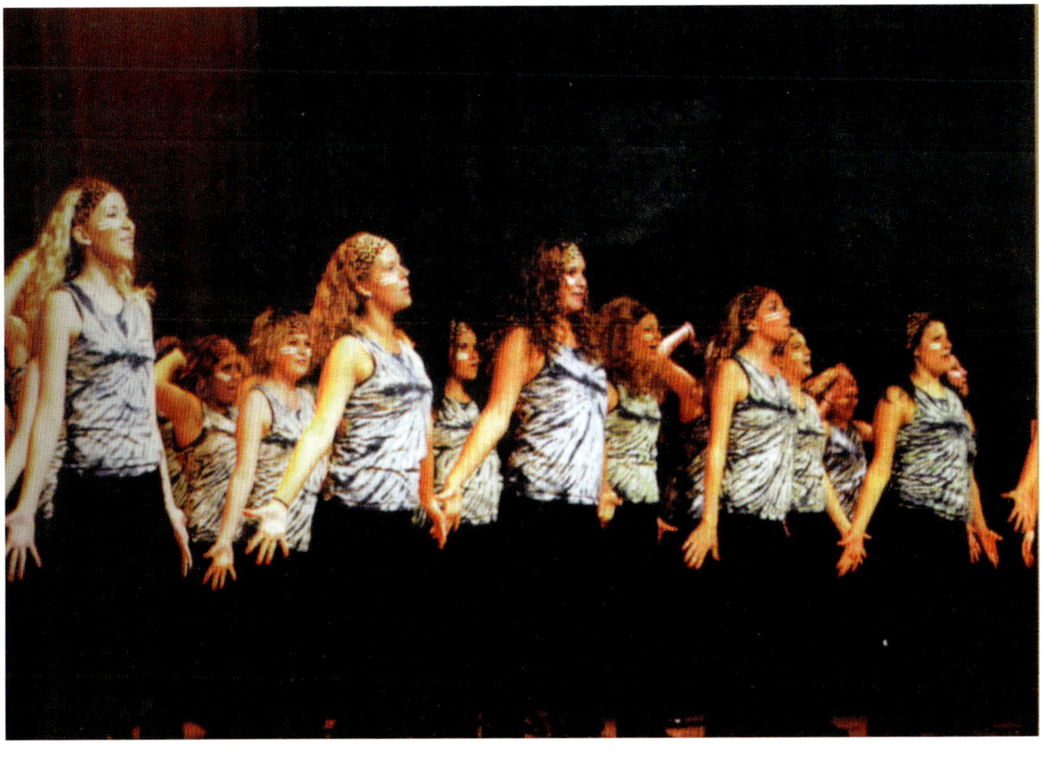

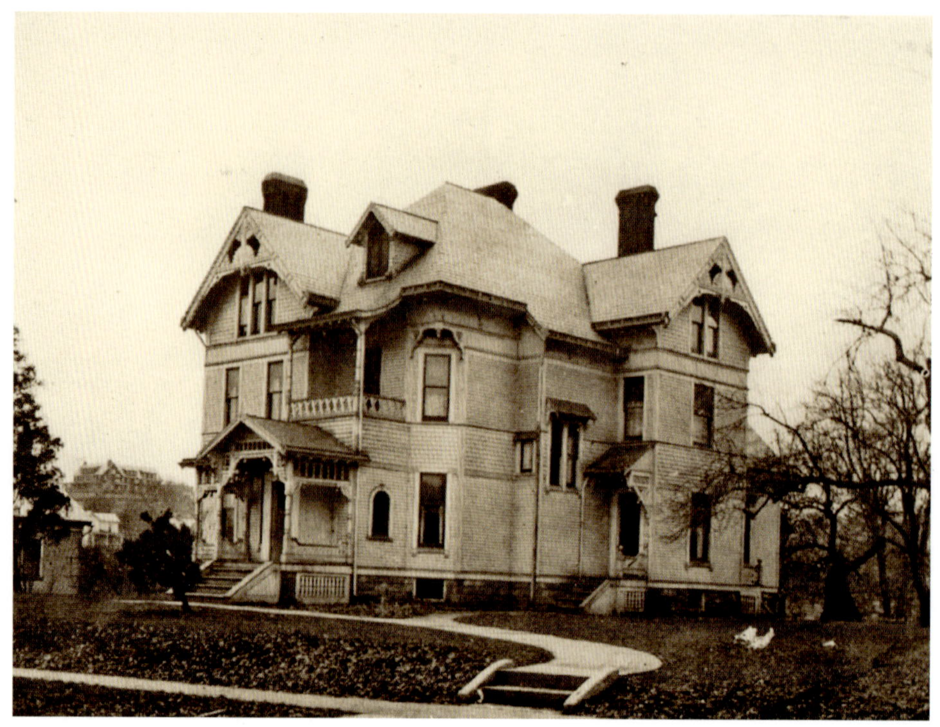

THOMPSON HOUSE: Located on the west side of South Market Street, diagonally across from the library, the wooden frame building was first leased by the college in 1920 to handle overflowing enrollment and housed women students. Later, the Thompson House accommodated sororities. In 2014, it houses only junior and senior women students.

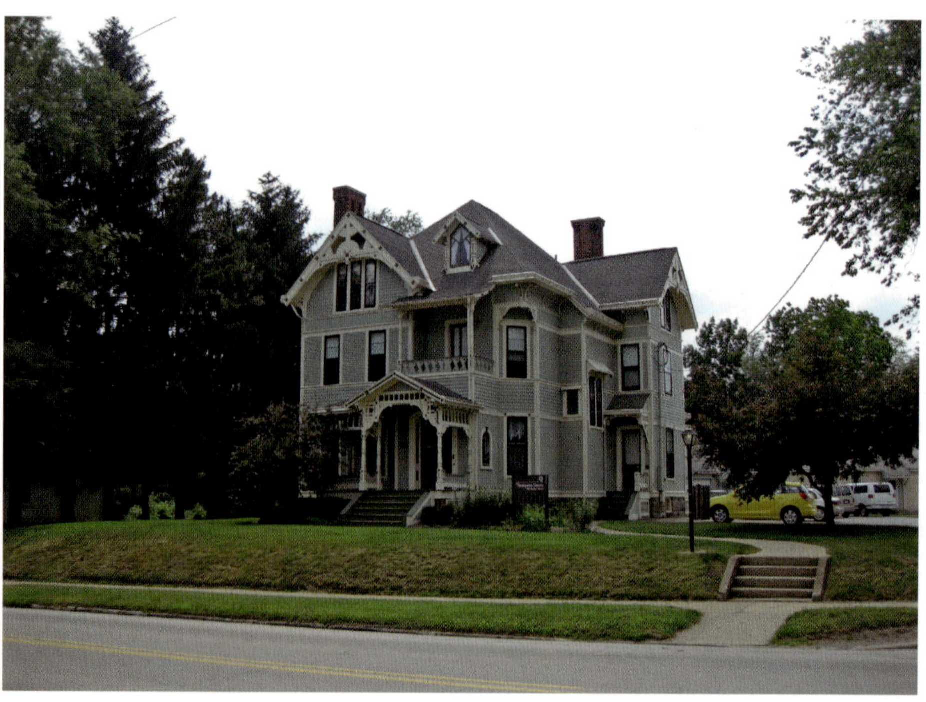

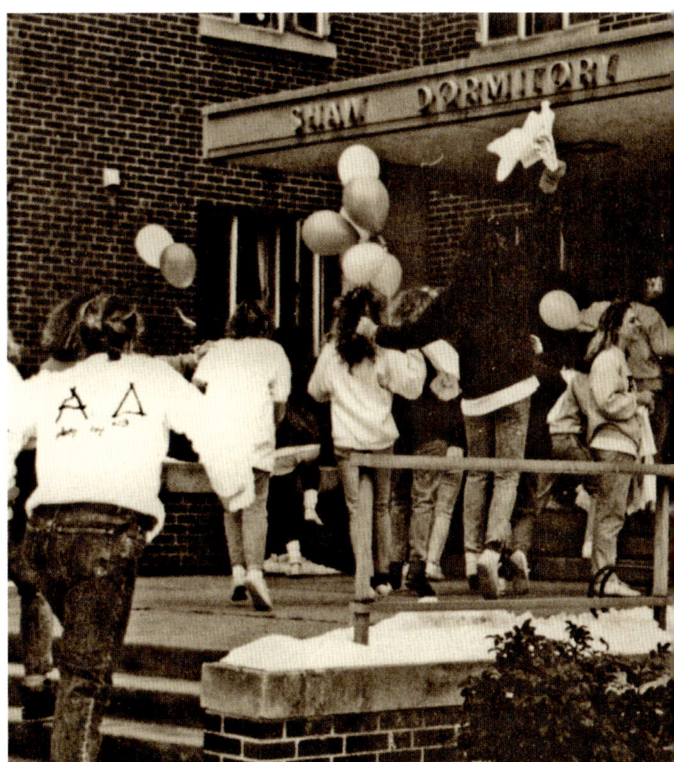

Greek Sorority Rush: Right after returning from winter break in early January, women rush for sorority membership in one of Westminster's five sororities: Alpha Gamma Delta, Kappa Delta, Phi Mu, Sigma Kappa, and Zeta Tau Alpha. The 1989 photo, left, shows "Girls Pick-up Day" where they are matched with their sorority. This event used to be called "Pledge Day." The 2013 photo below shows this same event being held in Orr Auditorium.

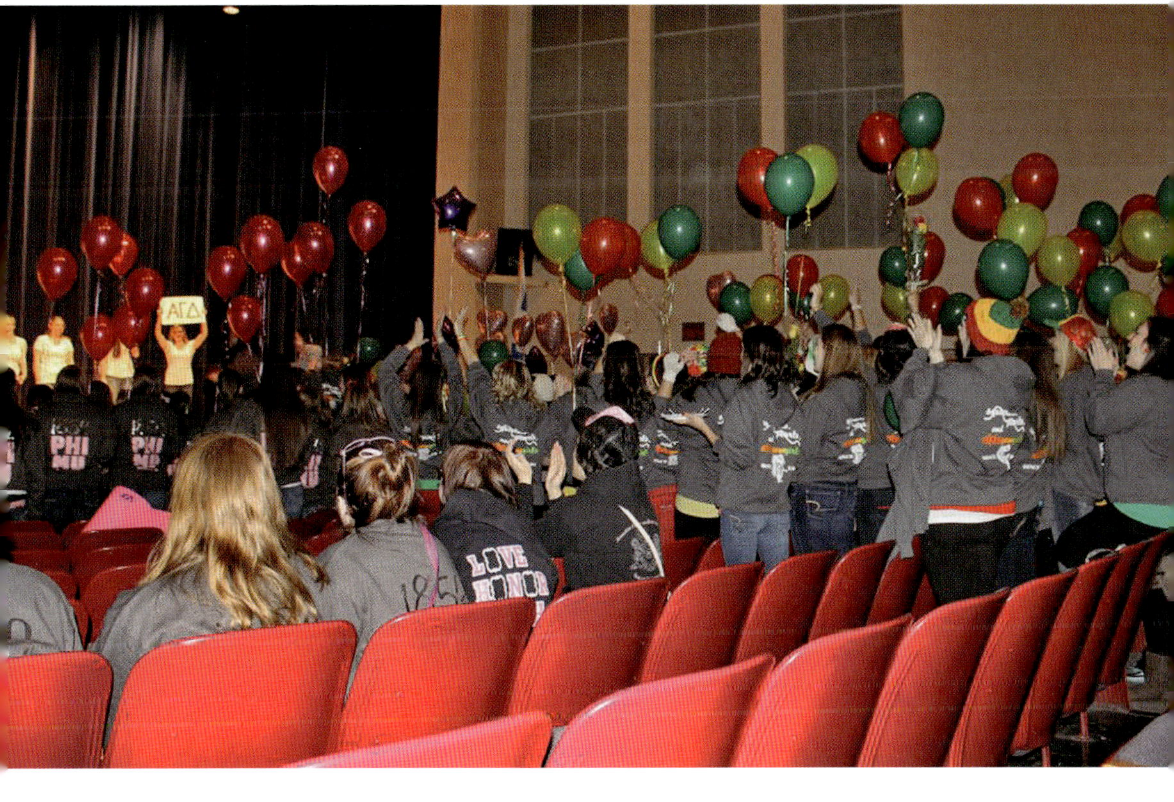

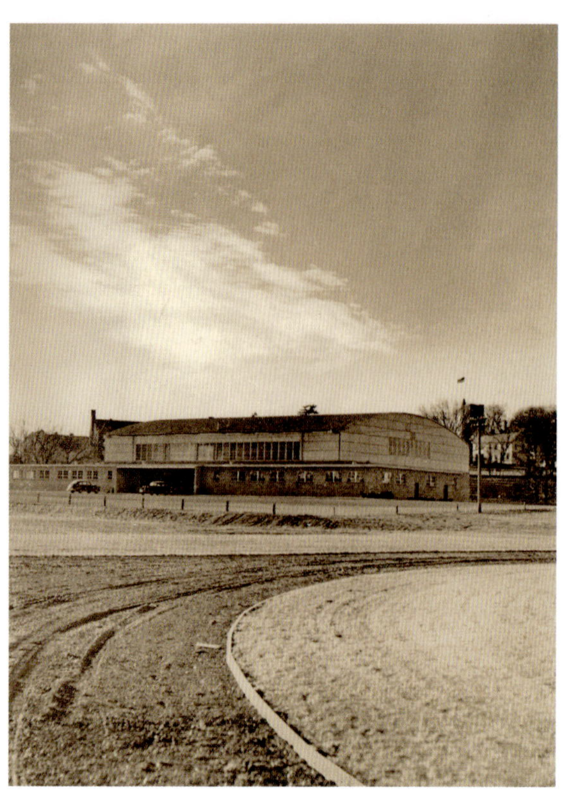

MEMORIAL FIELD HOUSE: Built in 1950 and completed in 1951 as a memorial to those who served and died in the two world wars. Built at a cost of $250,000 in 1950 dollars, it could seat 3,500 for basketball games and 5,000 when set up as an auditorium. The new field house saw the Titans play Geneva College for its first game. The field house reflects many renovations and additions made in 1999 and the early 2000s.

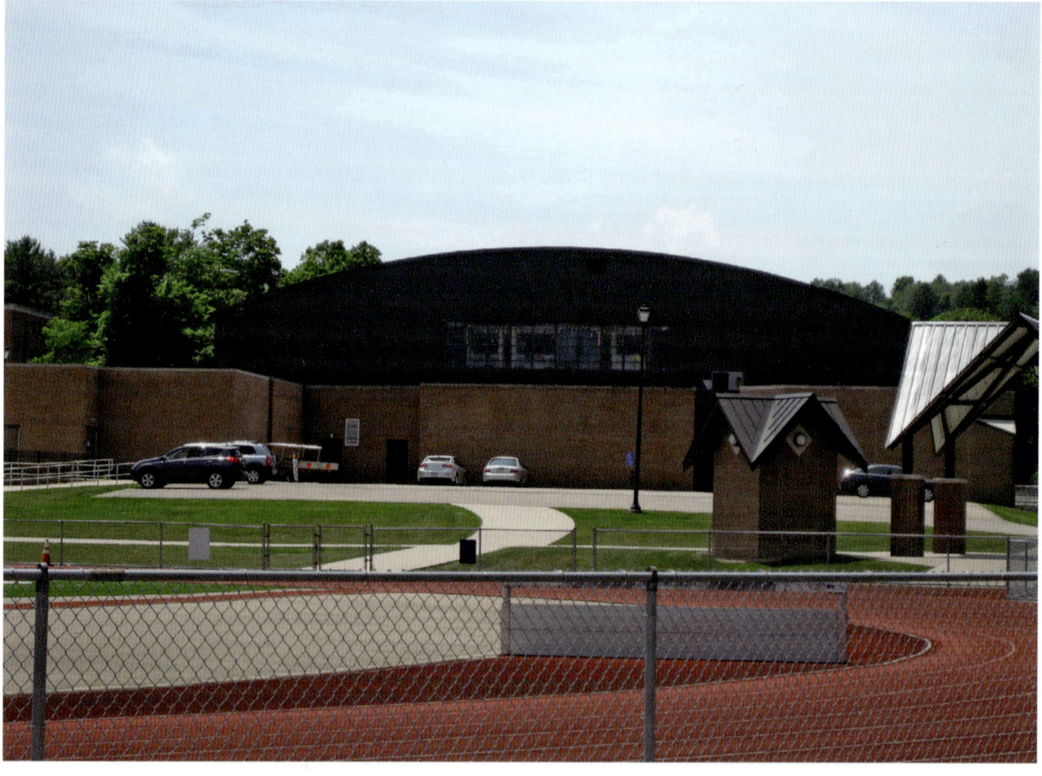

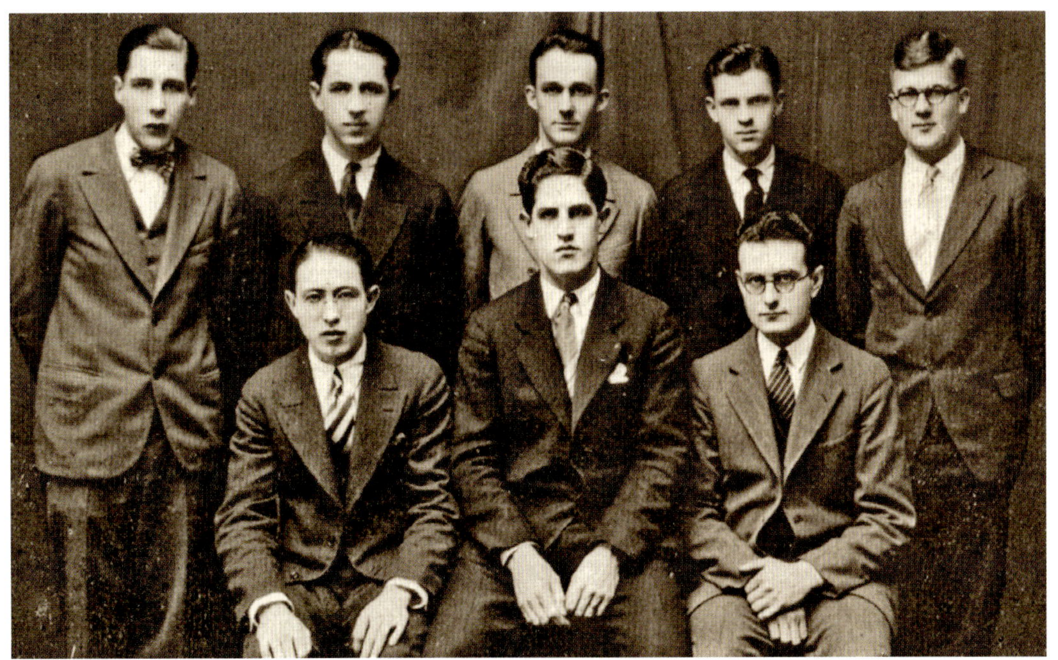

INTER-FRATERNITY COUNCIL: This organization coordinates all fraternity activities at the college. Participation prerequisites include membership in one of the campus fraternities and a minimum GPA of 2.0. The 1927 IFC and the 2011 IFC show a significant increase in active members and a significant change in attire, a sign of the less formal dress of the 2010s.

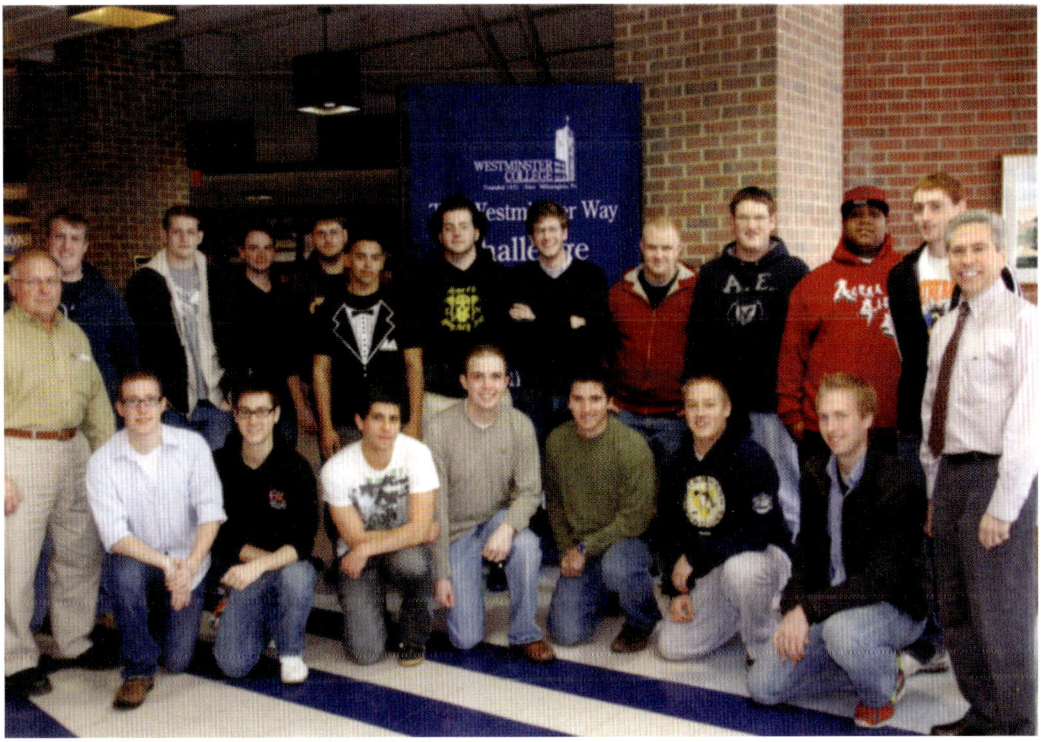

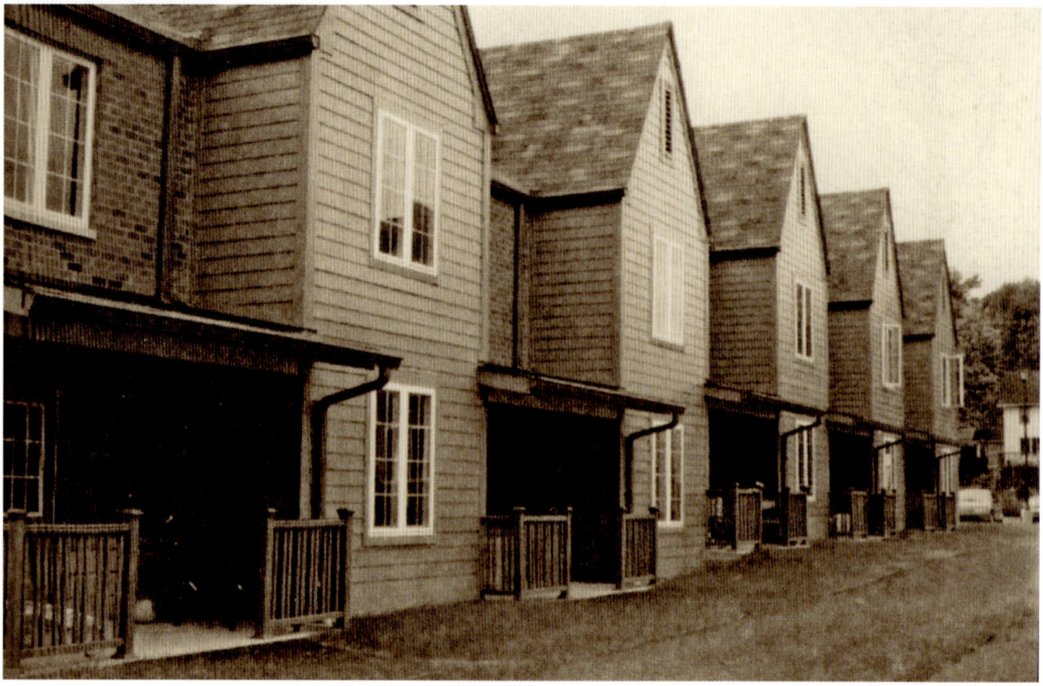

BERLIN VILLAGE: Opened in 2006, Berlin Village, is a unique feature of early twenty-first century student living on campus, where seniors apply for townhouse living instead of dormitory rooms. A complex of more than fifteen units overlook Brittain Lake, with each townhouse having four bedrooms, two baths, a living room, a kitchen, and laundry facilities. From its opening in 2006 to eight years later, the townhouses haven't changed much. Berlin Village is named after George Berlin, a trustee and generous benefactor to the college.

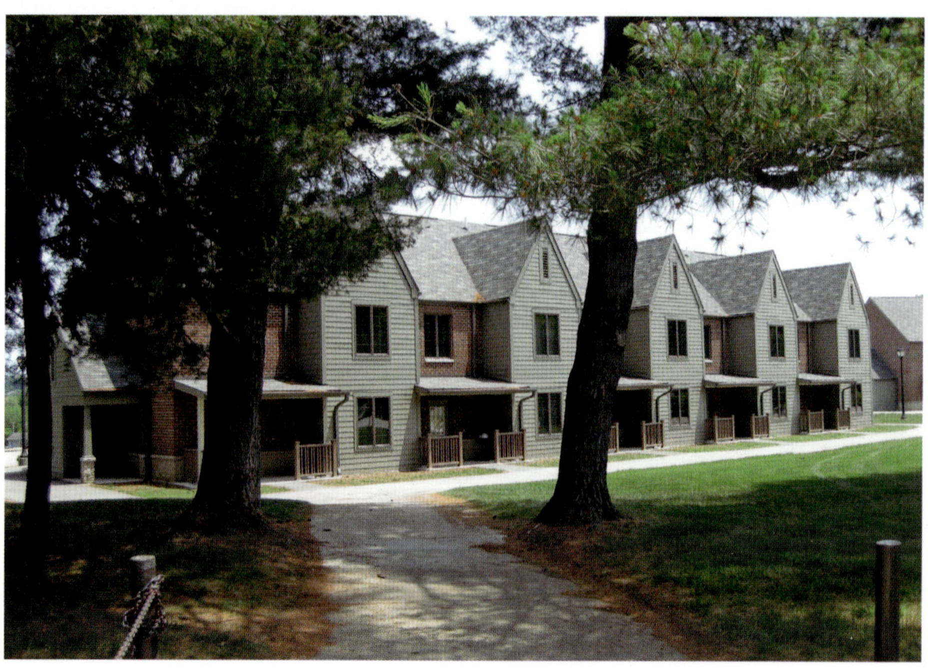

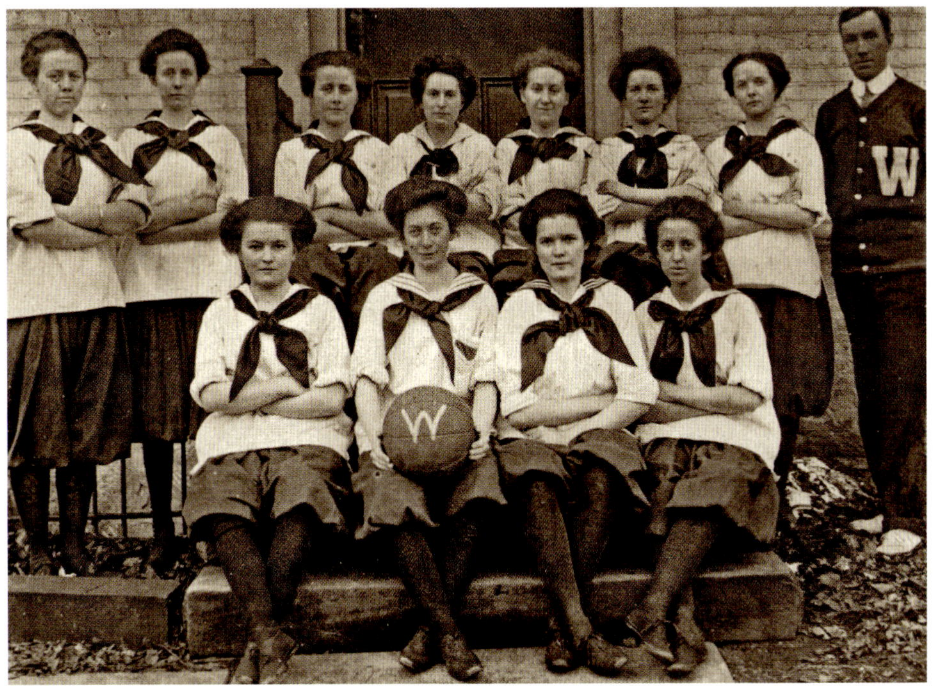

LADY TITANS BASKETBALL TEAMS: Long before the equal rights movement, Westminster College had equal rights for all its students, male and female. The 1910 photo, above, of the Lady Titans Basketball Team was the earliest photo of girls' basketball that we could find in the college's archives. Compare the uniforms from the 1910 team to that of the 2011 team. Uniforms for the Lady Titans certainly have changed.

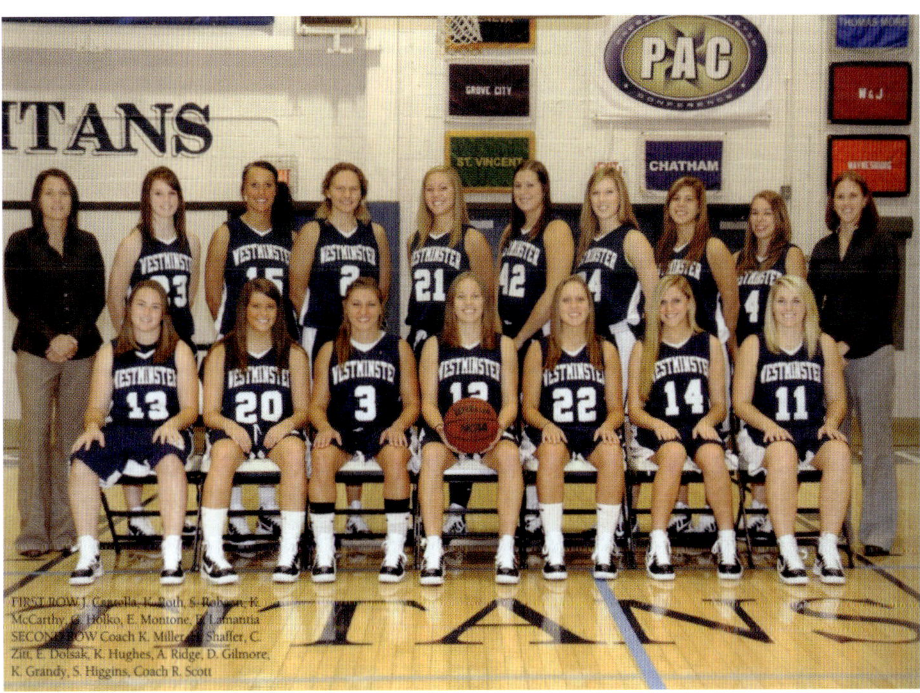

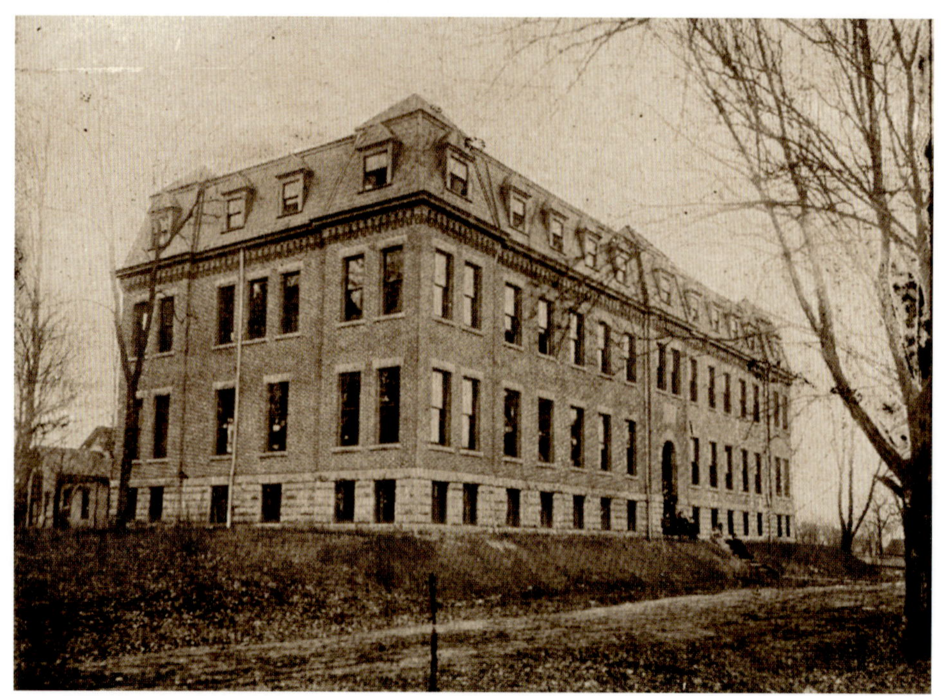

THOMPSON-CLARK HALL: Built and occupied in 1894 as the college's first science building. It was a gift of two men: Professor S.R. Thompson of the college's science department and W.A. Clark, prominent New Wilmington citizen. The building is the second oldest on campus after Hillside (1885). In 2001, $3 million in renovations brought new life to Thompson-Clark Hall, which houses the English, public relations, theatre, art, modern language, and communications departments.

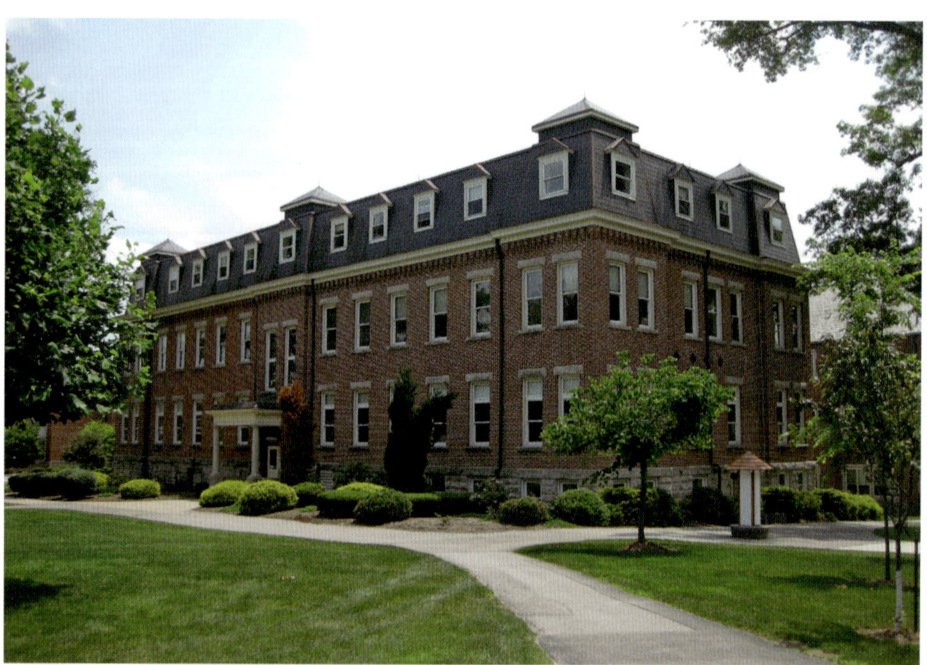

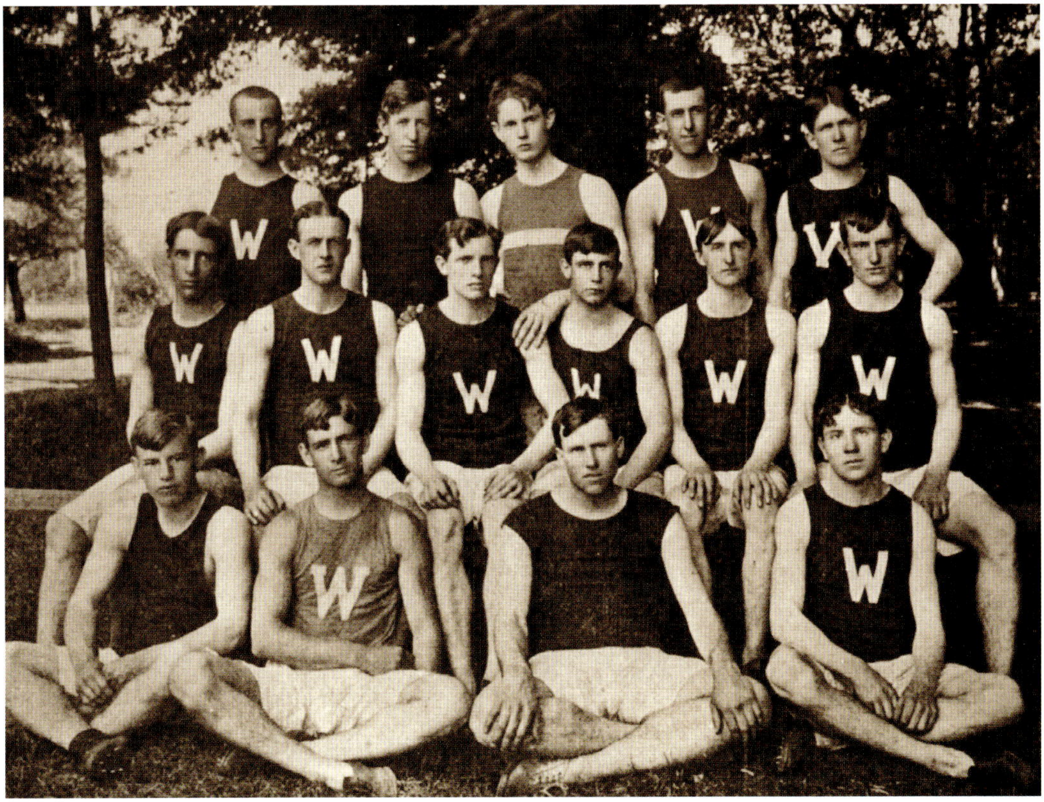

MEN'S TRACK: Can be traced all the way back to 1902 when Westminster track's relay team captured the mile event at the National Intercollegiate Field Meet in Philadelphia. The oldest track team photo on record was from 1904, shown above, and shown below is the college's 2010 track team. The men's track team still competes against the college teams of Oberlin, Mount Union. Juniata and Kenyon.

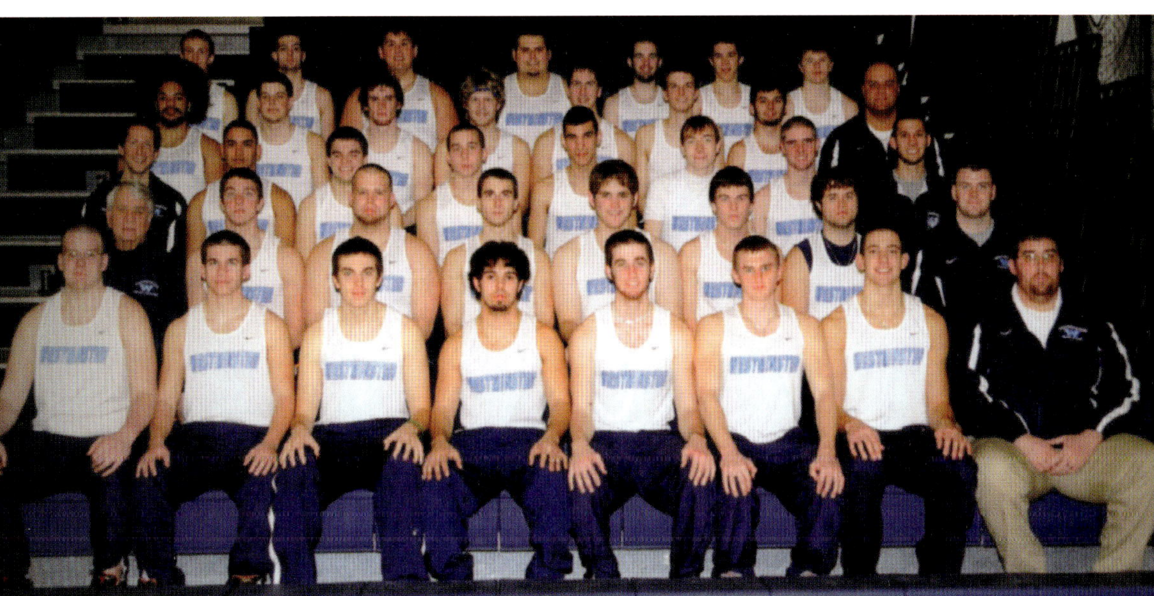

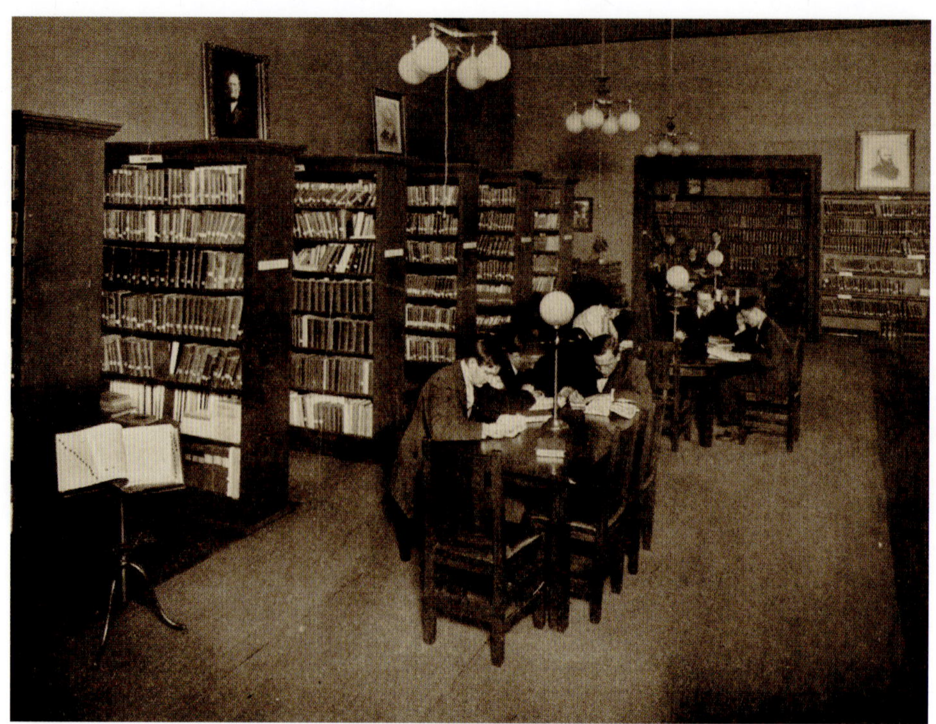

McGILL LIBRARY: Students, above, are using the library in 1930 to study and do research. The photo below shows students in 2014, still using the library for study and research, but, in modern times, students also use their lap-tops or use the computers in the library for accessing internet information.

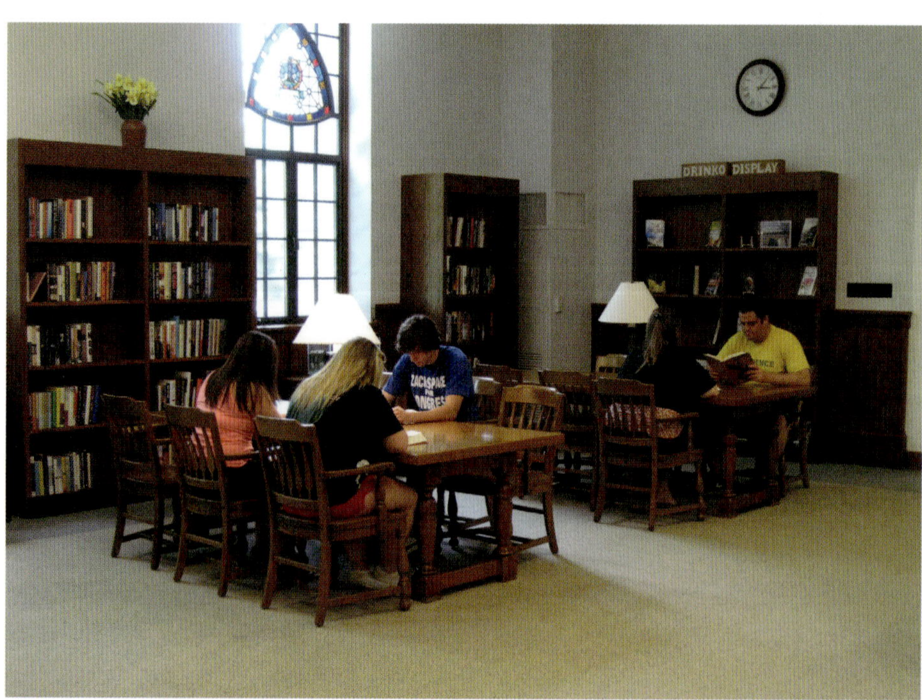

COLLEGE ID: A student ID card – complete with photo and student ID number – have been the norm for many years. Here, the 1982 student ID shows little change compared to the 2014-15 Titan Card. Student ID cards are still needed to take books from the library, eat in the cafeteria, enter sporting events, and – the biggest change – to access student housing-dorms by using the ID as a "swipe-card" to open the dorm's security doors.

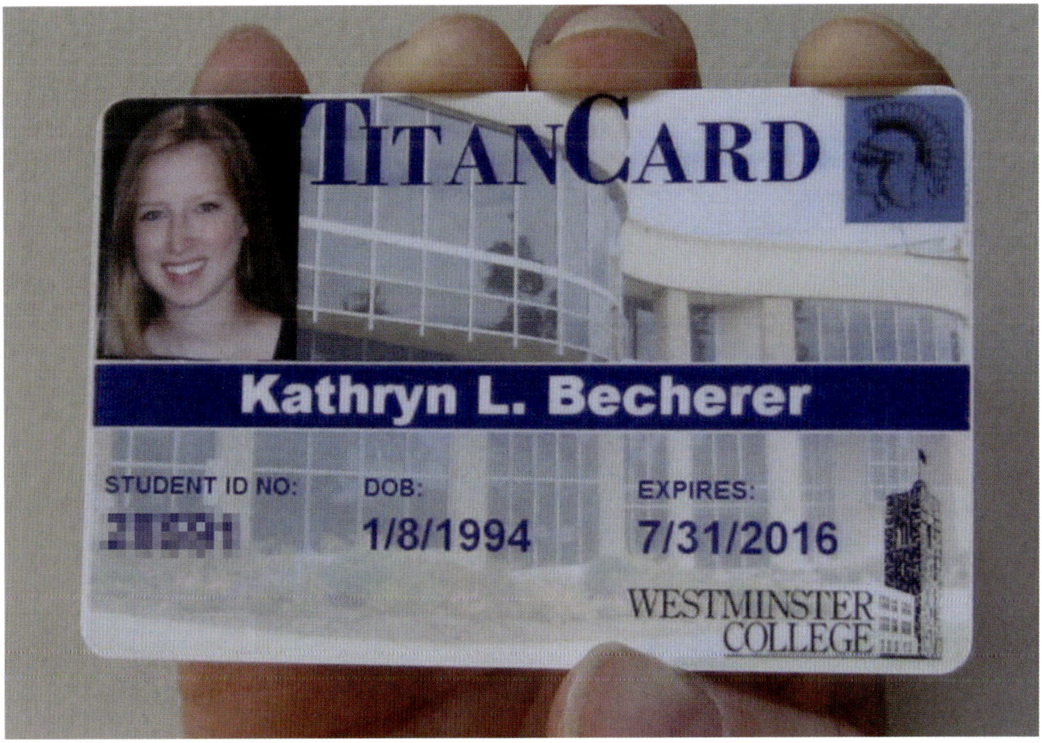

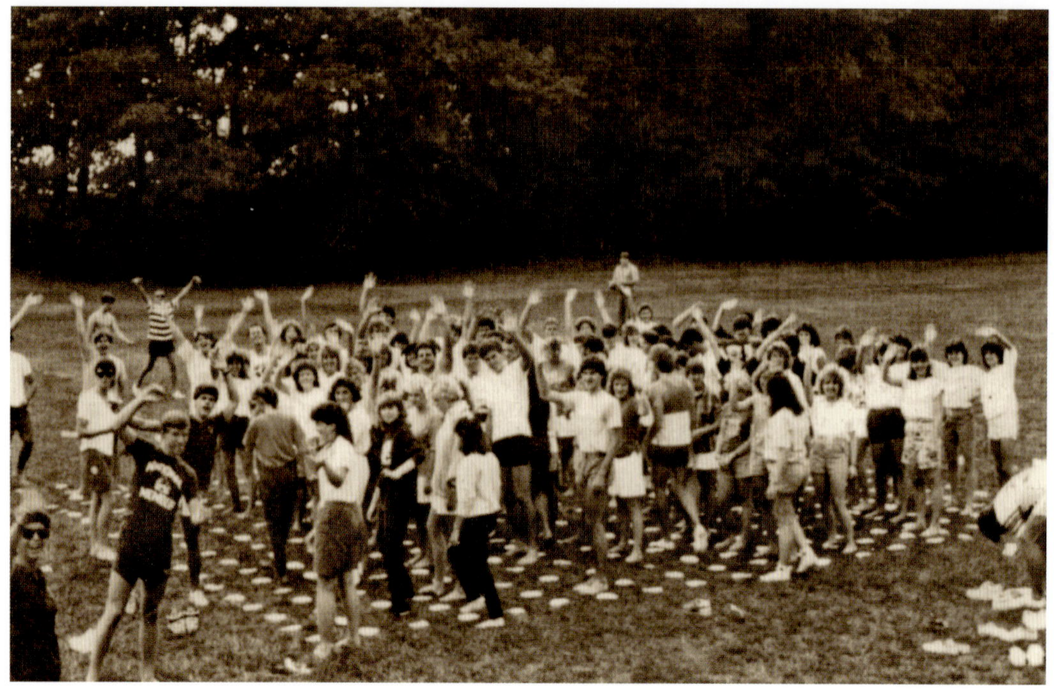

Fresh Start: During the freshmen orientation week, the college has a "fresh start" experience for new students where they meet their fellow classmates and get orientated to campus. The students enjoy picnics, attend information sessions, participate in skits, and ice-breaker activities like the one shown above in 1987 and one shown below in 2013.

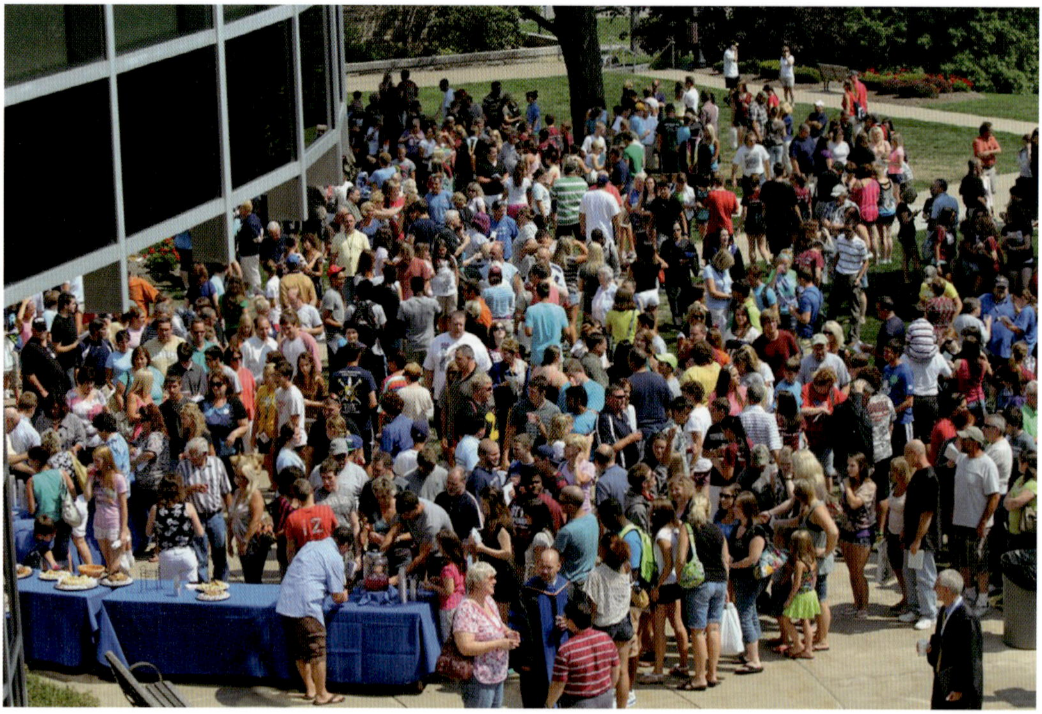

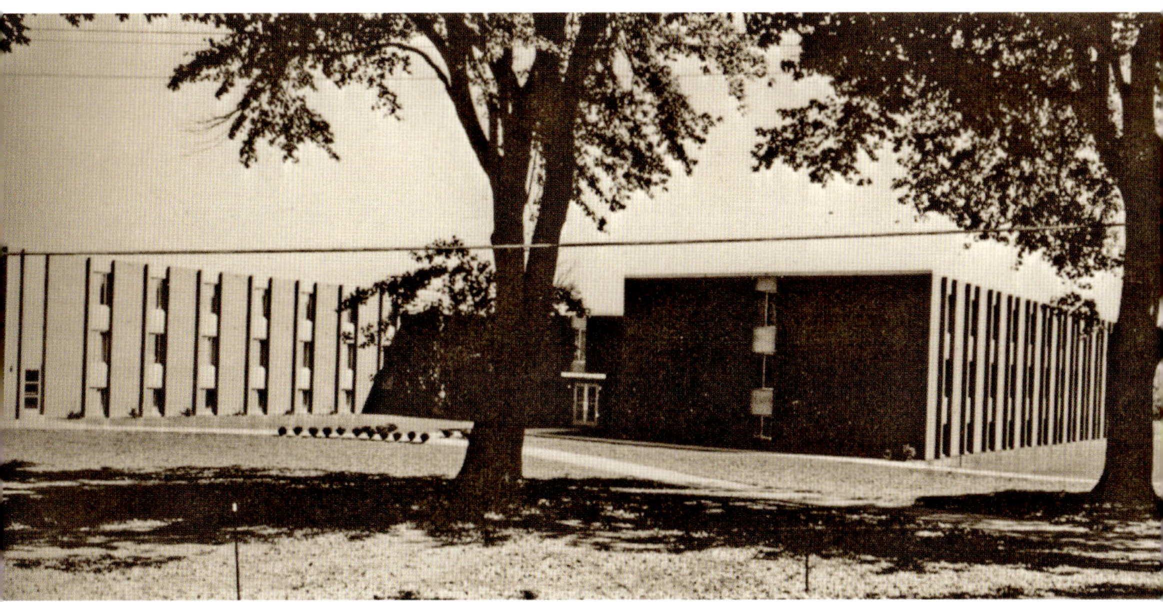

EICHENAUER HALL: This men's dorm was completed in 1966 and was named for John Eichenauer, a former Trustee and generous benefactor to the college. It faces South Market Street. It was built at a cost of $930,000 in 1965 dollars to house 260 men. The top photo shows how it looked in the late 1960s. The photo below shows how Eichenaur Hall looks in 2014, as it still serves as a men's dorm.

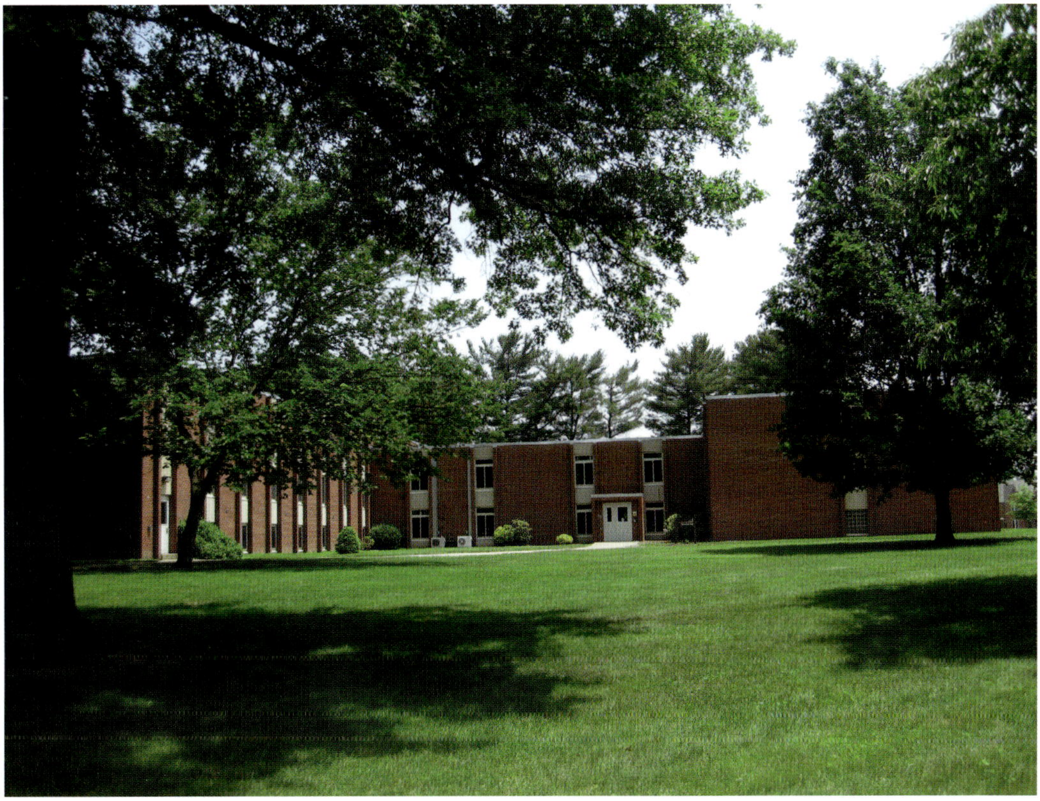

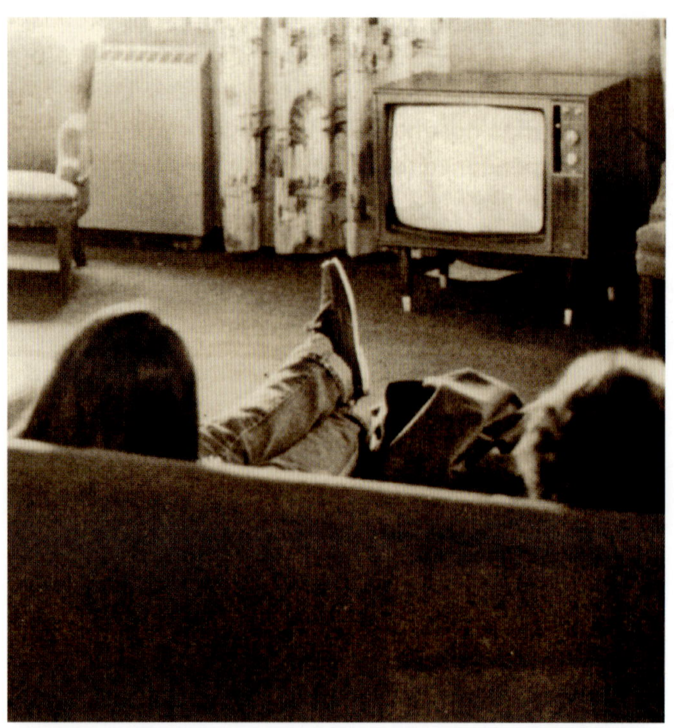

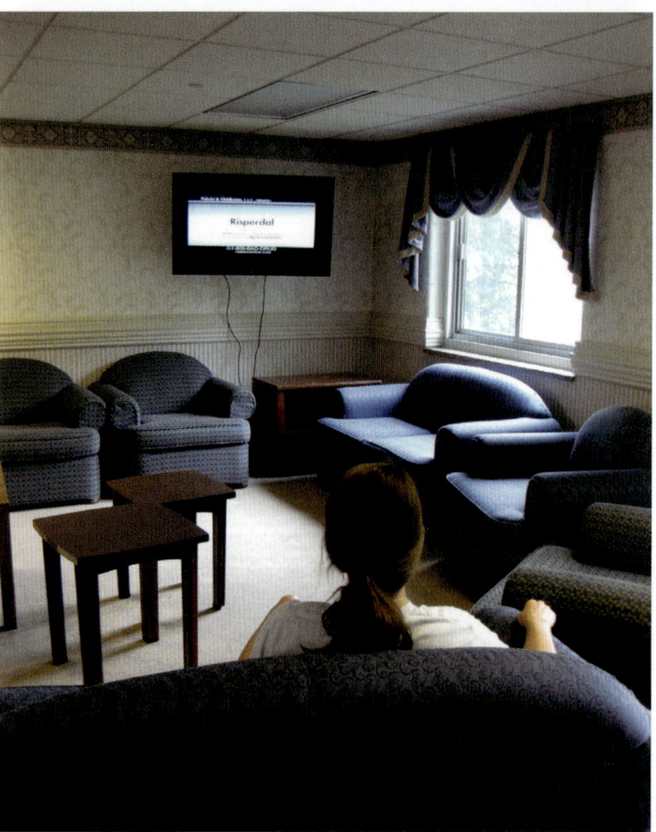

WOMEN'S DORM LIFE: Some things never change like watching TV in the lobby at Shaw Hall in 1982 and watching TV from the same spot in 2014. Only, in the more recent image, the furniture is newer and softer and the TV is a flat screen with cable channels.

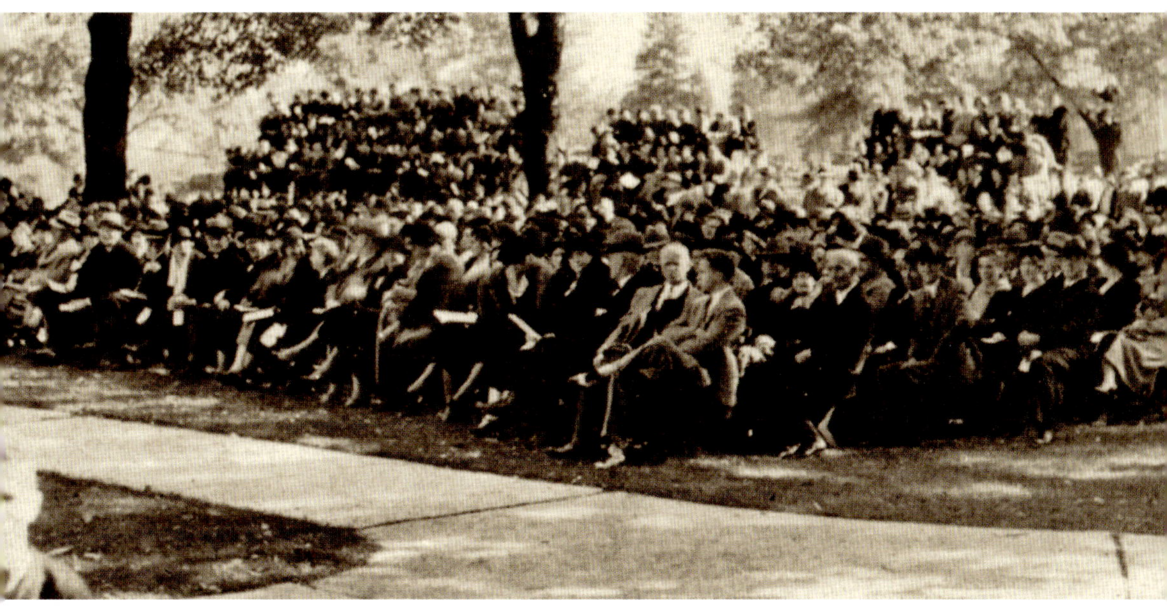

GRADUATION AUDIENCE: Proud parents, friends, and family members still gather and face Senior Terrace in anticipation of the arrival of that year's graduating class, weather permitting. Graduation audiences in 1932 and 2012, at the same spot, illustrate how the custom continues – arrive early and find a good seat, preferably under one of the shade trees.

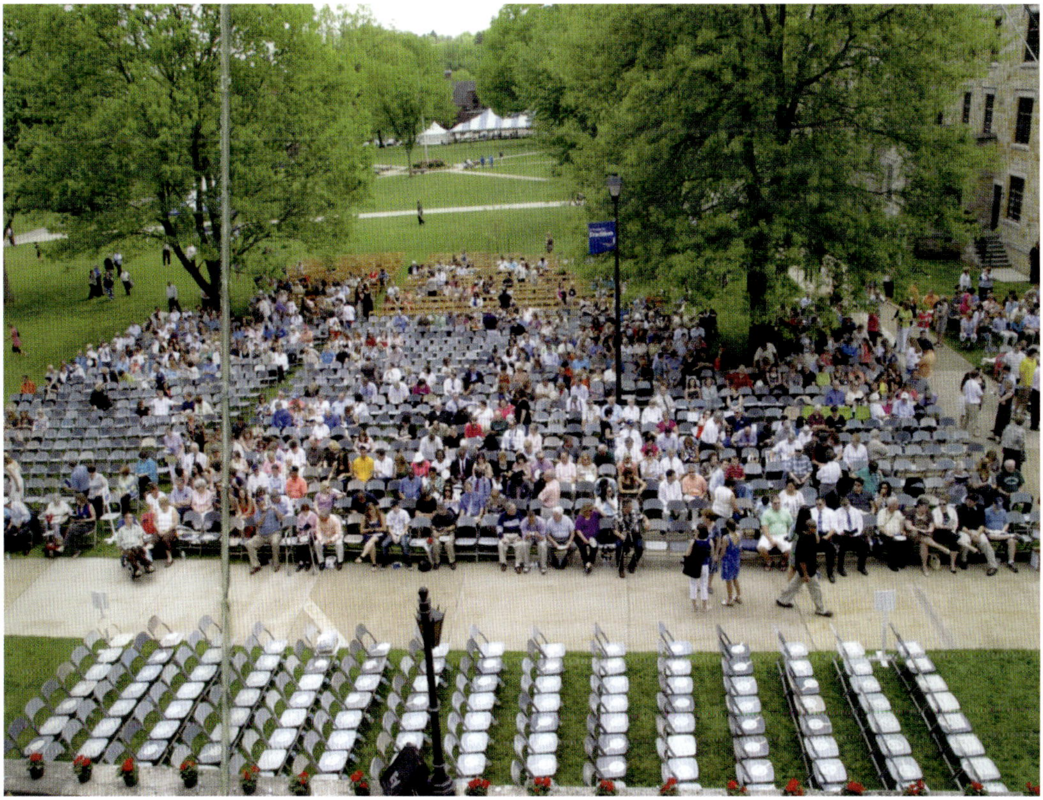

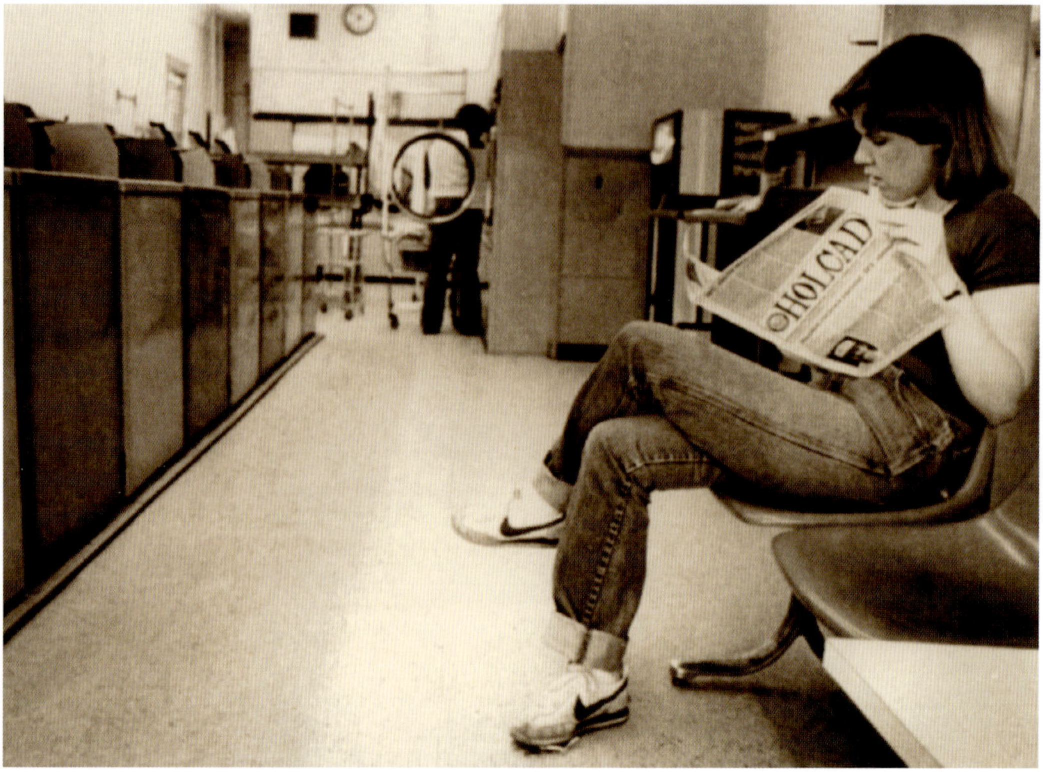

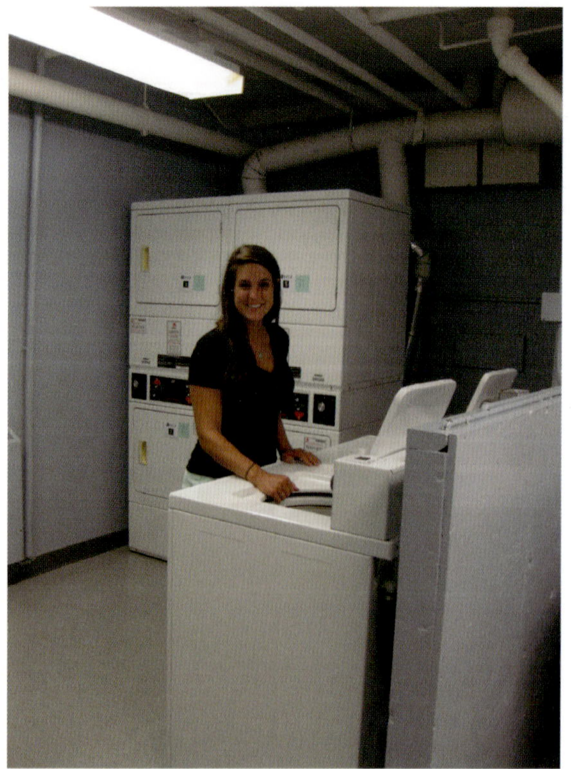

LAUNDRY: Doing laundry away from home is still a part of college life for most students. The laundromat in the center of town is still there and still charges for machine usage. However, in the early twenty-first century, all the college's dorms have free washers and dryers for dorm residents. The photo above is thought to be from the town laundromat in the 1960s. The photo, right, shows the washers and dryers in Shaw women's dorm in 2014.

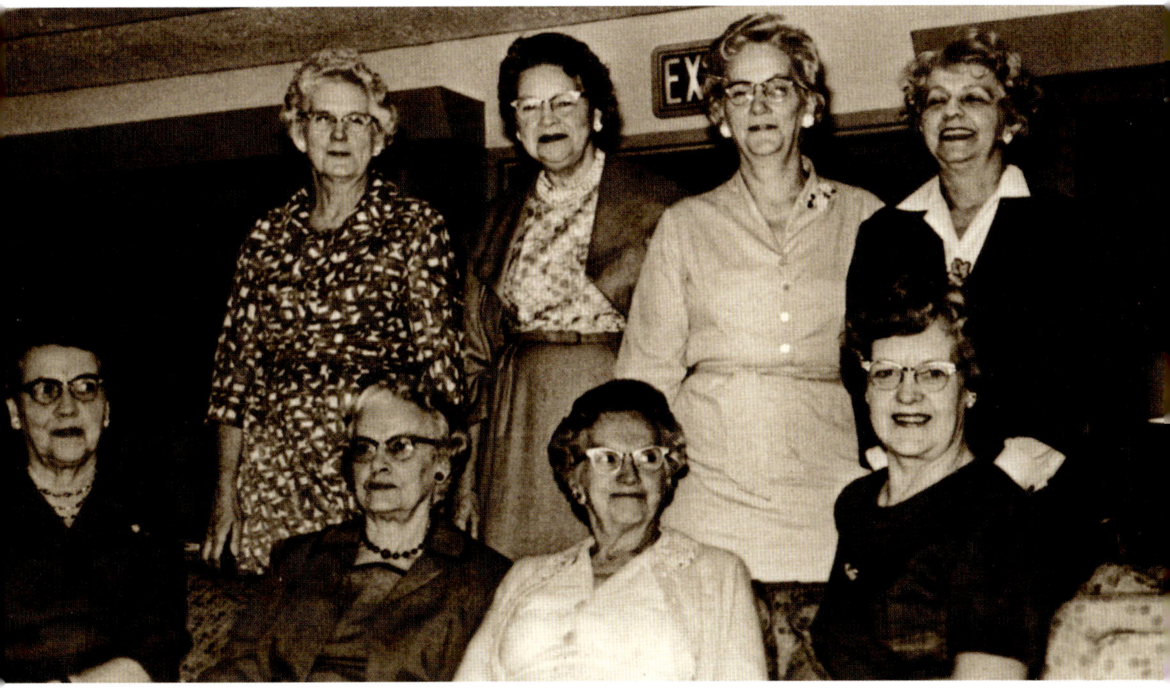

RESIDENCE DIRECTORS: The RDs in charge of the dorms have changed considerably over the years, as evidenced by those in the photo above, compared to the 2014 Residence Directors, shown in the photo below. This is another sign of changing times at the college.

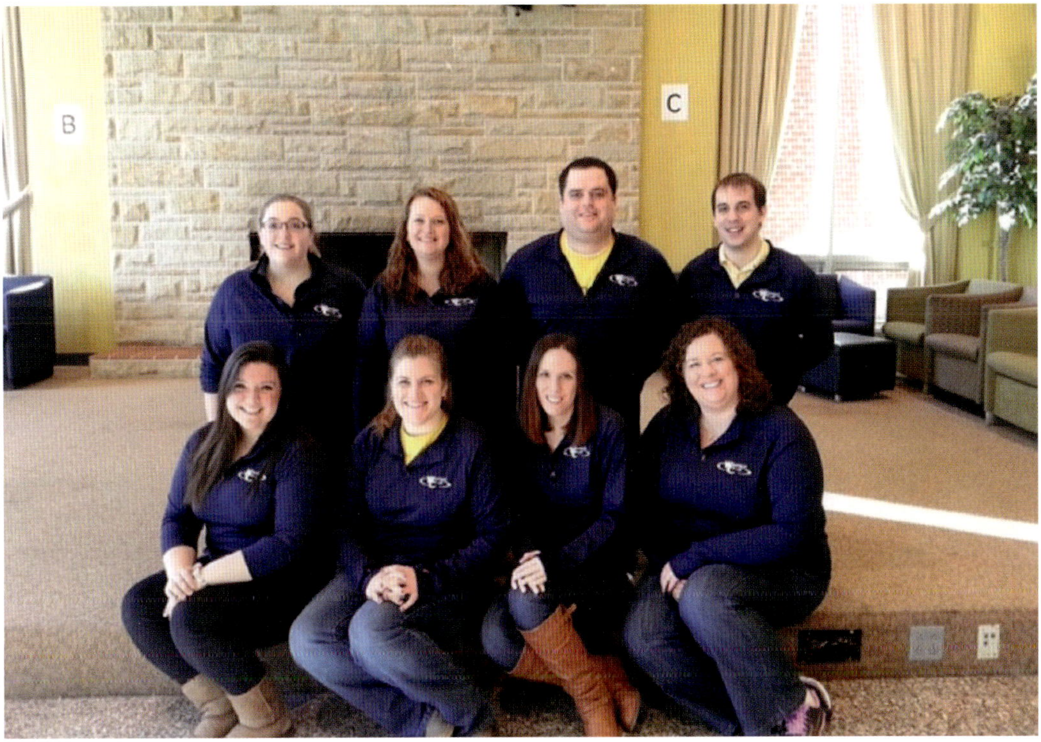

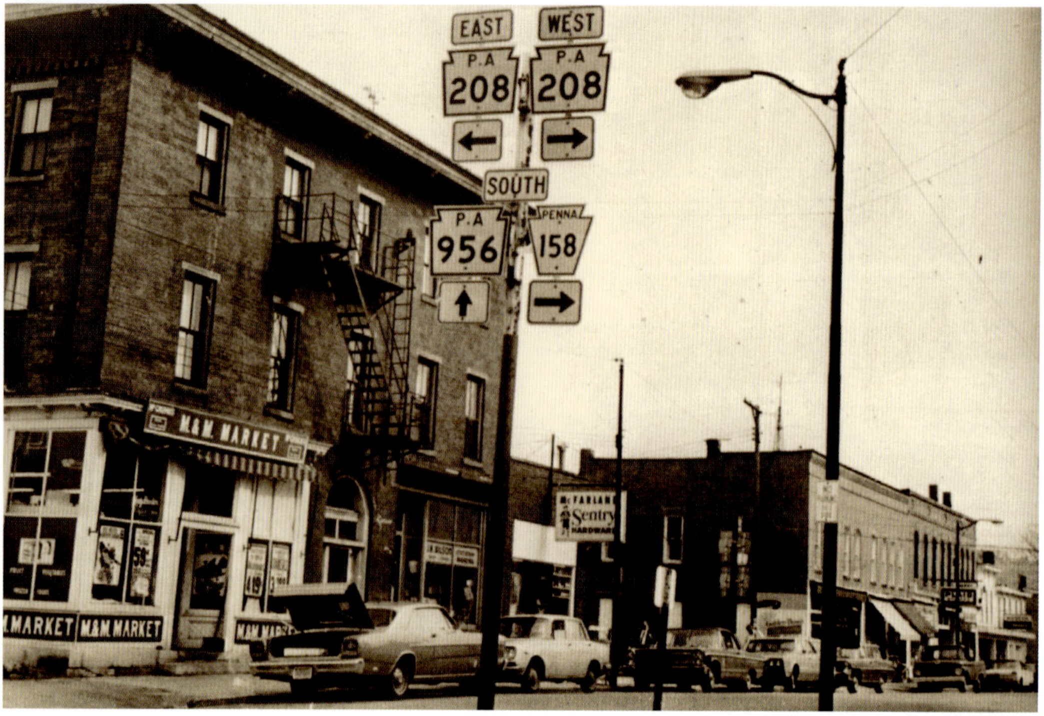

DOWNTOWN NEW WILMINGTON: Still looks familiar as one compares the view in the center of town in 1967, shown above, to the same site, shown below, in 2014. A grocery store is still on the corner, far left. The highway signage is the same. Store signage and fronts have changed a little, but the buildings are recognizable.

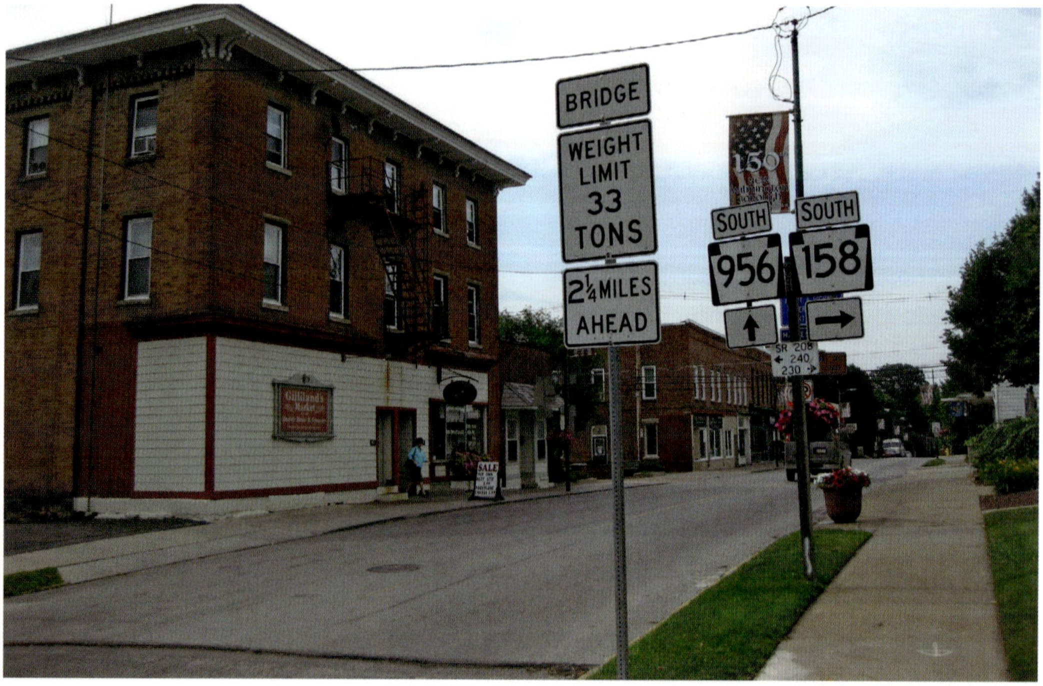

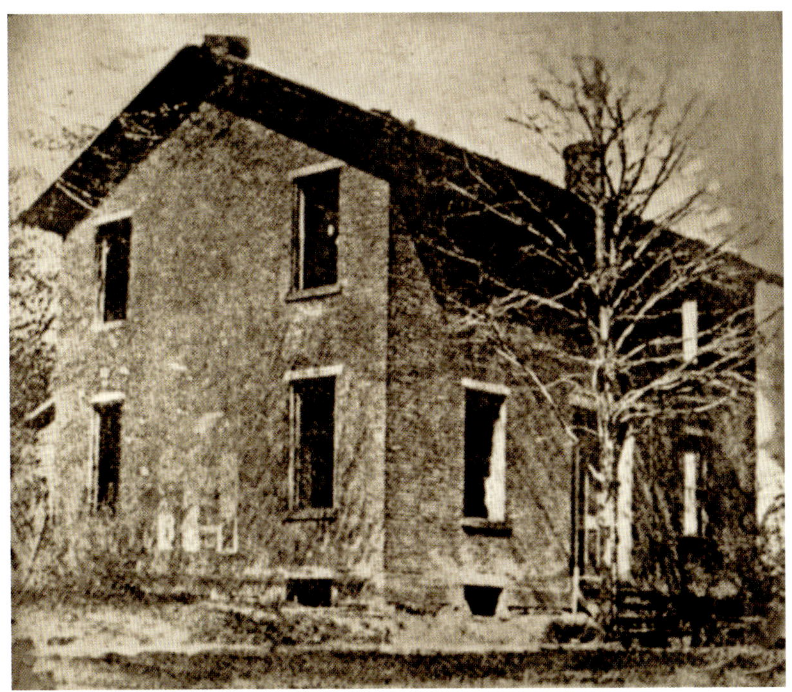

MAPLE STREET: The street runs in front of the exterior entrance to the chapel. The first Westminster College building, shown above, was used from 1853 to 1855 and stood along Maple Street in the area that came to be occupied by the south wing of the United Presbyterian Church. The smoldering ruins shown in the photo below was the college's second building, also located along Maple Street on the site occupied by Old Main in 2014. From the ashes of this January 1927 fire, a new Old Main Memorial was built and is the Old Main we know in the early twenty-first century.

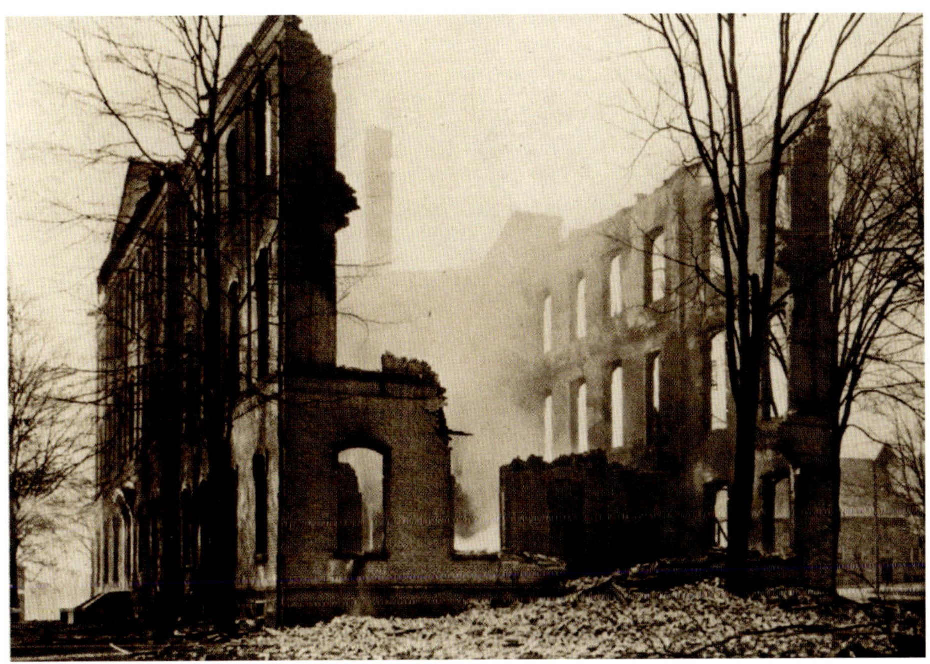

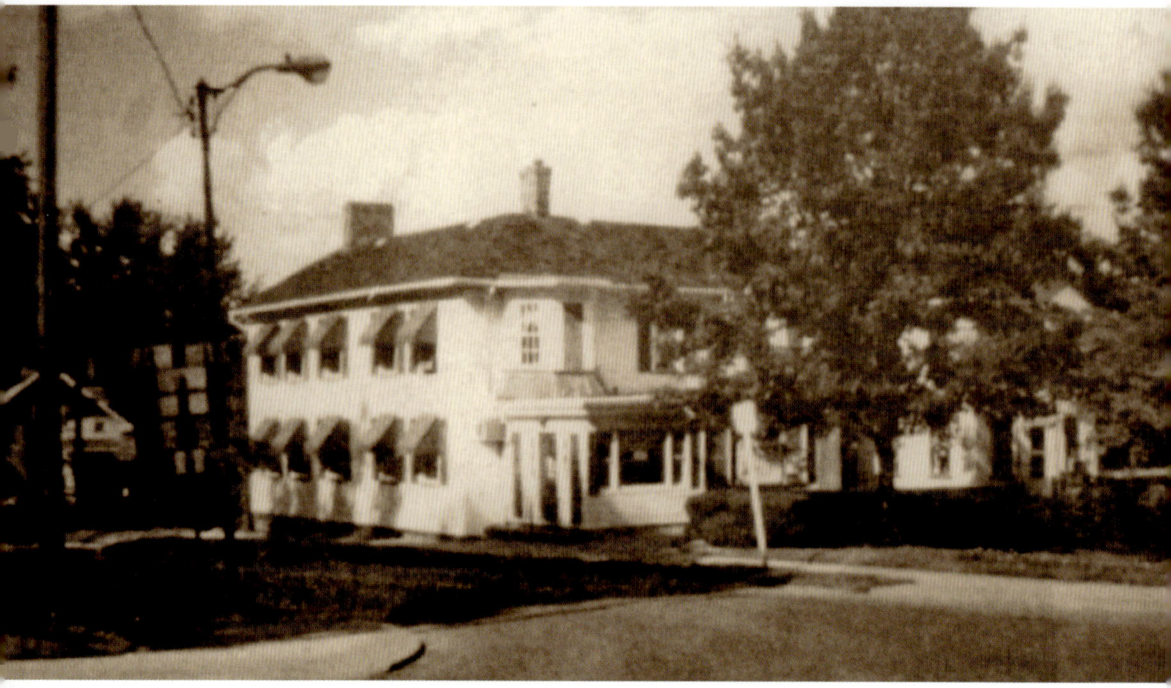

The Tavern: Anyone who has gone to Westminster or visited the campus has probably dined at The Tavern in the center of town. Here's how it looked in 1935 compared to 2014. It is still a great place for dinner, especially noted for its sticky buns. Good back then. Good decades later. Notice the oak tree in front is much bigger in 2014 compared to 1935.

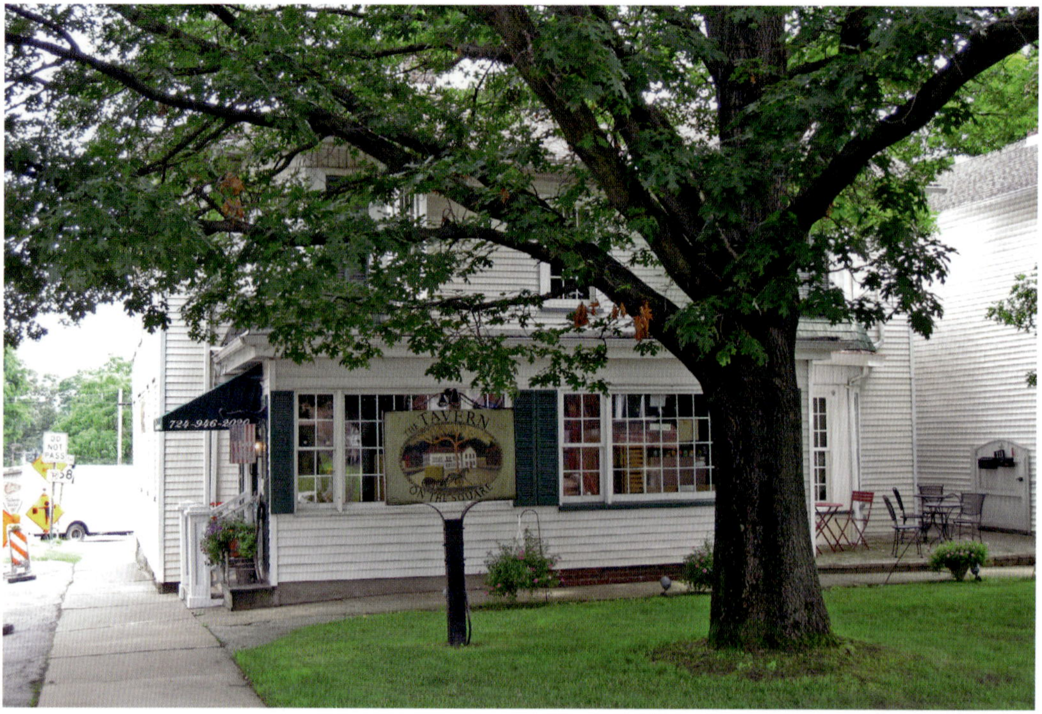

STUDENT GOVERNMENT ASSOCIATION: This association is called SGA by students. It functions in a manner similar to the US Congress and the executive branch of the US government. The executive branch in SGA includes the student body president, vice president, secretary and treasurer, and an appointed cabinet. The SGA legislative branch consists of senators who are elected each year to represent the students of the college. The senators work with the administration and faculty of the college to help determine the policies and concerns of the Westminster students. The 1963 SGA officers are shown above, and the photo below shows the 2013 SGA members.

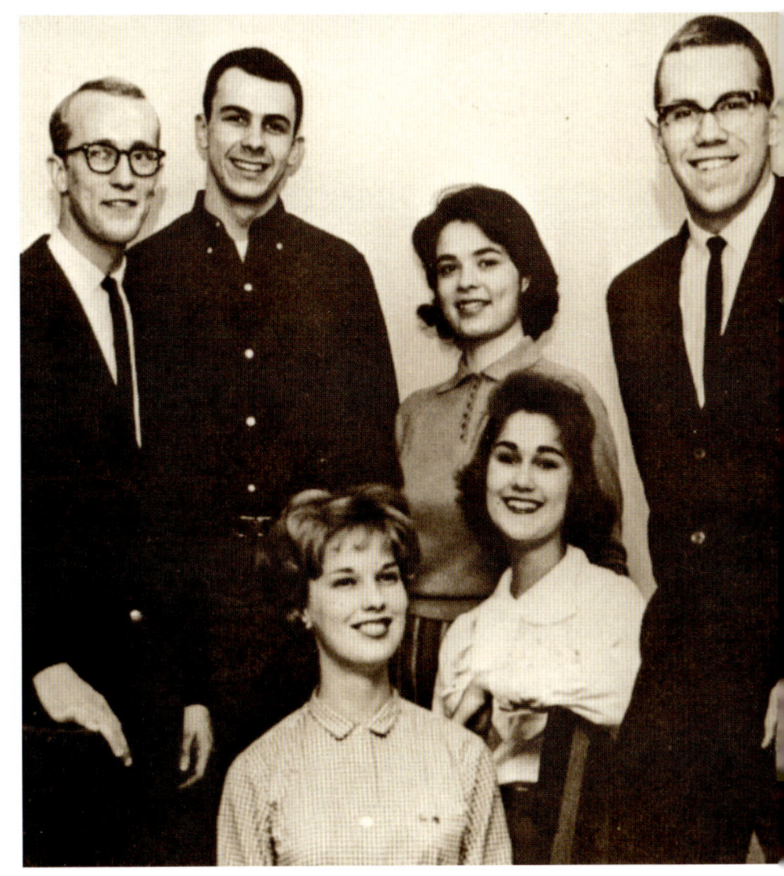

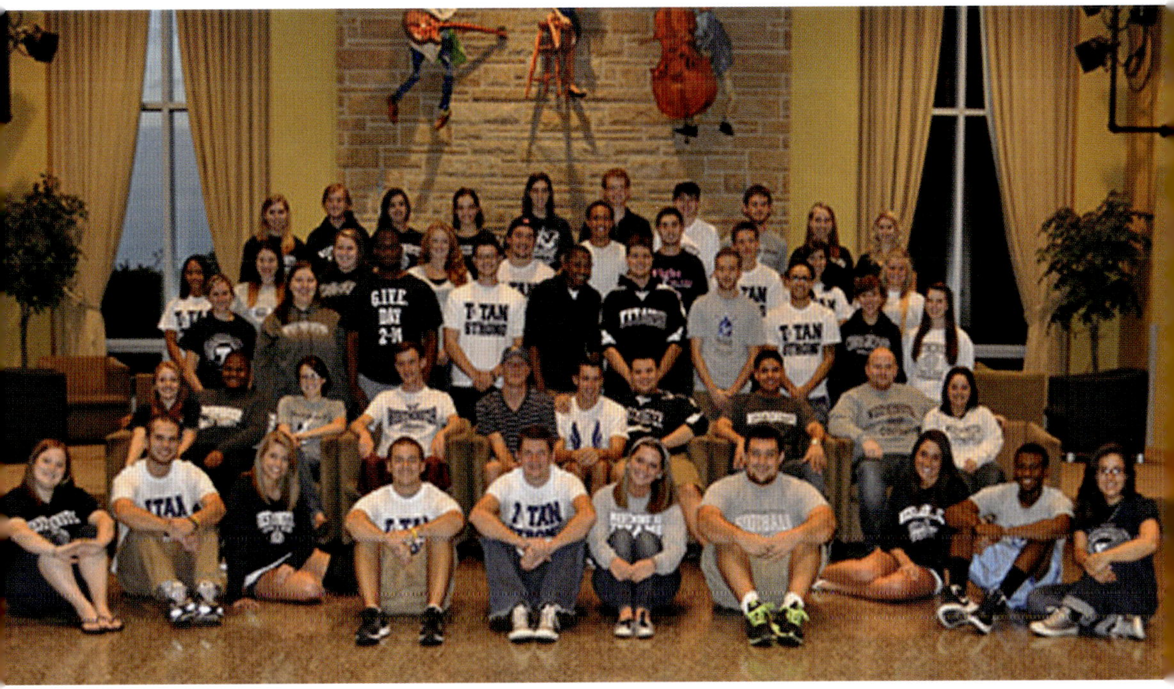

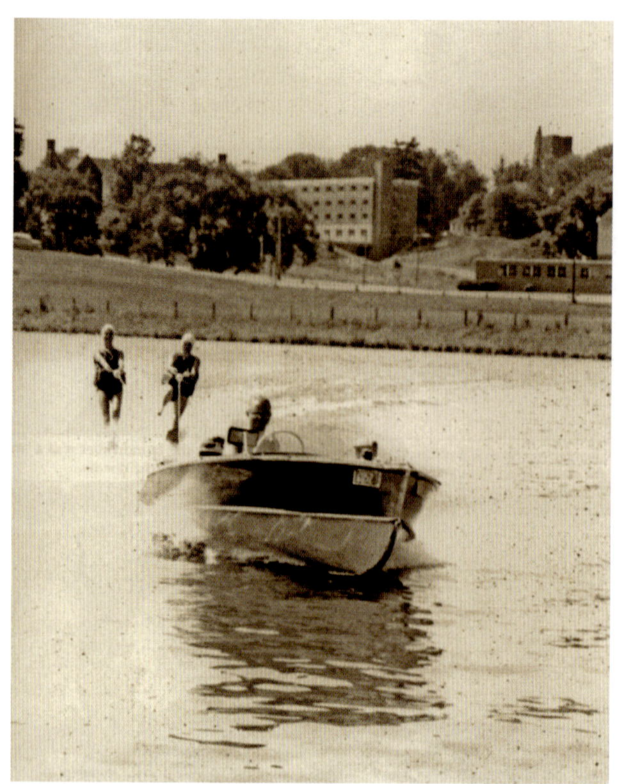

BRITTAIN LAKE: The lake was built in 1951 on five acres, and named for J. Frank Brittain, whose gifts financed the project. In the background of the top photo is Russell Hall, men's dormitory, also completed in 1951 as part of the college's expansion in the southeastern portion of the campus that year. In the foreground is President Orr and his boat, kept at the lake. He towed students, friends, and family including his daughter Arlis and her friend Biz Ellis Hines. The photo taken about 1957 can be compared to 2014 photo of Brittain Lake.

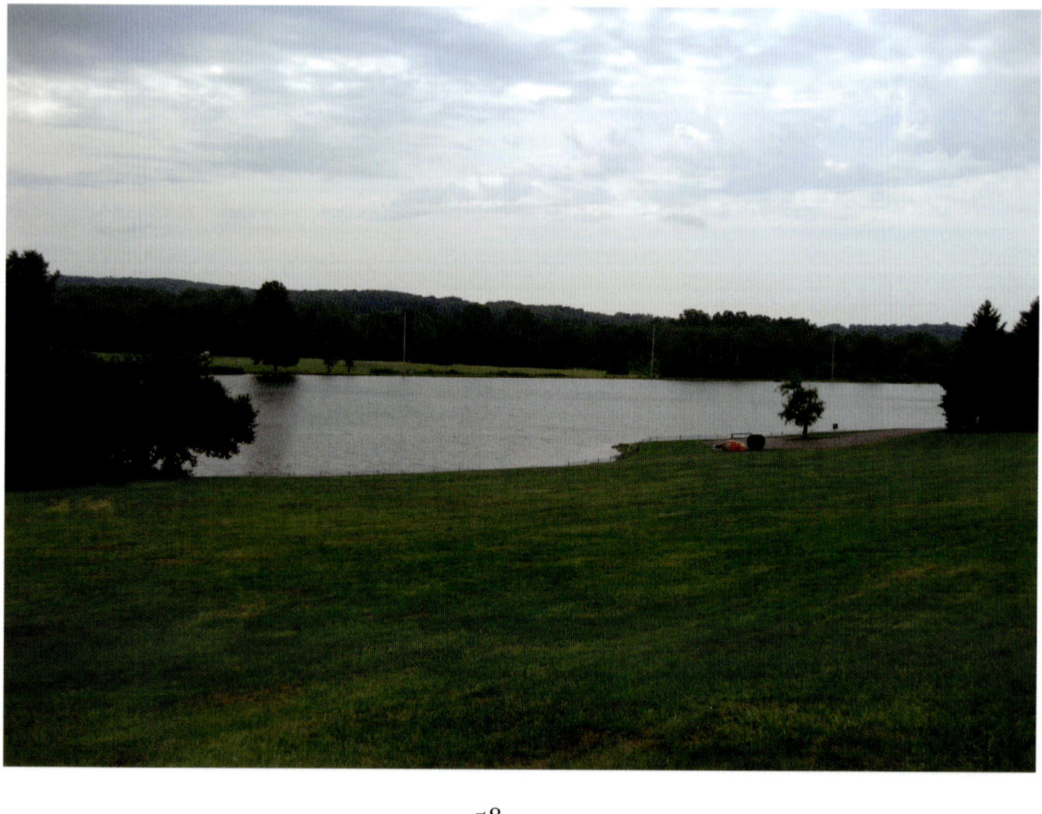

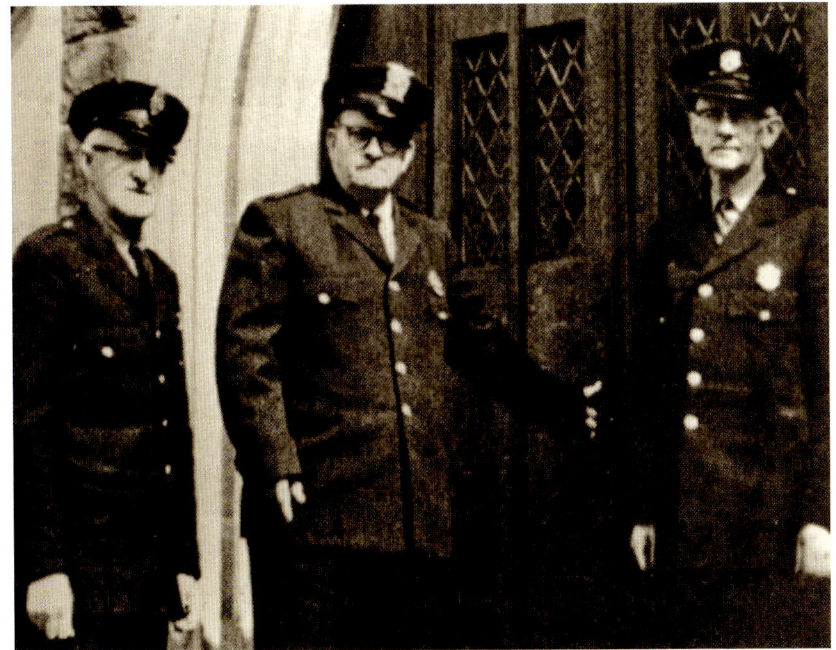

Public Safety: The 1967 photo, above, shows what was then referred to as the Campus Police. In 2014, this component of campus staff is called Public Safety. This department provides safety and security services to the campus community twenty-four hours a day, seven days a week, throughout the year. The department, in 2014, consists of nineteen members, the majority of whom are retired from public emergency services agencies. Some of the services provided by the Public Safety Department include campus-wide patrol, escort services, transportation for sick or injured persons, security for special events and traffic control.

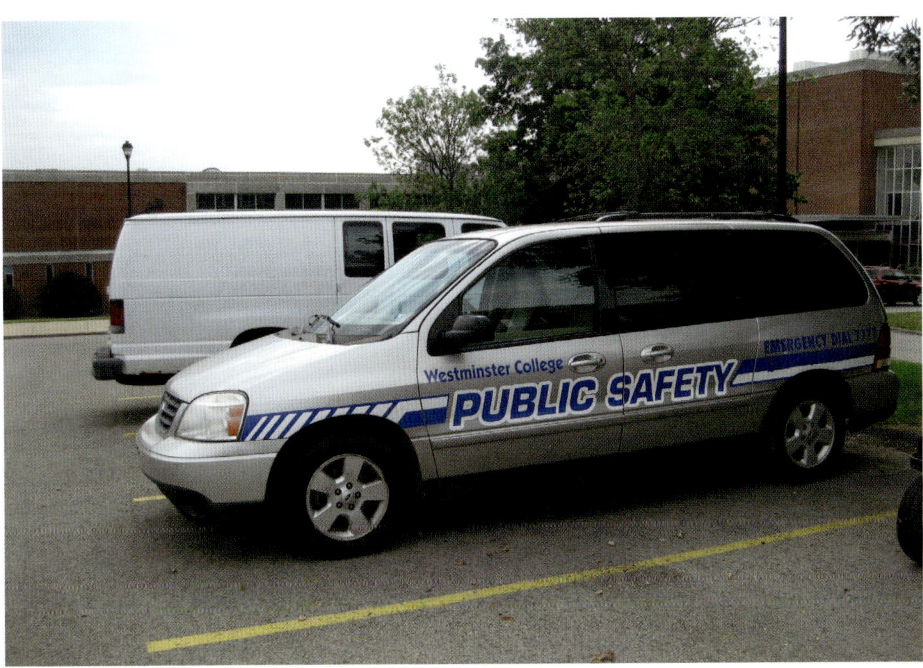

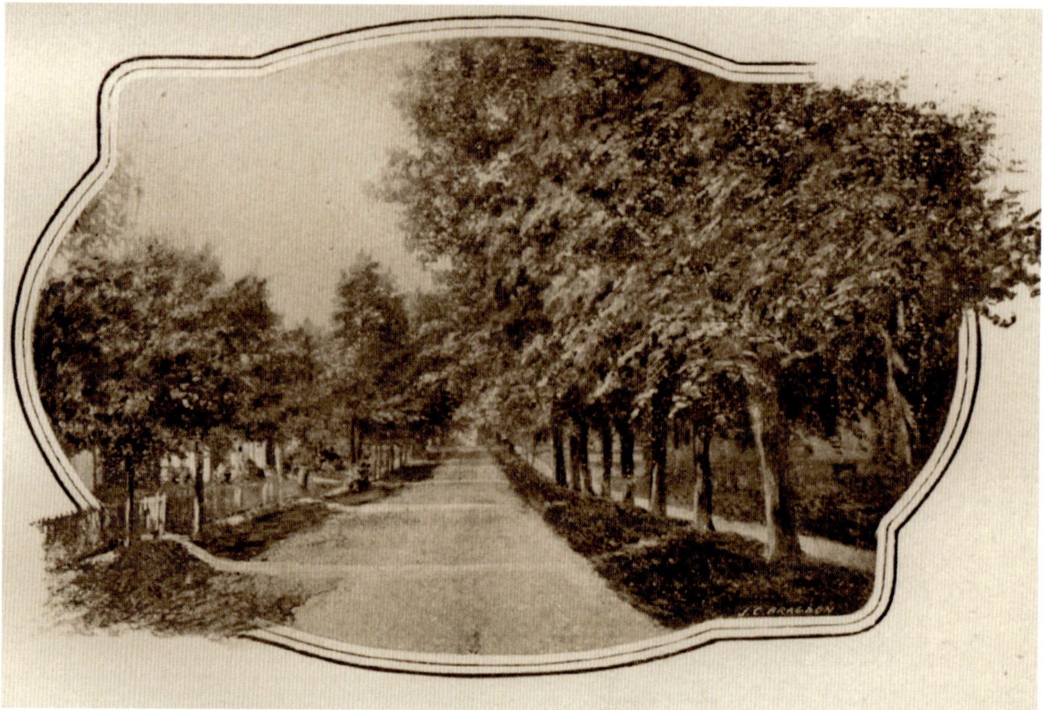

APPROACH TO THE COLLEGE FROM SOUTH MARKET STREET: The photo above shows what a driver would see approaching the college from South Market Street in 1906. The photo below shows the same approach to the college in 2014, still pleasantly situated in a rural setting, free from inner-city traffic, blight, and congestion.

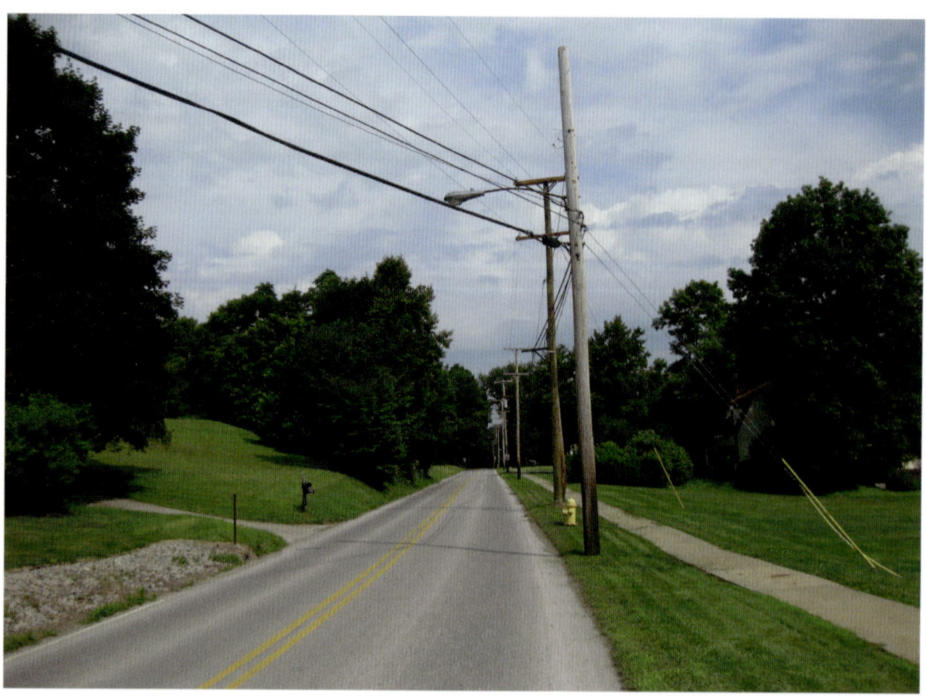

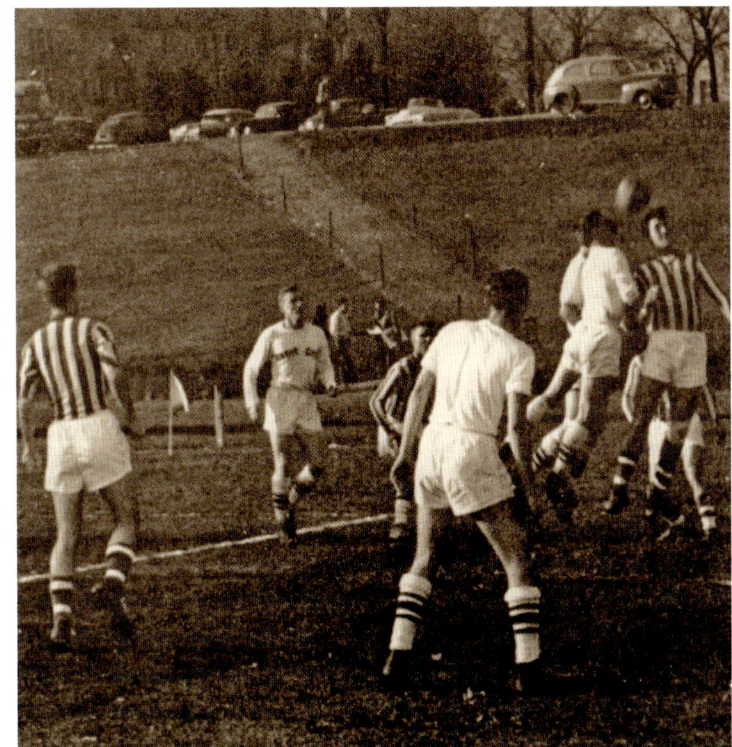

Men's Soccer: College records show this sport as far back as 1946. The program was discontinued from 1952-85 and resumed in 1986. The 1950 soccer team, shown in an action shot above, can be compared to that of a 2011 game shown, below. Overall, the thirty-year winning record is fifty percent. Opponents still include teams like Washington & Jefferson, Thomas Moore, Waynesburg and Saint Vincent Colleges.

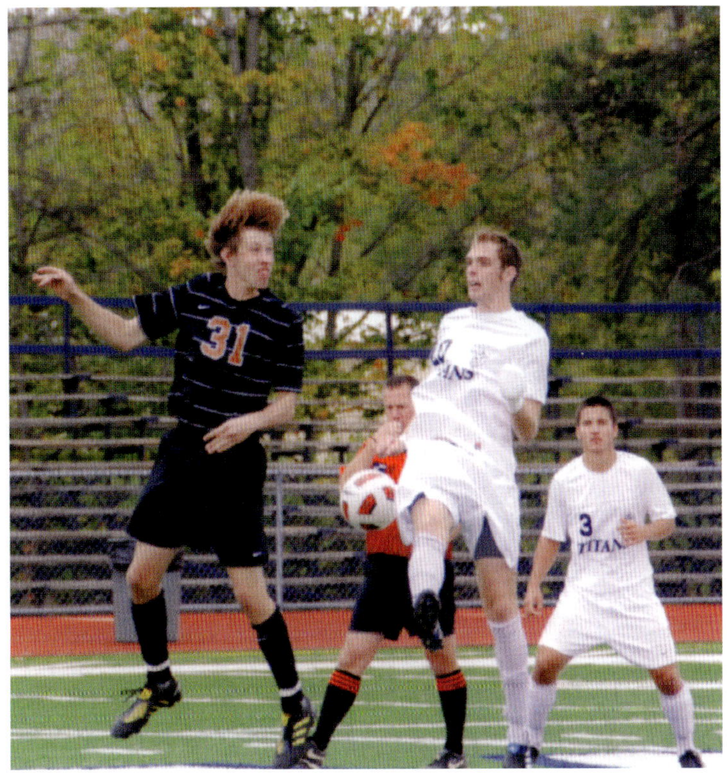

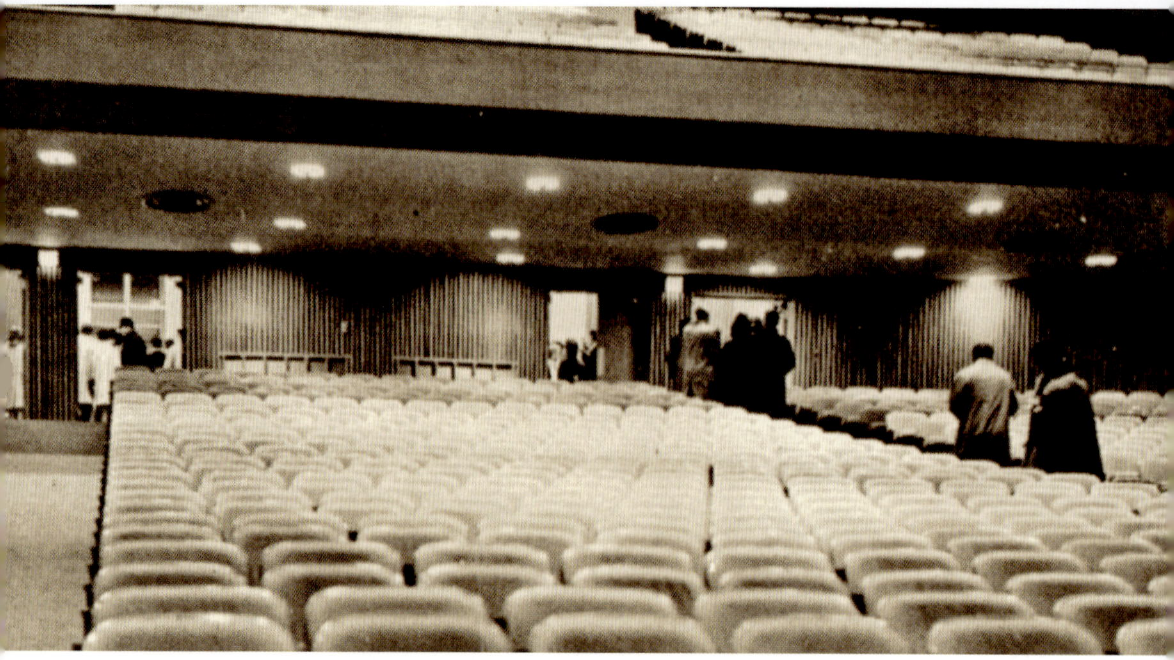

INSIDE ORR AUDITORIUM: It was built in 1966 to seat 1,750. The top photo shows how it looked shortly after its opening. The photo below shows the recent remodeling, which included new seating, lighting, sound systems, and carpeting. The auditorium is used for many campus activities and community events, such as the college's "Celebrity Series," which is popular for the public from the area of western Pennsylvania and eastern Ohio.

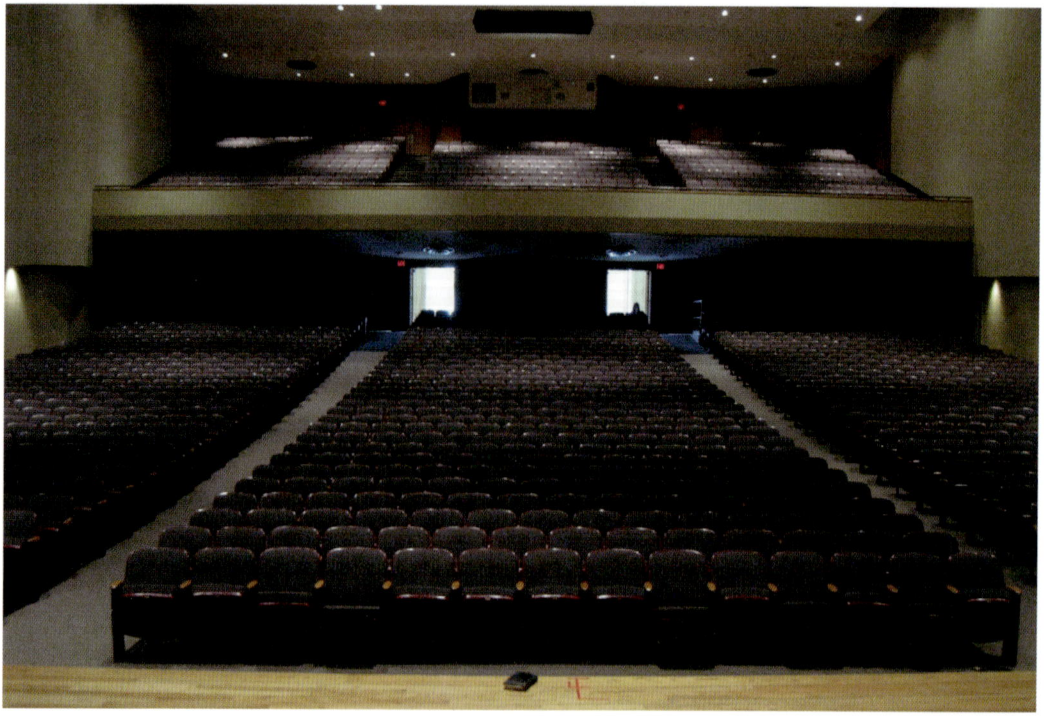

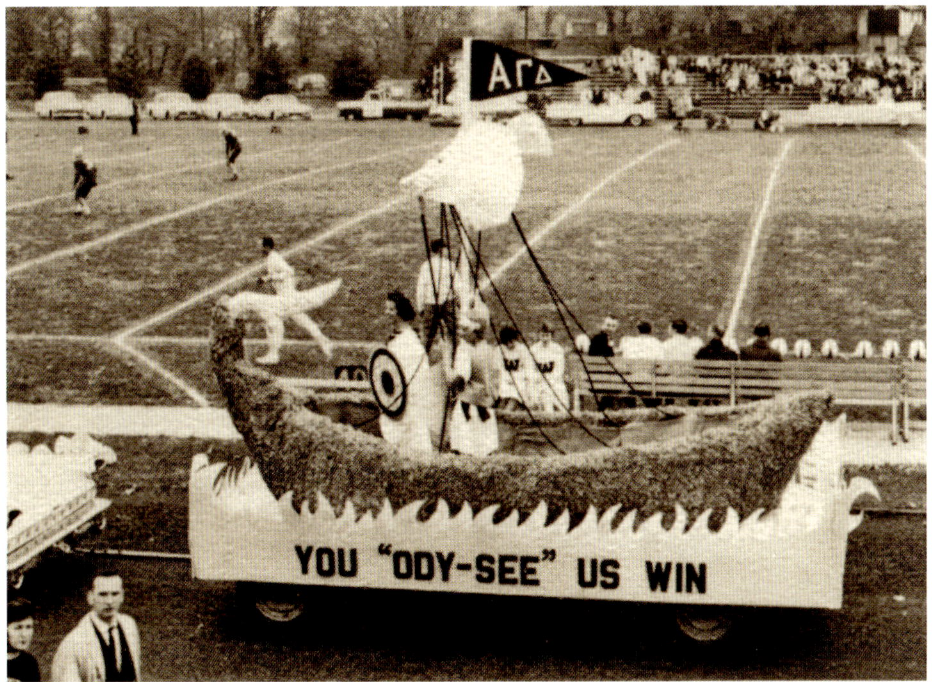

HOMECOMING FLOATS: The floats are still a fall tradition at Westminster College as an integral part of Homecoming festivities. The photo to the right is a homecoming float from years past when the floats went by the home-side stands for spectator viewing. In the 2010s, the floats are still a key part of homecoming, but use a different parade route, going up South Market Street, as seen below in 2012.

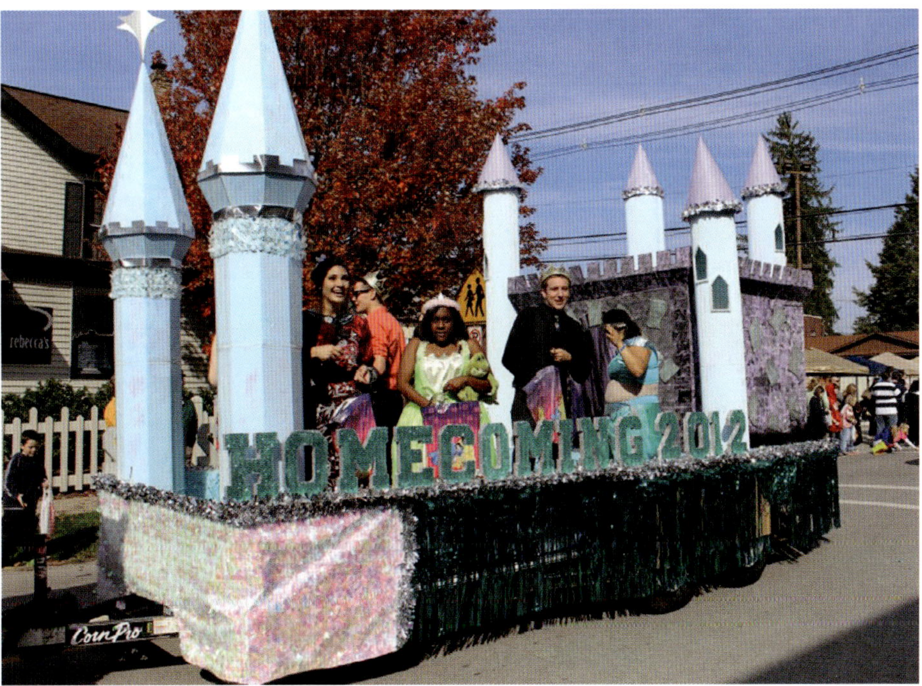

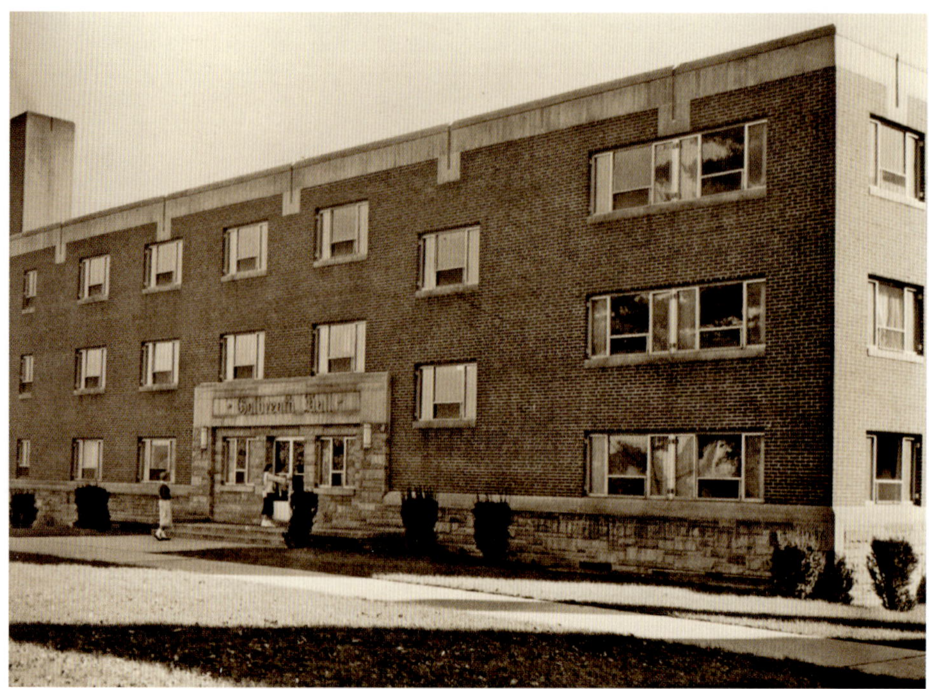

Galbreath Hall: The hall is a women's dorm facing the McKelvey Campus Center. This is how it looked when it opened in 1957. It was named for Dr. Robert Galbreath, a former president, and cost $1.4 million at the time. The campus dining hall is housed in the lower level of Galbreath. The photo below shows Galbreath in the summer of 2014. This three-floor dorm houses up to 152 women in the 2010s. The dorm has a kitchenette with a stove/oven for student use.

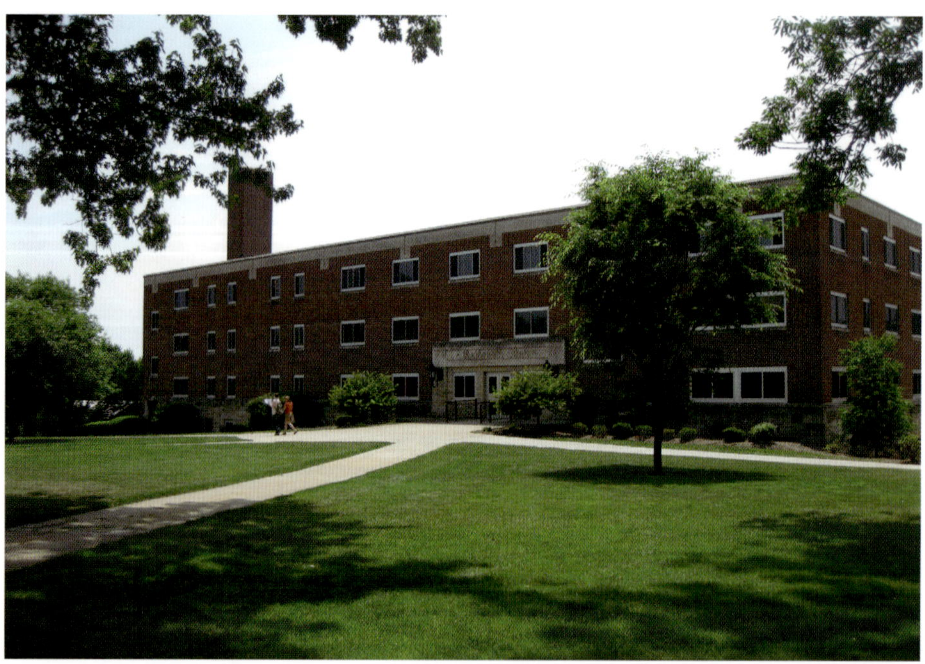

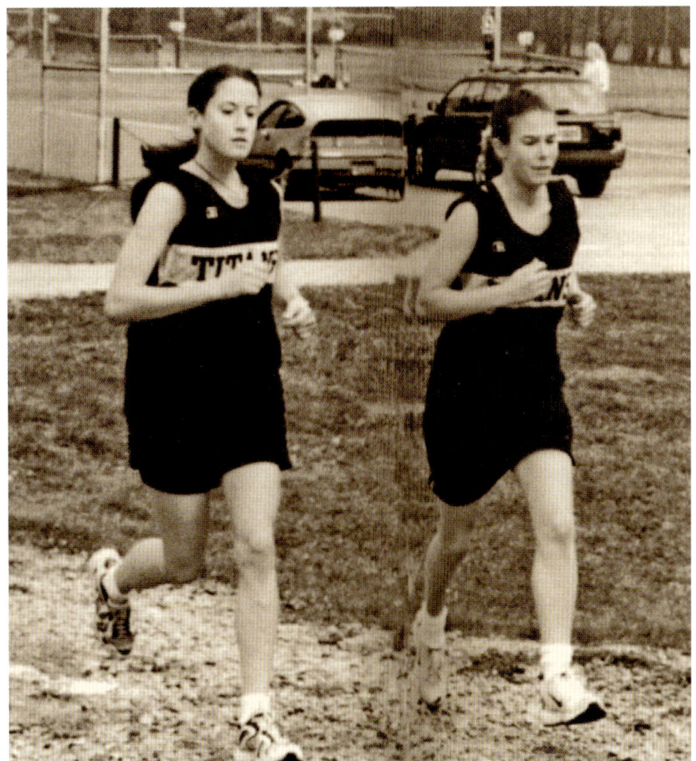

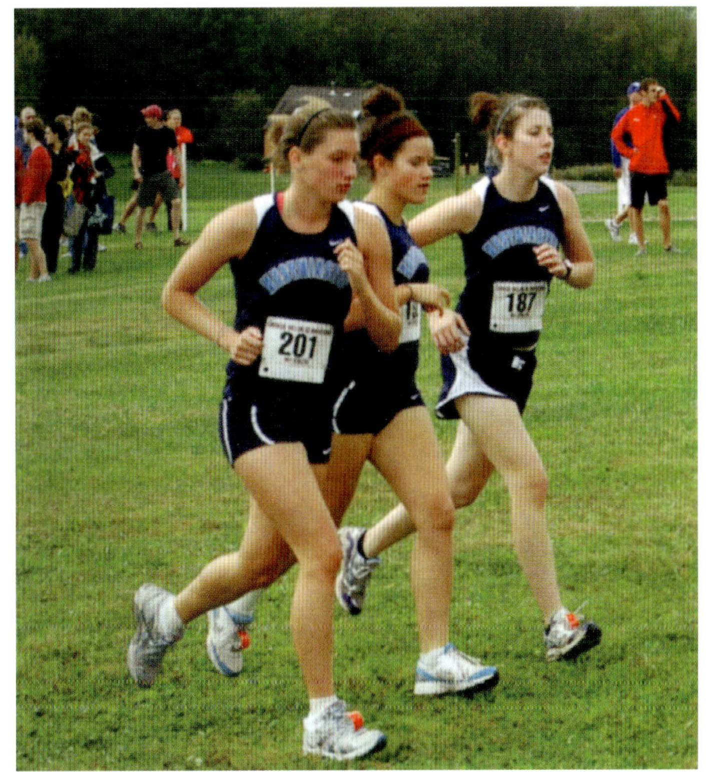

WOMEN'S CROSS COUNTRY: Introduced at Westminster in 1988. College records for this sport, going back to 2002, show the women's cross country all-time PAC League often finishes the season in the top three. The photo above shows several of the 1999 team members, while the photo at the right shows some team members of the 2011 team on a cross country run.

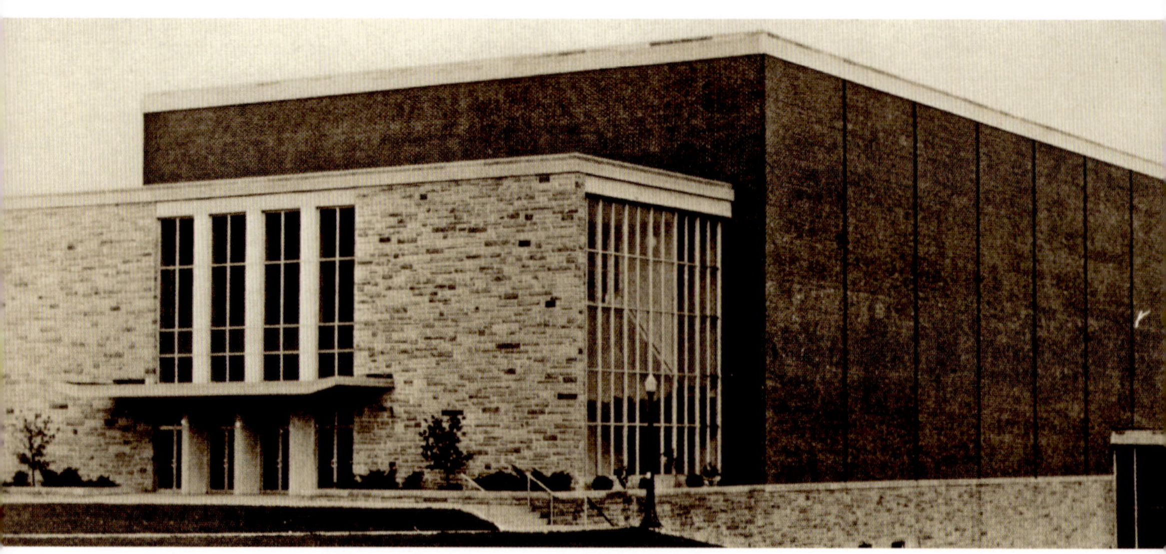

Arts and Sciences Building: Built in three stages in the 1960s, as funds became available. Shown above is the first section that was built when it opened in 1961, Orr Auditorium. The building was named after Dr. Will Orr, one of the college's former presidents. In 1966, the Patterson Hall classroom wing was added, followed by the Beeghly Theatre addition. Shown below is Orr Auditorium in 2014. The auditorium is used for many college activities, while Patterson Hall classrooms are utilized daily, and Beeghly Theatre is used for college plays and theatre activities.

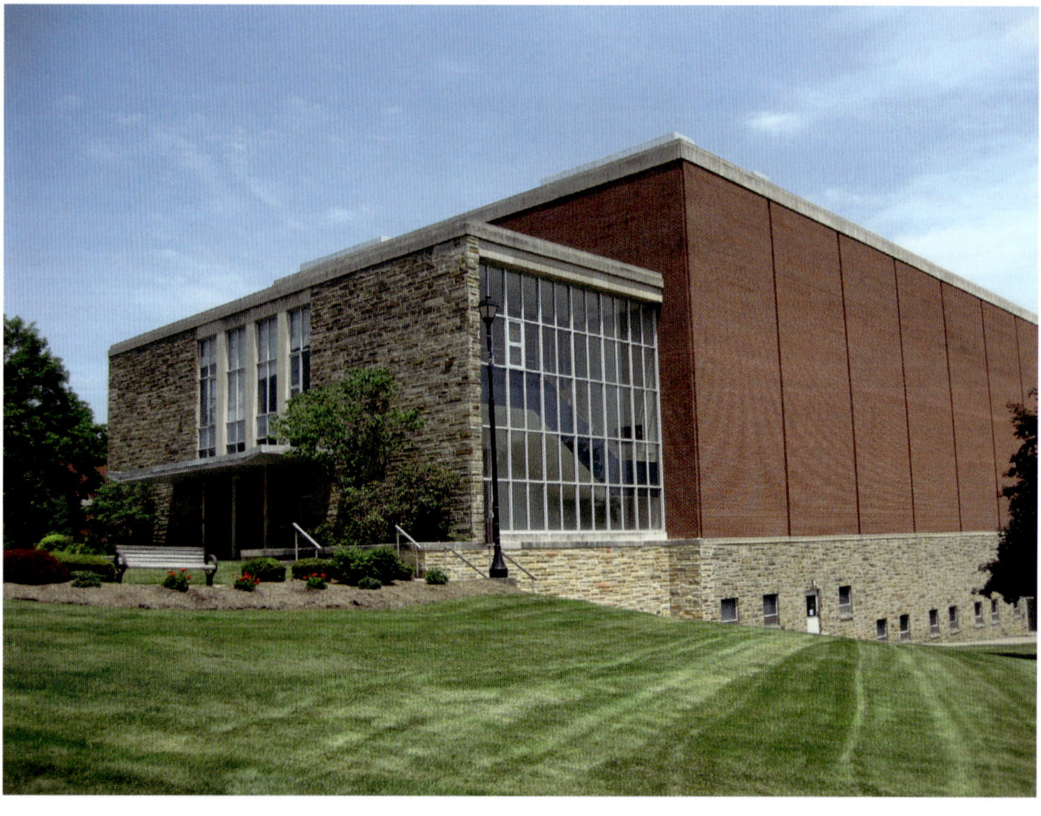

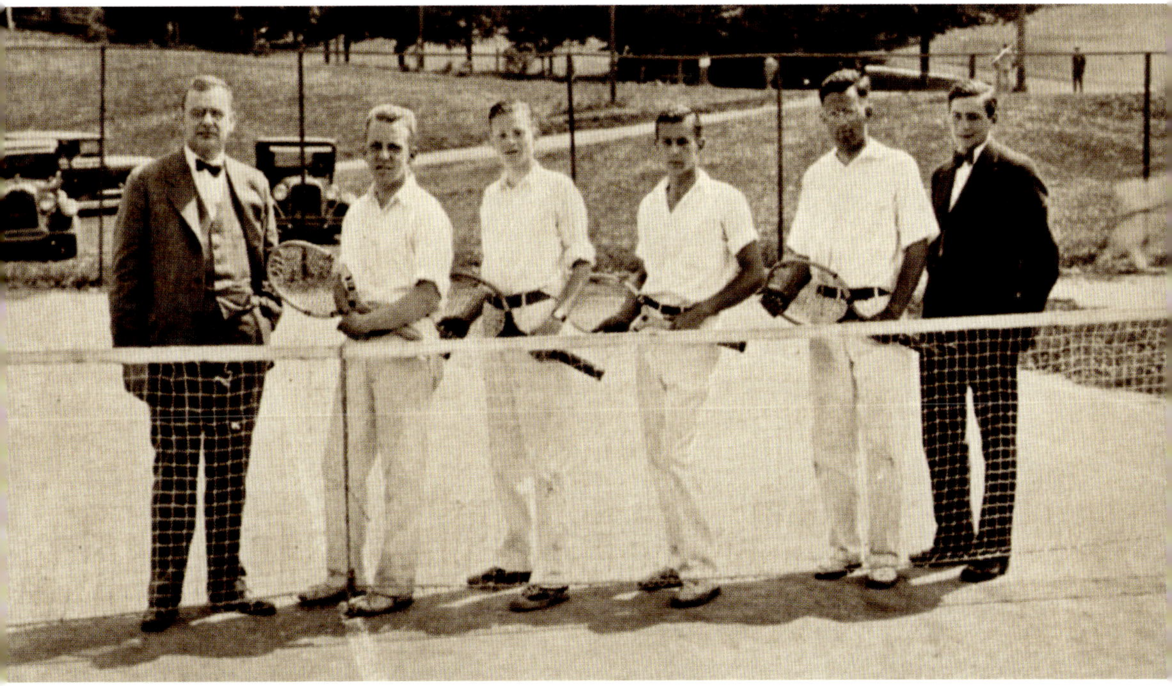

MEN'S TENNIS: The 1930 team, above, and the 2011 team, below, show the enthusiasm continues for this sport. Competition still includes teams like Grove City, Washington and Jefferson, Bethany, Thomas Moore, Waynesburg and Thiel Colleges. The 1930 team would have liked the warm-up jackets of the 2011 team. Note the old Model A 1930 Ford in the background of the top photo of the 1930 team.

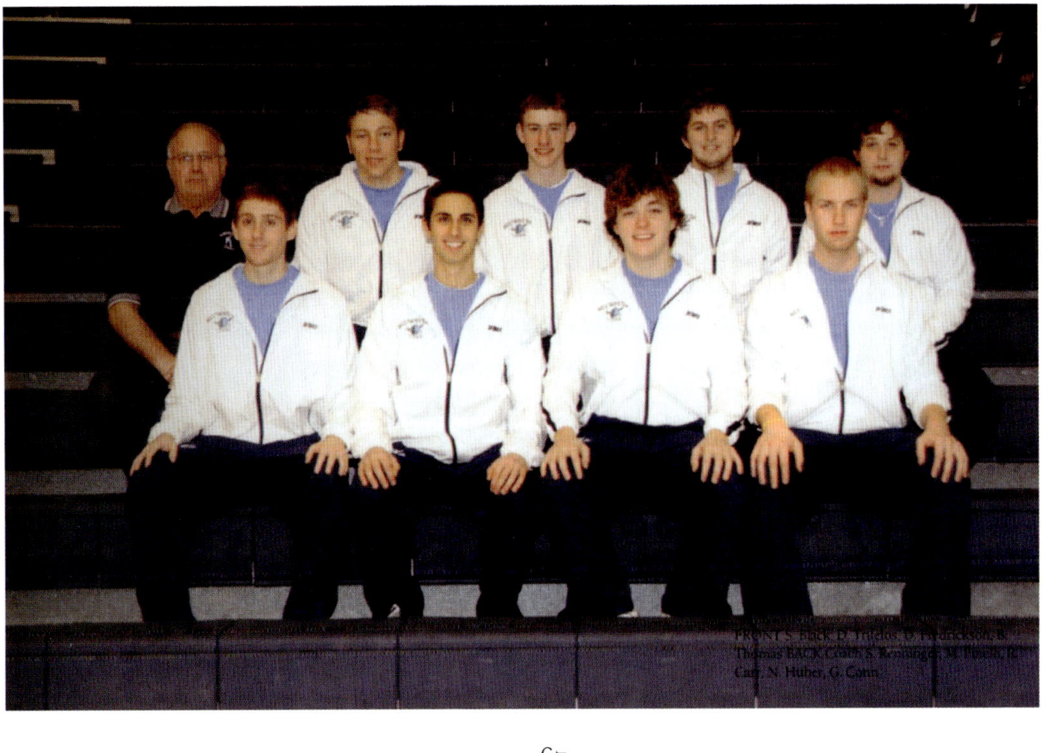

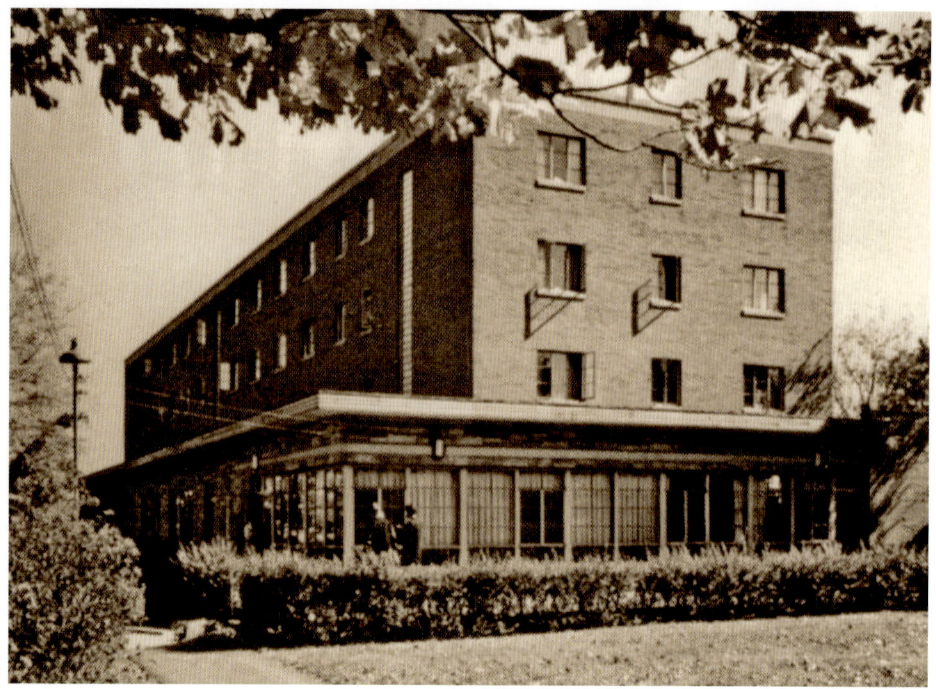

RUSSELL HALL: Built in 1950 at a cost of $500,000 to house approximately 150 men. It was first occupied in 1952. Named after one of the college's presidents, the dorm was part of the Centennial Campaign to celebrate the college's 100th anniversary. In 2014, Russell Hall is a freshmen men's dorm. This dorm, Brittain Lake, and the Memorial Field House were all completed in 1951-52.

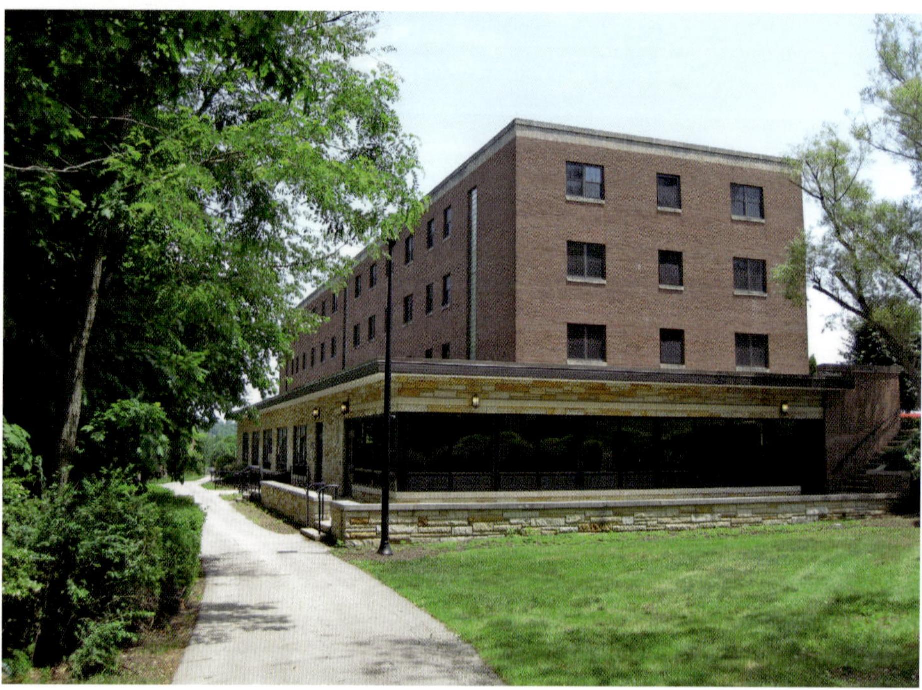

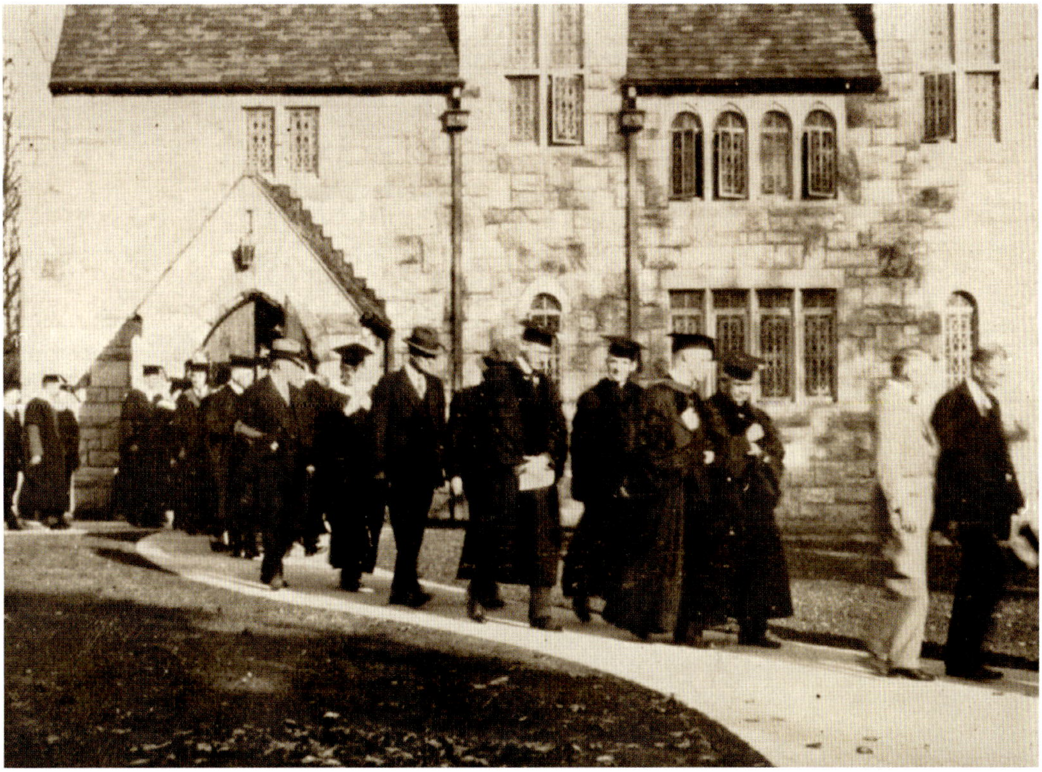

Faculty Processional: Part of Westminster's graduation tradition is the colorful processional of the faculty as they come two-by-two into the graduation ceremony in the field house or on Senior Terrace. It's colorful due to the varied and bright colors of the academic regalia worn by the faculty: mortar-board caps, berets, academic hoods indicating degree fields, and gowns designating the colleges-universities from which they graduated. The top photo is from the 1930s whereas the bottom photo is thought to be from the early 2000s. The location is the same in both photos – outside Old Main approaching Senior Terrace.

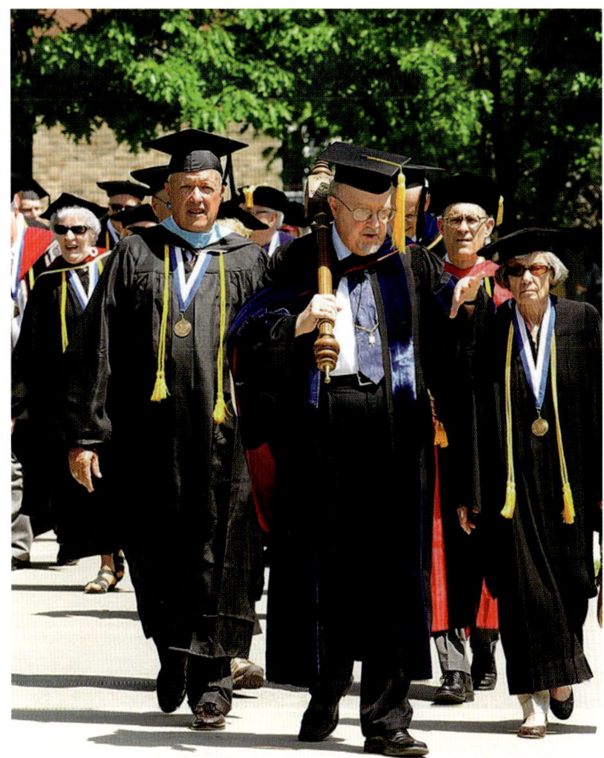

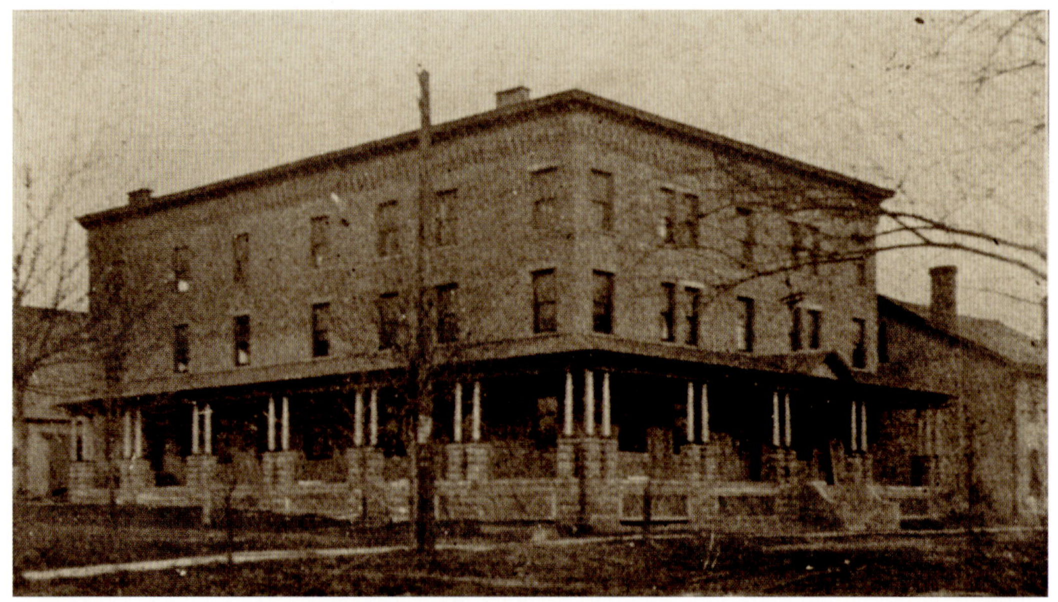

ONCE A HOTEL: You can't miss this building in town and it is clear it was once a hotel. During World War II it housed soldiers in training at Westminster and had no vacancies. The photo above shows how it looked in 1906. Check the rates. The photo below shows how it looks in 2014. It is used for student apartments in the more recent image.

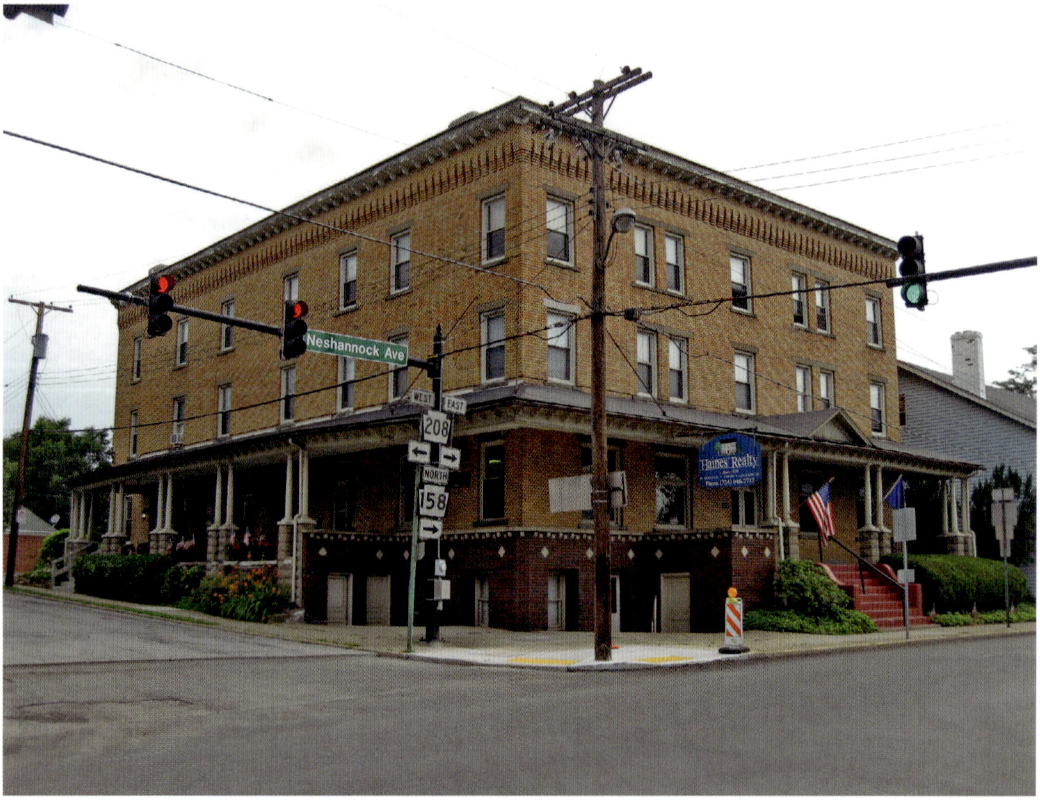

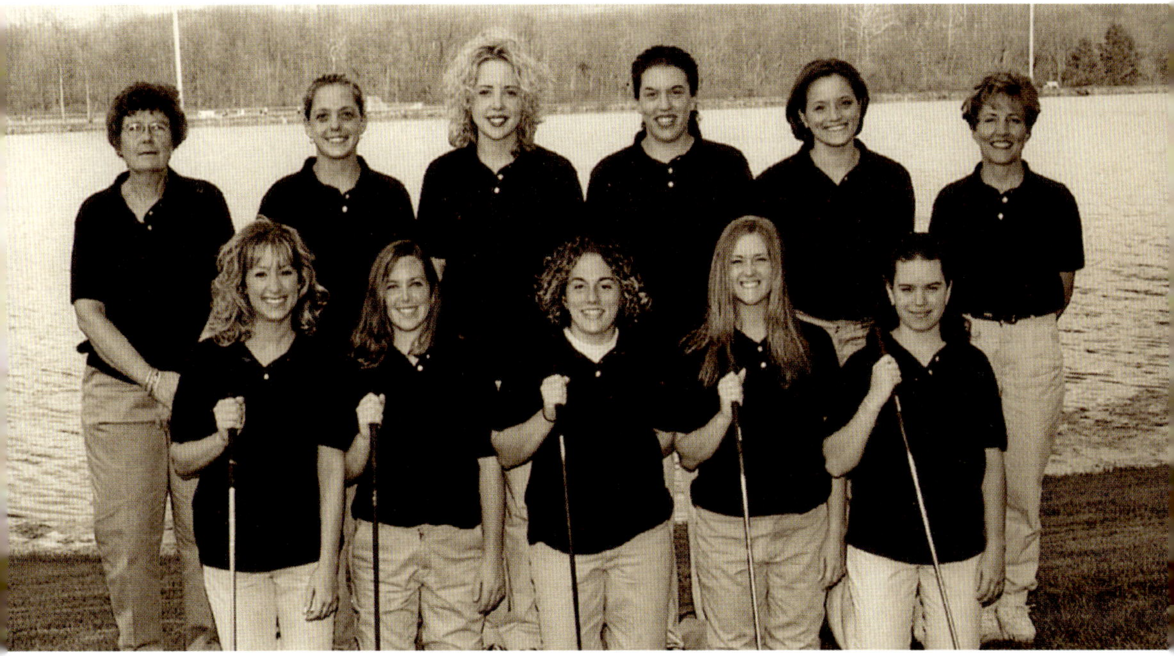

Women's Golf: Westminster garnered its third PAC (Presidents' Athletic Conference) women's golf crown since 2005. Westminster women's golf teams were eligible for PAC championships for the first time in 2002-03. Above is the 2002 team and below is the 2010 team. The team uniforms look similar.

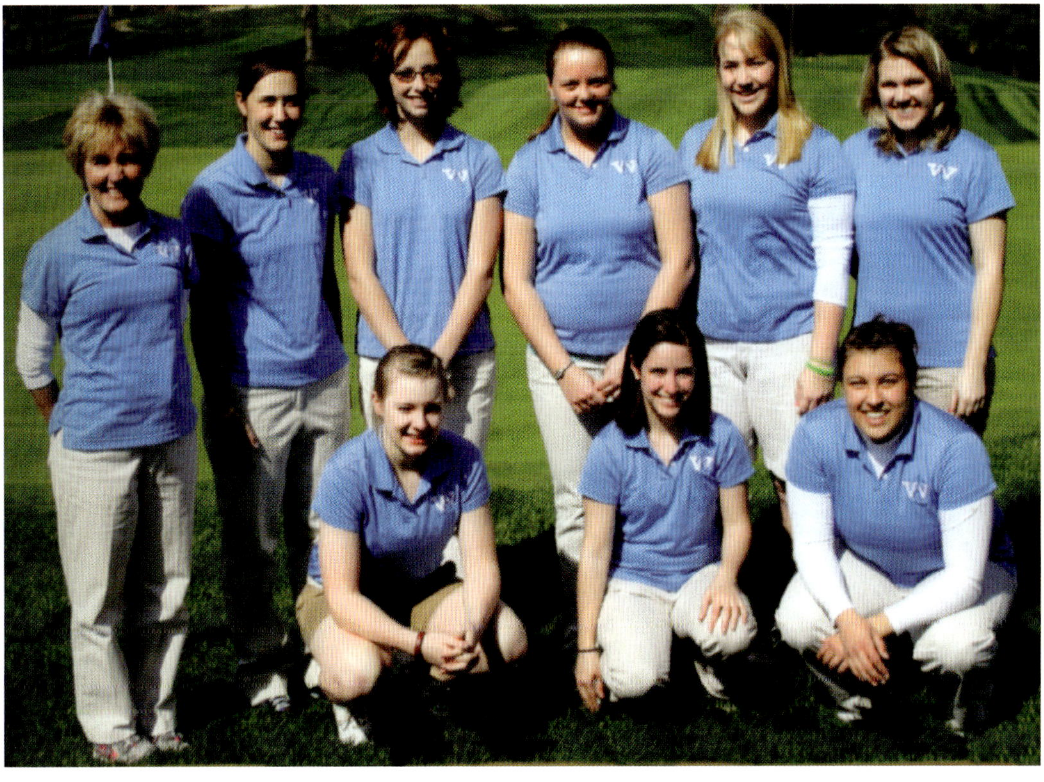

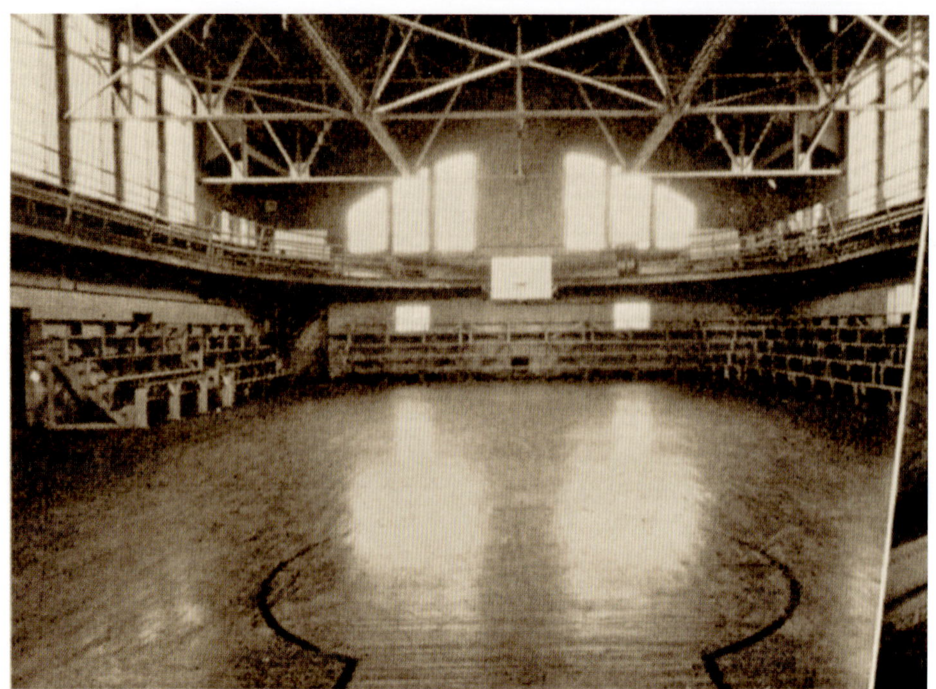

BALCONY TRACK INSIDE OLD 77: If you look closely you can see the balcony track above the gym floor in Old 77 as it looked in 1932 when it was fairly new. Balcony tracks, as they were called, were popular back then. In 1932 this building was simply called the gym. After it closed in 1951, it was called Old 77. The photo below, taken in 2014, shows the balcony track and gym floor used for recreation and physical fitness. This fitness center is equipped with state-of-the art weight and aerobic equipment, racquetball courts, locker rooms, and shower facilities.

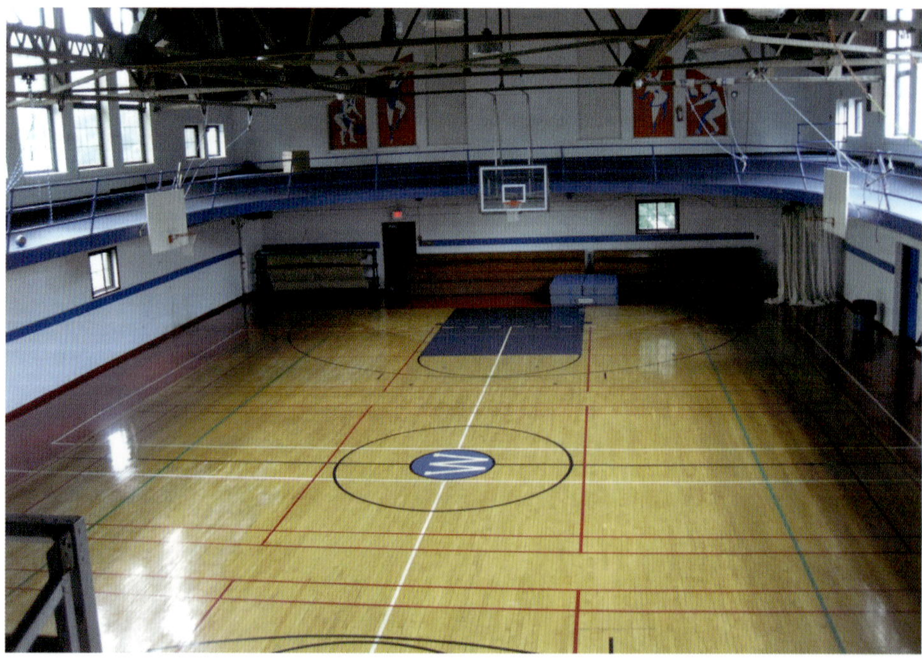

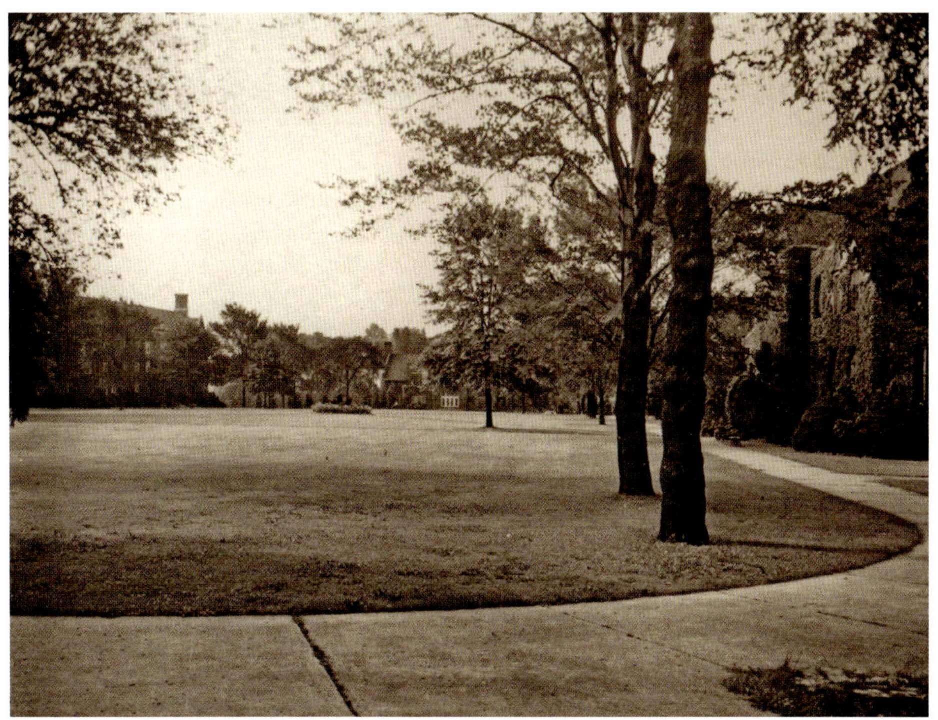

THE QUAD: The center of the campus is officially called the quadrangle, but the students call it "the quad." Here's how it looked in 1954 compared with 2014. The trees are bigger, and it is still a beautiful setting for a college campus.

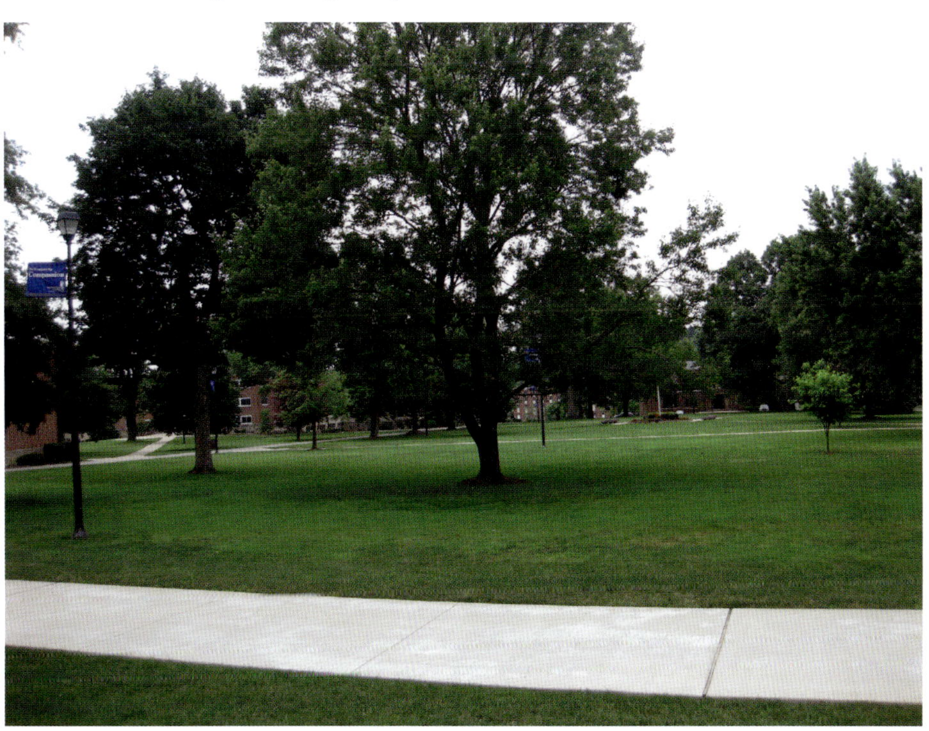

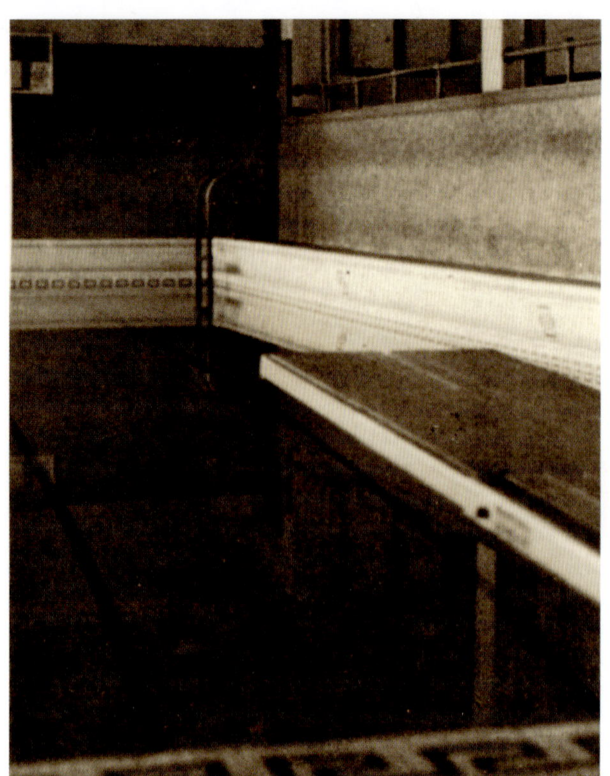

College Swimming Pool: The top photo shows the old pool in the Old 77 building in 1963, affectionately called "the bath tub" by students back then. The bottom photo shows the new pool-natatorium in the new Memorial Field House in 2014. The natatorium was dedicated in 1976 with Olympic Gold Medalist Micki King as the featured speaker. Westminster, since the advent of the new pool, has proven very successful in collegiate swimming, winning national titles in the 1980s and 1990s. This past season the natatorium saw the women's and men's swimming and diving teams break eight pool records. The natatorium was built as an addition to the Memorial Field House.

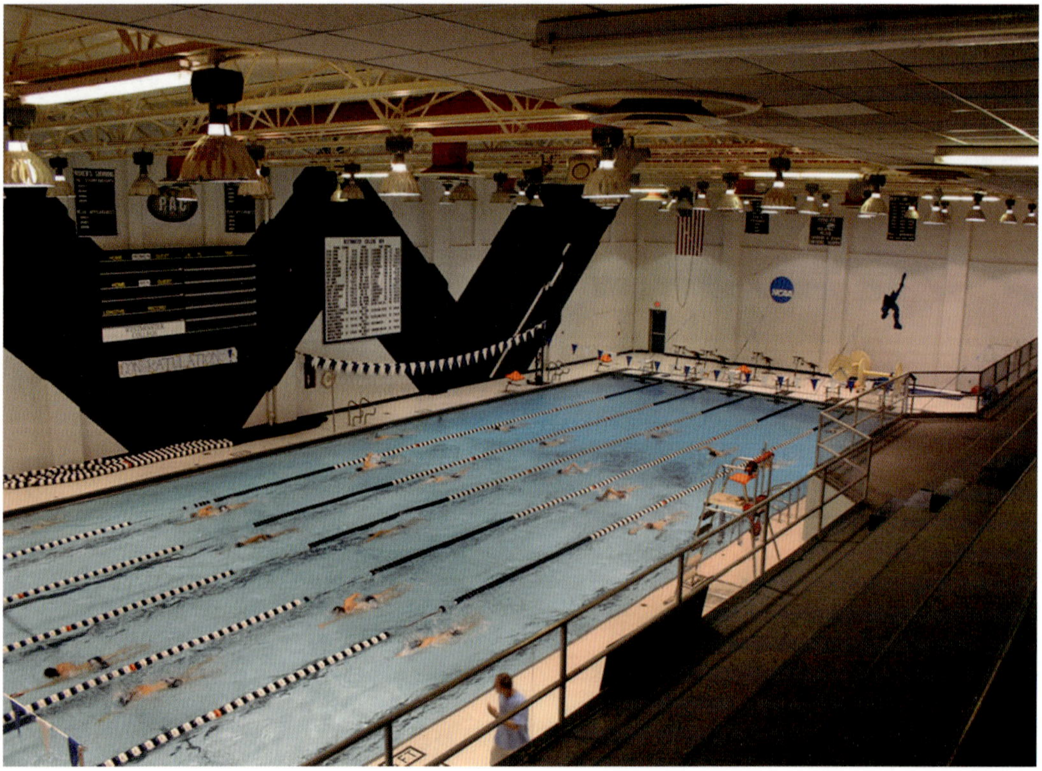

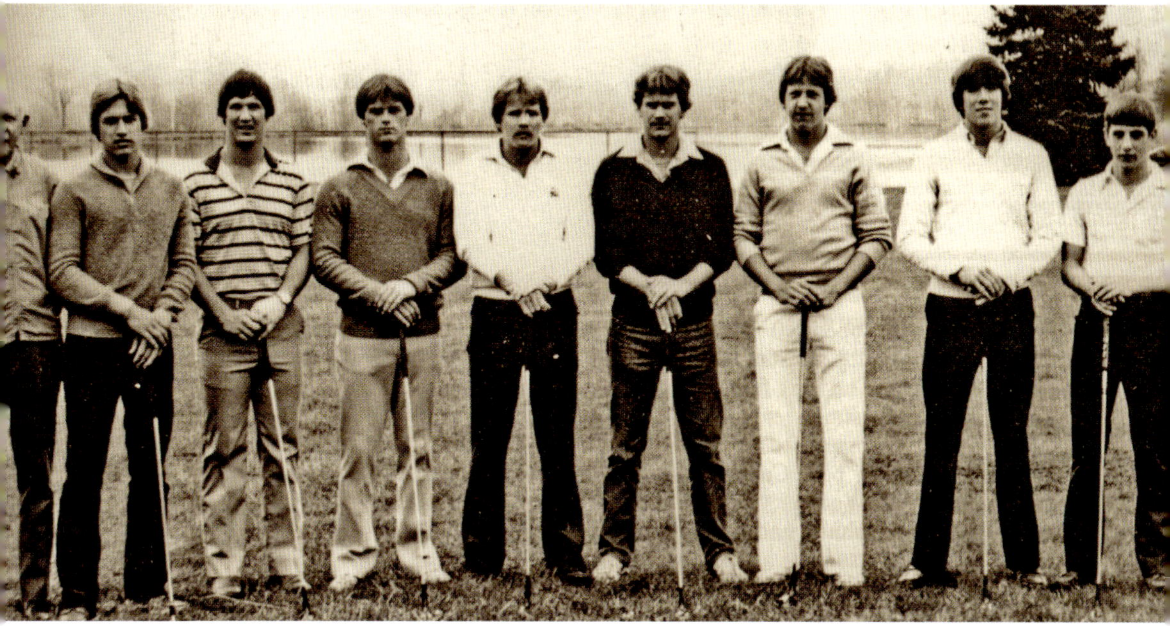

MEN'S GOLF: The 1981 team, above, and the 2011 team, below, share many things in common, such as a fondness for the links and a pride in being Titans. Westminster men's golf records show an amazingly small number of coaches from 1969 through 2013 – only four – in this order: Harold Burry, Buzz Ridl, Joe Fusco and Gene Nicholson. The 2005 team placed 18th at the NCAA Division III Championships.

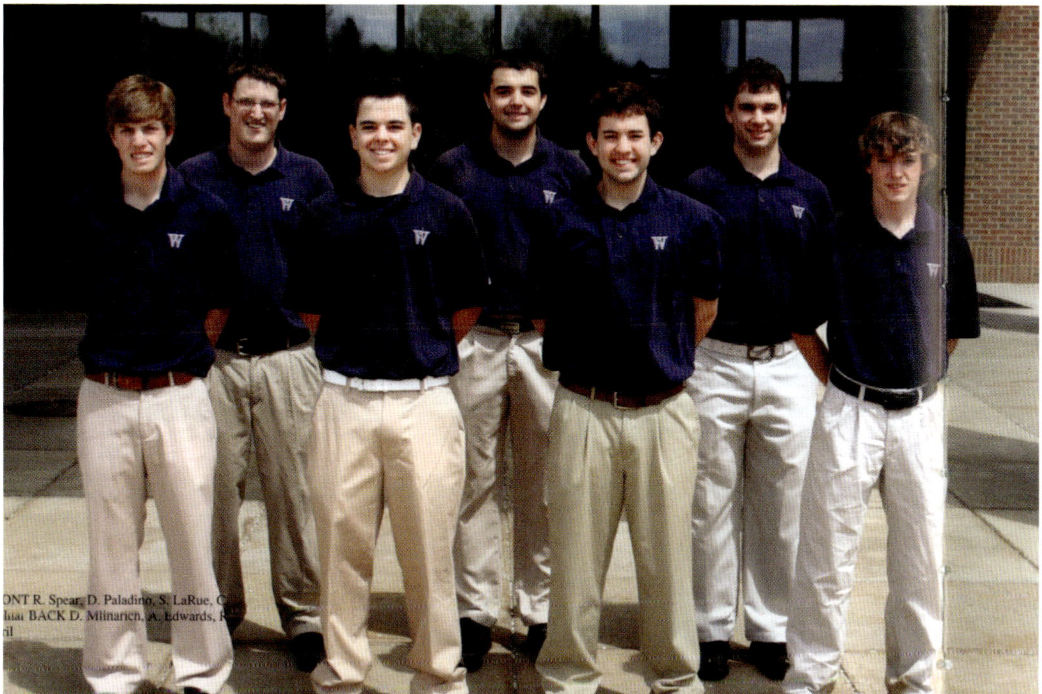

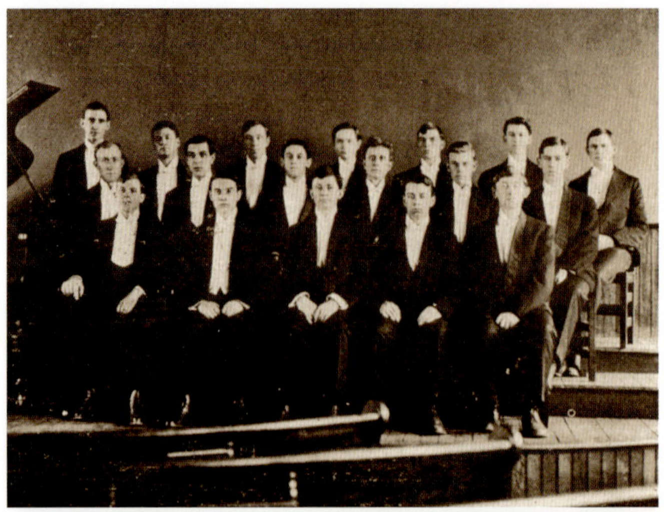

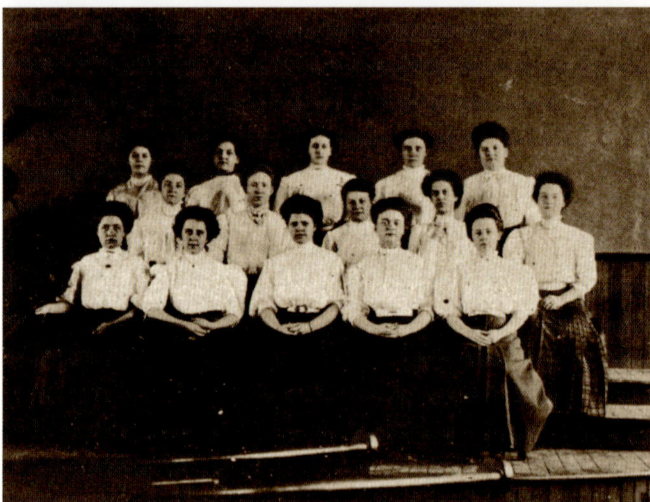

CHOIR: Above is the 1909 choir group. Below is the 2010 choir. In the 2010s, Westminster College's Chamber Singers and Concert Choir have tours that take them to churches in Maryland, Virginia and Washington, DC. The tour, in 2014, included performances at the National Presbyterian Church and the National Cathedral. Their music includes a variety of classical, traditional and contemporary works. Reverend James Mohr, Westminster chaplain, travels with the group and offers an introduction at each concert.

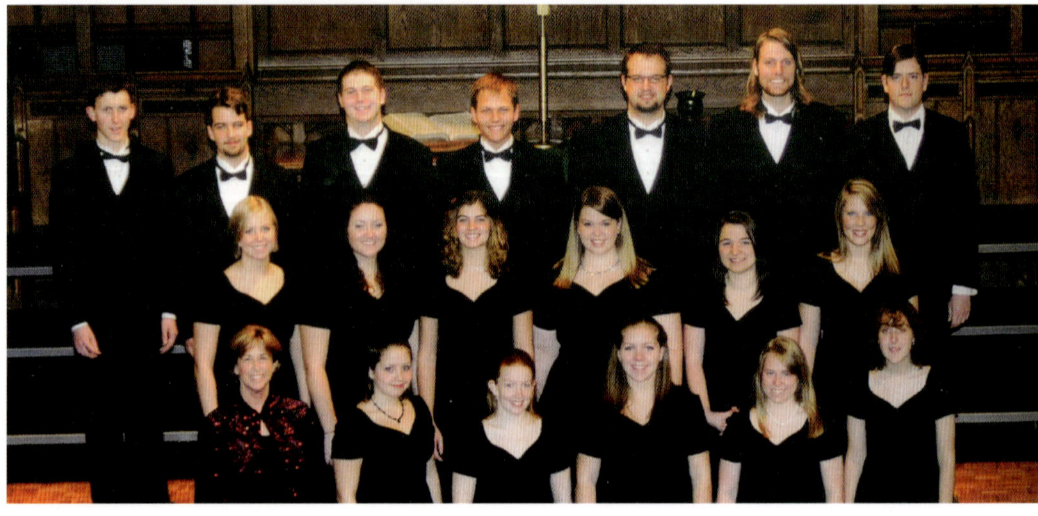

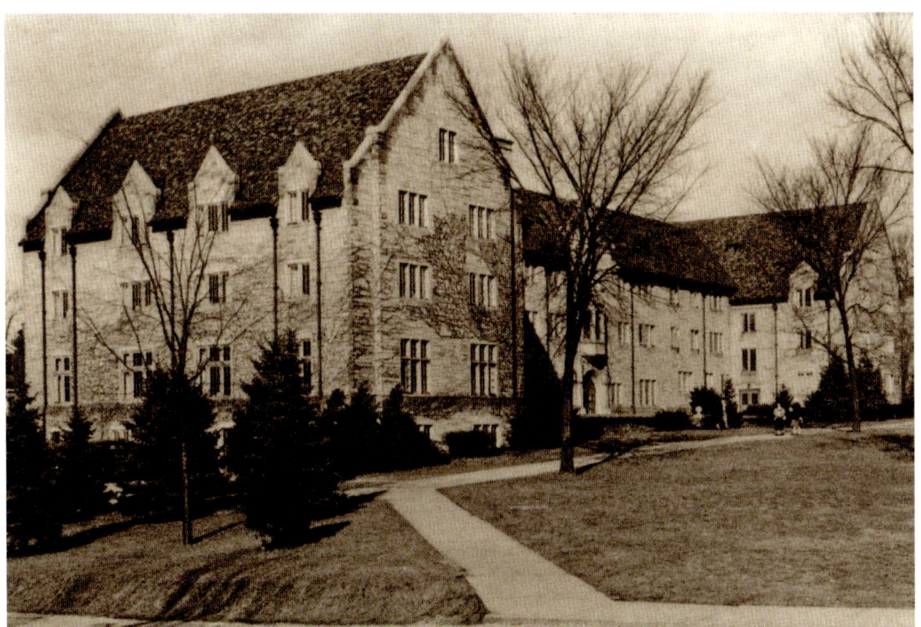

FERGUSON HALL: The students call it "Ferg" in the 2010s. This women's dormitory was completed early in 1941 at a cost of approximately $350,000. It was named Ferguson Hall in honor of Dr. Robert Ferguson, Westminster's fourth president. Like the other buildings facing the quadrangle in the center of campus, it is constructed of native sandstone in collegiate Gothic architecture. The dorm is directly across the quadrangle from Browne Hall. In the early twenty-first century, it is sometimes called the "sorority dorm" as it houses sorority women. The photo above is how the dorm looked in the late 1940s. The photo below shows how this dorm looks in 2014.

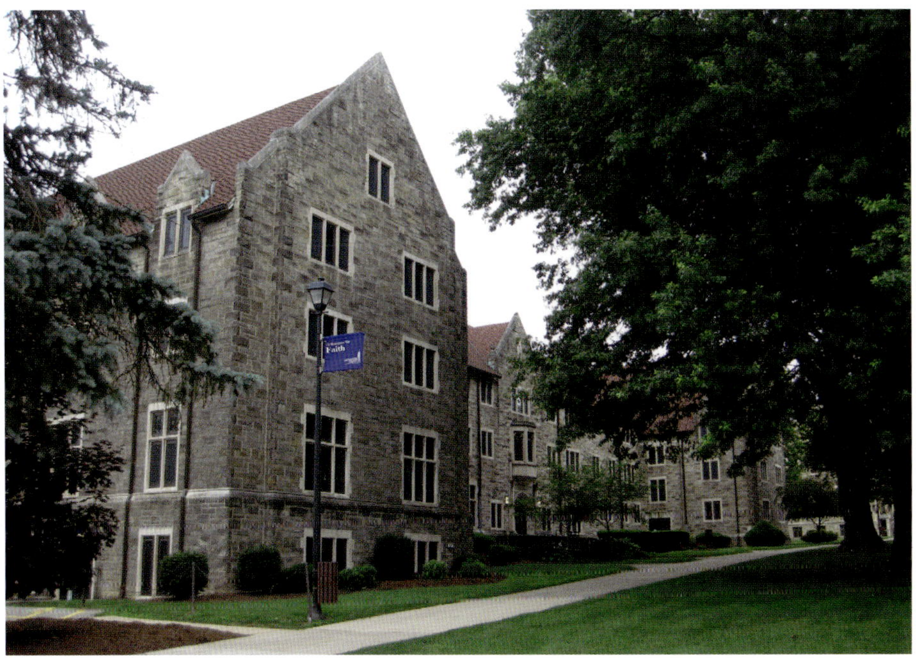

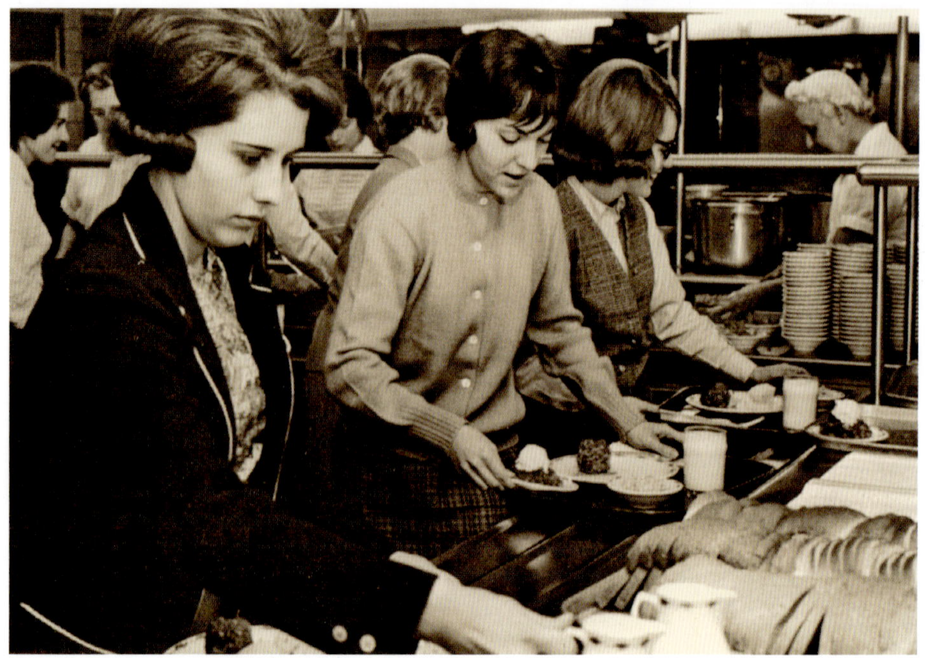

CAMPUS DINING HALL: The hall is located below Galbreath Hall. Shown above, students are going through the "cafeteria line," as it was called in 1960. In 2014, there is a new approach to food services, as shown below. Students in the modern era have the option for "all you can eat" and a new buffet style. The photo below shows this new dining hall in summer 2014 shortly after summer break started.

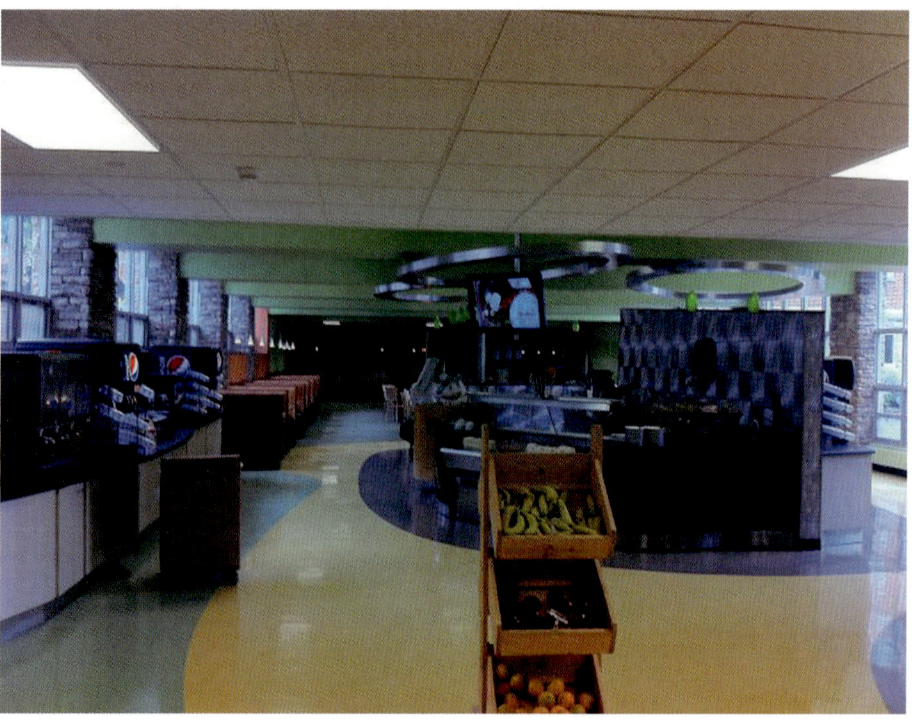

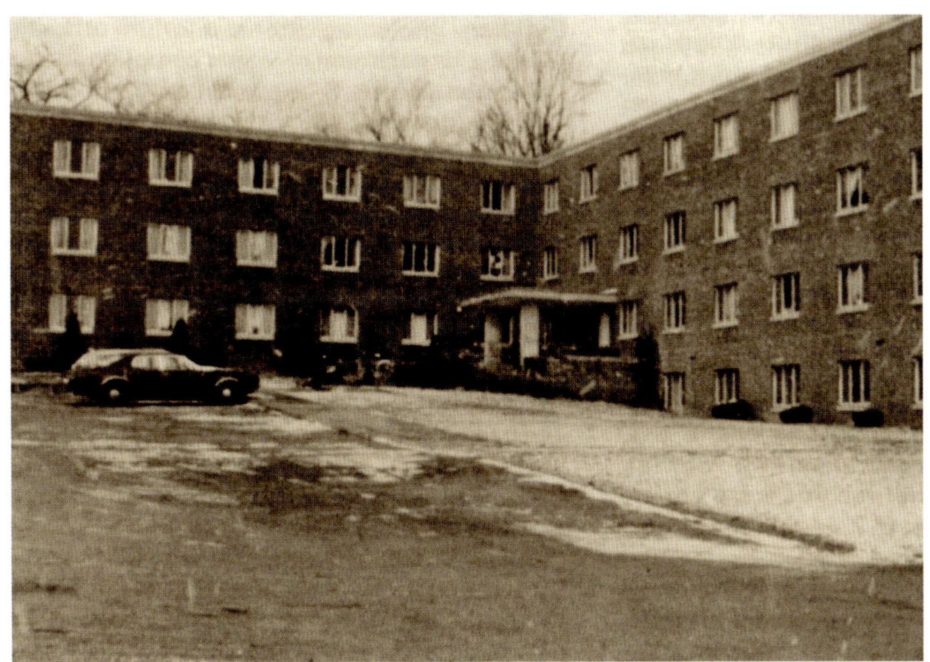

SHAW HALL: Opened in early 1960 as a women's dormitory and named after Walter Shaw, a generous benefactor of the college. The college's infirmary was incorporated in one wing of the ground floor back then, and was named for Mr. Shaw's late wife. The dorm is predominately for first-year women. Each of the three floors contains single and double bedrooms. In 2014, the college's Health Center is located on the ground floor. The residence life staff at Shaw focuses on assisting first-year residents in their transition to college life. The photo above shows Shaw Hall in the 1960s. The photo below shows Shaw Hall as it looks in 2014.

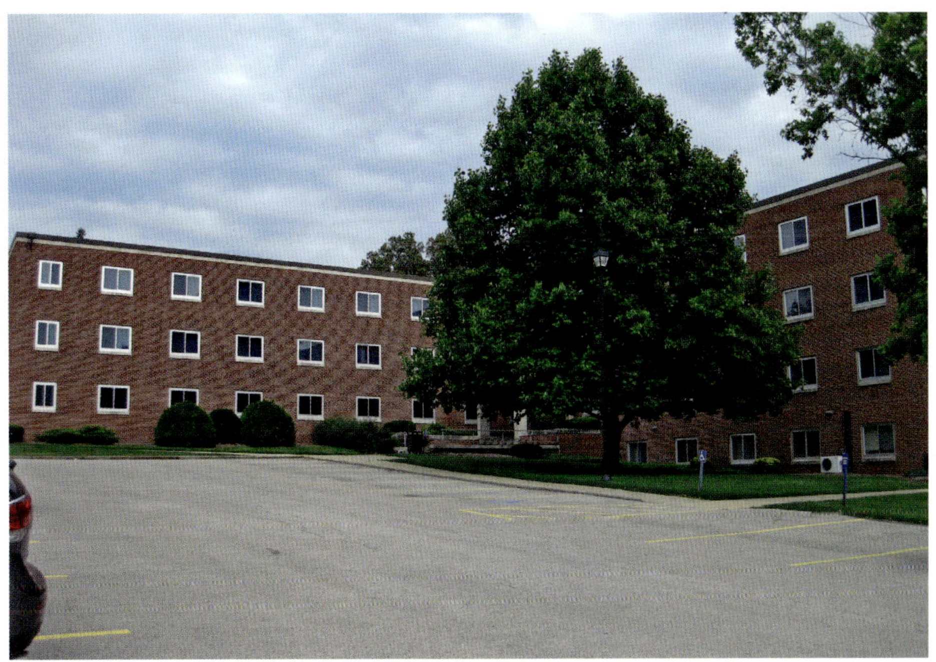

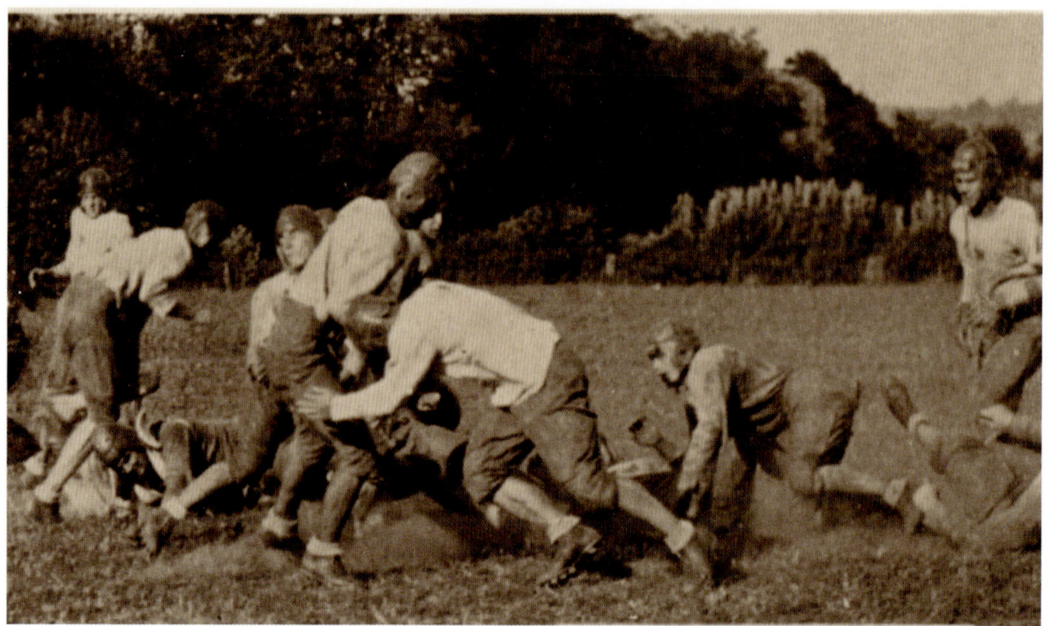

Football Scrimmage: The top photo is a football scrimmage in 1930 on the Westminster campus practice field. Note the leather helmets, lack of padding, and the type of athletic shoes and socks worn. The photo below is a 2012 football scrimmage with Thomas Moore College. Look at the changes in helmets, jerseys, shoes, socks, padding, and that gloves are worn by the runner with the ball.

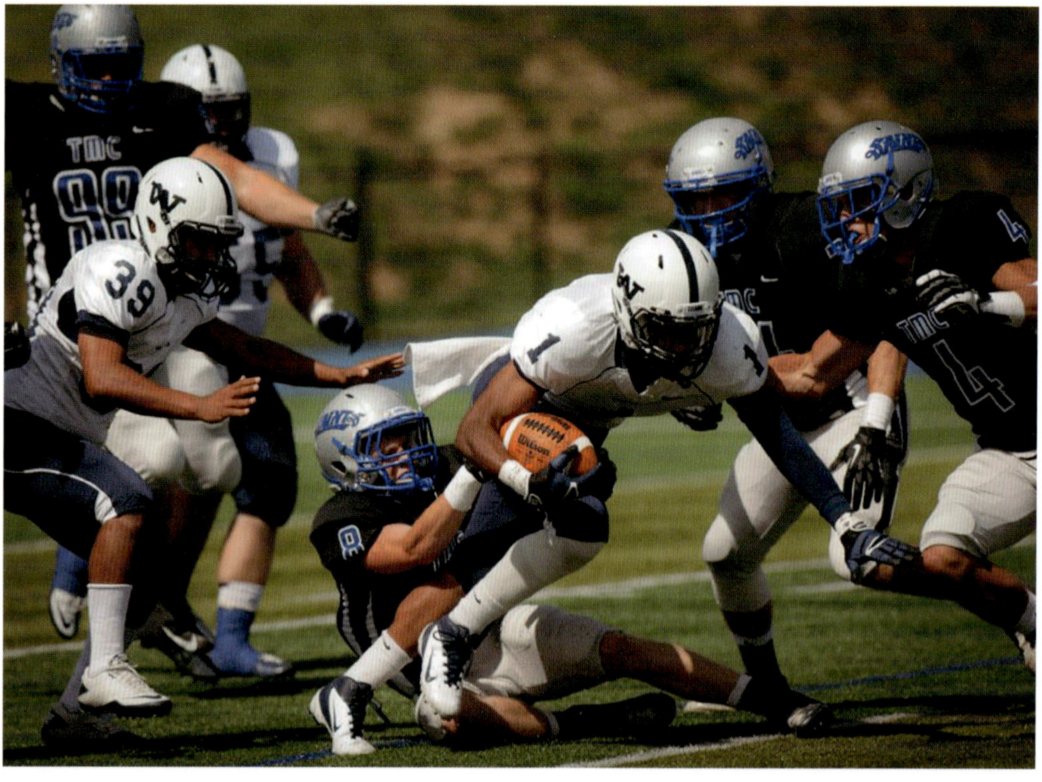

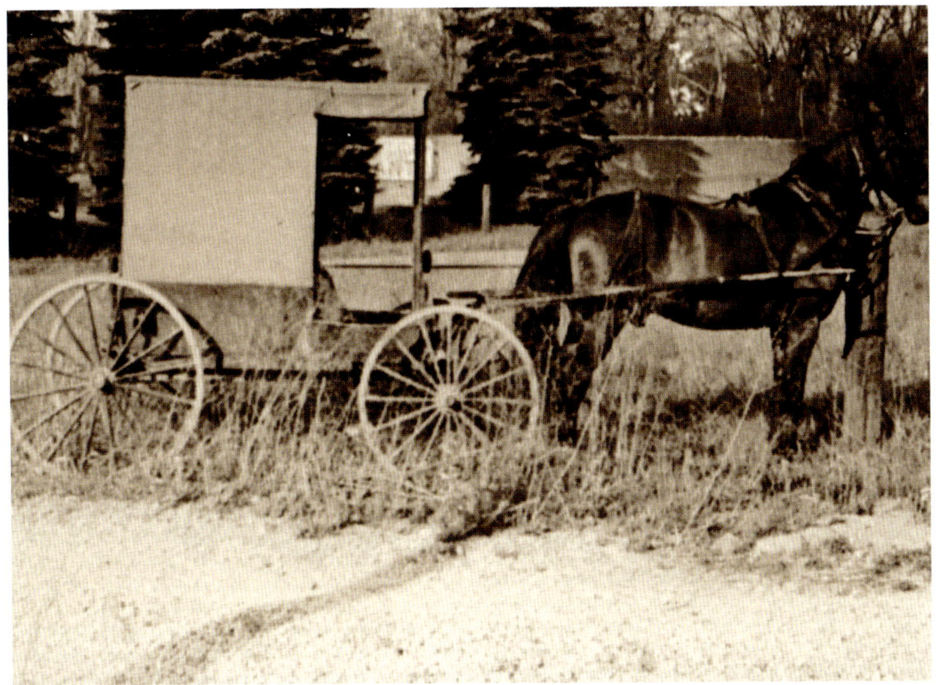

AMISH HORSES AND BUGGIES: What's the difference here? The answer is sixty-seven years. The photo above was taken in 1947 where the Amish parked their horses and buggies, in the lot behind the stores on South Market Street. The bottom photo is this same site in 2014. Amish horses and buggies in town are a familiar site to Westminster students. What college students see horses and buggies near their college campus in the twenty-first century? Westminster students do.

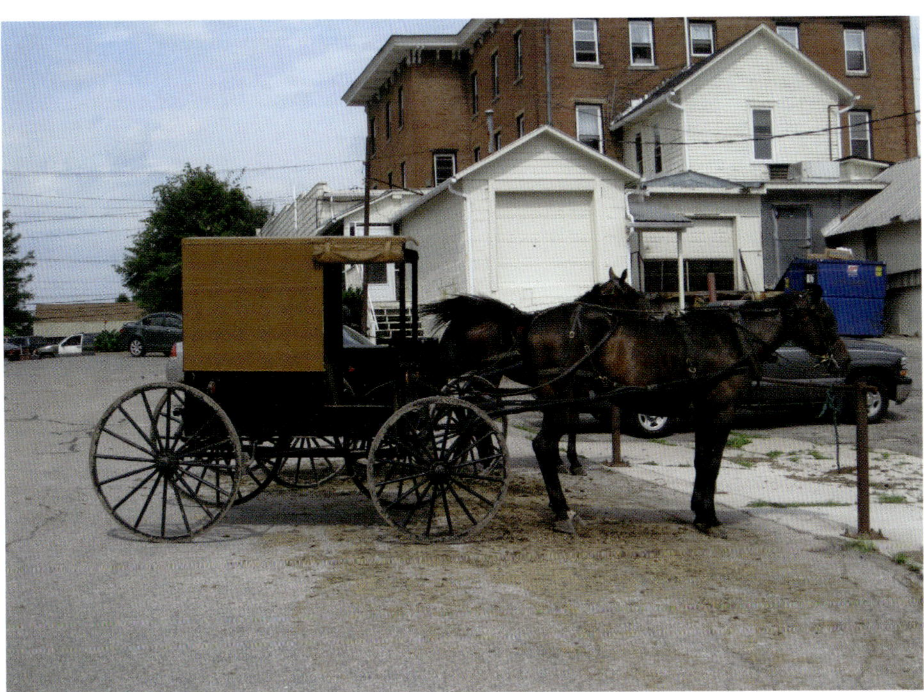

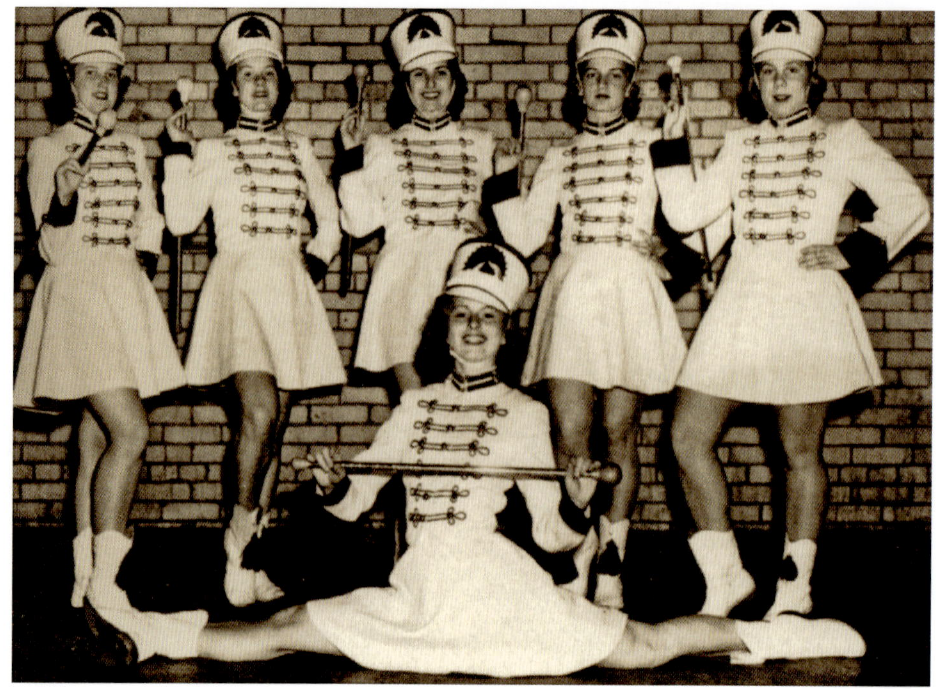

MAJORETTES TO COLOR GUARD: The majorettes, shown above, are from the 1954 majorette line of the Westminster Marching Band. In the 2011 photo, below, is the Titan Marching Band color guard and dance line. The marching band performs both corps and traditional style shows at all home games and some away games in the 2010s. The Titan Marching Band provides pep and music for spectators in the stands. The color guard and dance line members are selected each year by on-campus tryouts. Pregame and half-time entertainment are still part of Titan football games.

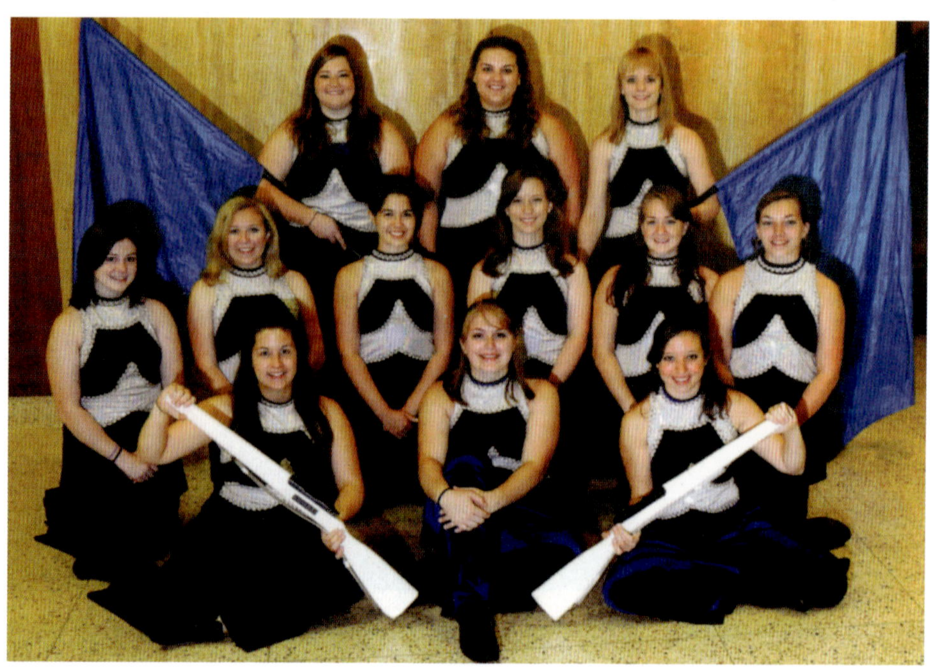

BEEGHLY THEATRE: Built in 1965-66 and opened in 1966. This state-of-the-art theatre was made possible by Leon Beeghly, a Youngstown industrialist and generous benefactor to the college. Most of Westminster's theatre classes are taught right in the theatre complex itself. The stage is equipped with traps and a counterweight fly system. There is an adjoining scene shop that provides space for the construction of scenic units and easy access to the stage. The theatre is equipped with a lighting console, sound mixer, mini-disc desks and a multi-path amplification system. The photo below shows Beeghly Theatre in 2014.

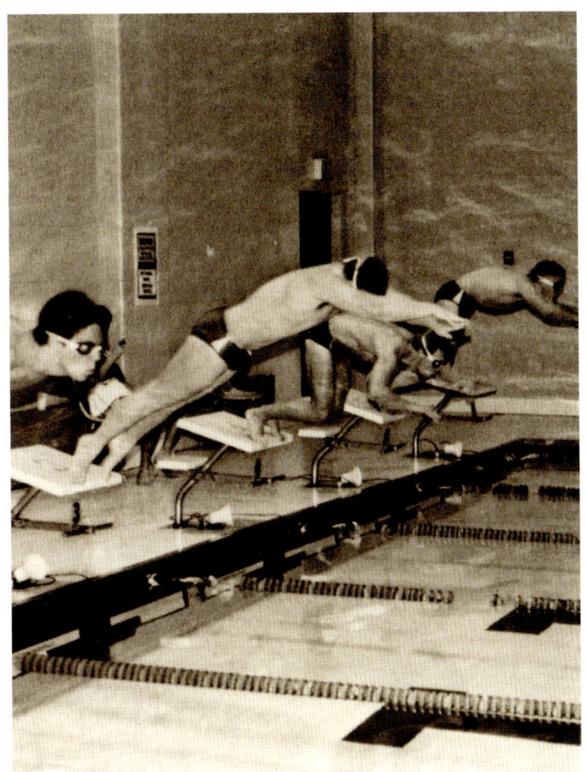

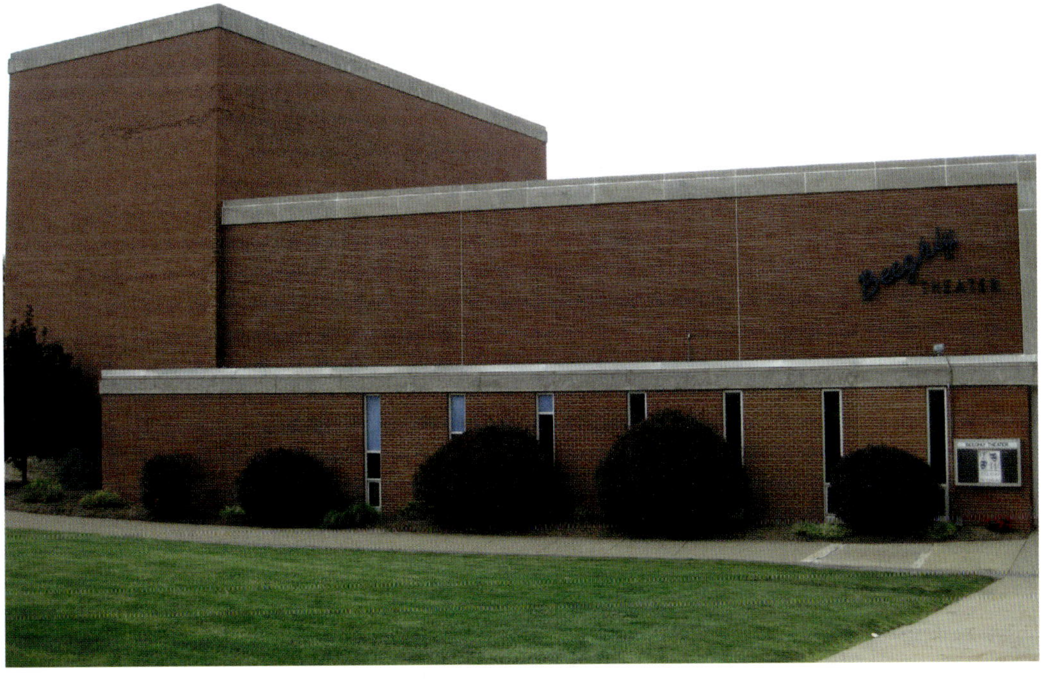

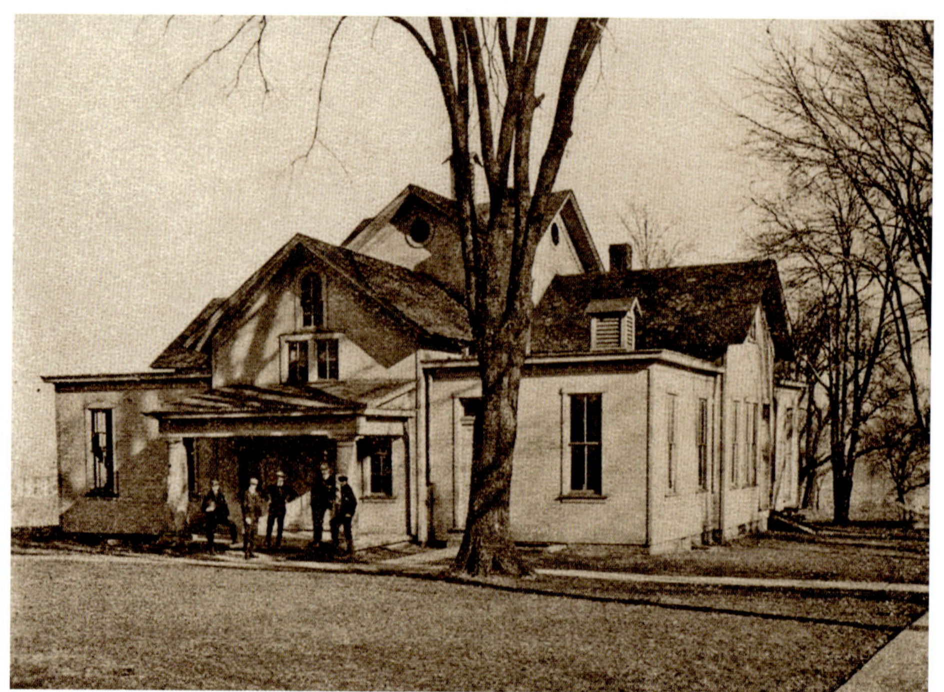

GYMS: The top photo shows Westminster's first gym. It was a wooden frame building built in 1878 with funds largely raised by students. It was used for more than forty years until the "Old 77" gym was built in 1920 as the college's second gym. It was used from 1921-1951 when the Memorial Field House was opened as the college's third and present gym. This Field House, since then, has been remodeled and expanded with additions in 1975, 1994, 1999, and 2001. The new entrance to the Field House, shown below, is part of renovations and expansions made in 2001.

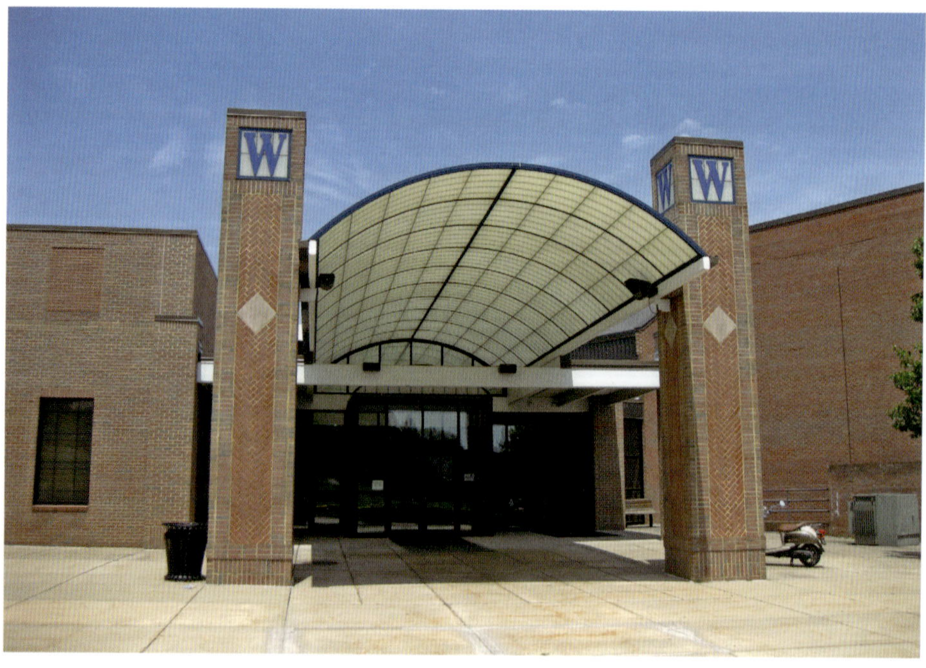

STUDENT MEDIA: The earliest edition of the college's newsletter, *The Holcad*, on file is dated September 26, 1941 and is shown here. The latest edition at the time of publication of this book is May 2, 2014. All Holcad editions, going all the way back to 2004, are available online at holcad.com. Other student media at Westminster in the 2010s include: the yearbook, *The Argo*, the SCRAWL, a literary journal published bi-annually, the Titan Radio station at digital 88.9 FM, and the Westminster Cable Network.

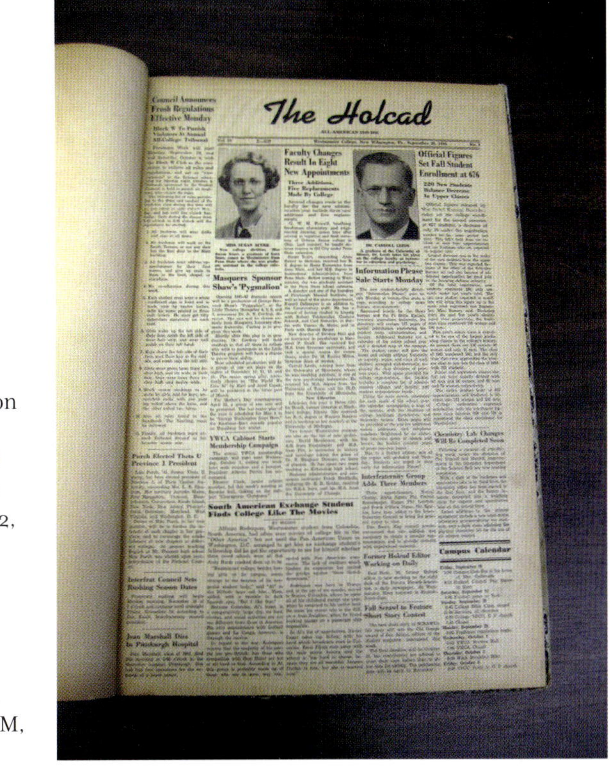
The Holcad

Council Announces Frosh Regulations Effective Monday

Faculty Changes Result In Eight New Appointments

Official Figures Set Fall Student Enrollment at 676

Masquers Sponsor Shaw's 'Pygmalion'

Information Please Sale Starts Monday

YWCA Cabinet Starts Membership Campaign

South American Exchange Student Finds College Like The Movies

Campus Calendar

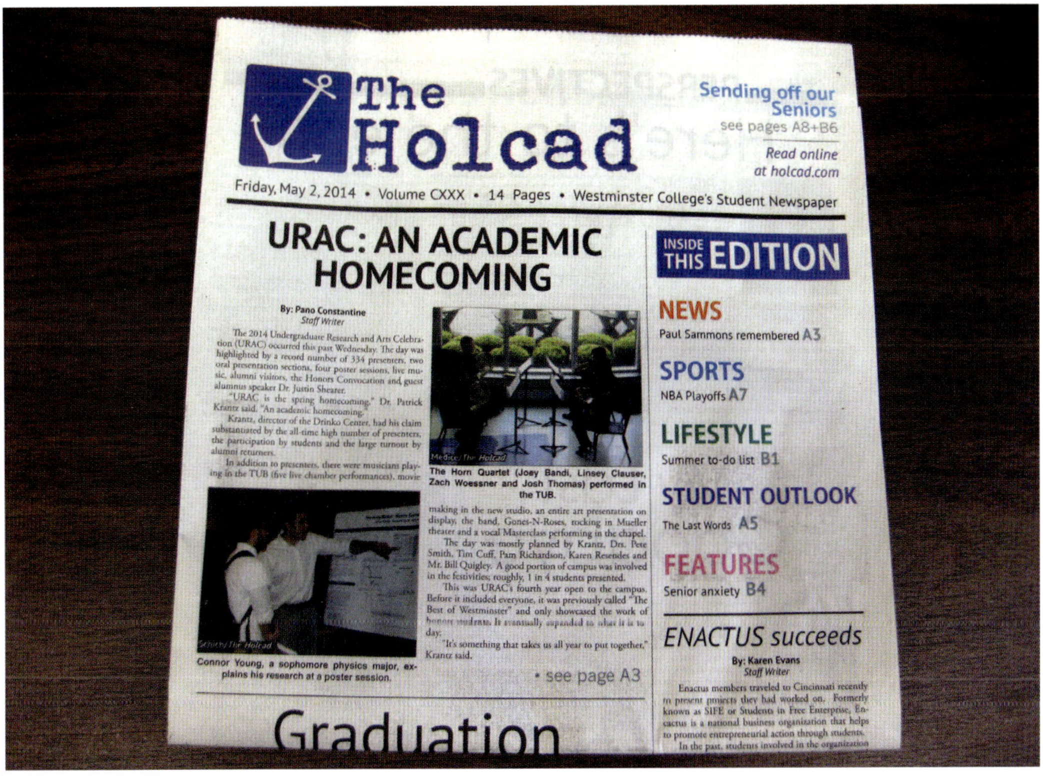

The Holcad

Sending off our Seniors
see pages A8+B6

Read online at holcad.com

Friday, May 2, 2014 • Volume CXXX • 14 Pages • Westminster College's Student Newspaper

URAC: AN ACADEMIC HOMECOMING

By: Pano Constantine
Staff Writer

The 2014 Undergraduate Research and Arts Celebration (URAC) occurred this past Wednesday. The day was highlighted by a record number of 334 presenters, two oral presentation sections, four poster sessions, live music, alumni visitors, the Honors Convocation and guest alumnus speaker Dr. Justin Shearer.

"URAC is the spring homecoming," Dr. Patrick Krantz said. "An academic homecoming."

Krantz, director of the Drinko Center, had his claim substantiated by the all-time high number of presenters, the participation by students and the large turnout by alumni returners.

In addition to presenters, there were musicians playing in the TUB (five live chamber performances), movie making in the new studio, an entire art presentation on display, the band, Gones-N-Roses, rocking in Mueller theater and a vocal Masterclass performing in the chapel.

The day was mostly planned by Krantz, Drs. Pete Smith, Tim Cuff, Pam Richardson, Karen Resendes and Mr. Bill Quigley. A good portion of campus was involved in the festivities; roughly, 1 in 4 students presented.

This was URAC's fourth year open to the campus. Before it included everyone, it was previously called "The Best of Westminster" and only showcased the work of honors students. It eventually expanded to what it is today.

"It's something that takes us all year to put together," Krantz said.

Medice/The Holcad

The Horn Quartet (Joey Bandi, Linsey Clauser, Zach Woessner and Josh Thomas) performed in the TUB.

Connor Young, a sophomore physics major, explains his research at a poster session.

• see page A3

INSIDE THIS EDITION

NEWS
Paul Sammons remembered A3

SPORTS
NBA Playoffs A7

LIFESTYLE
Summer to-do list B1

STUDENT OUTLOOK
The Last Words A5

FEATURES
Senior anxiety B4

ENACTUS succeeds

By: Karen Evans
Staff Writer

Enactus members traveled to Cincinnati recently to present projects they had worked on. Formerly known as SIFE or Students in Free Enterprise, Enactus is a national business organization that helps to promote entrepreneurial action through students.

In the past, students involved in the organization

Graduation

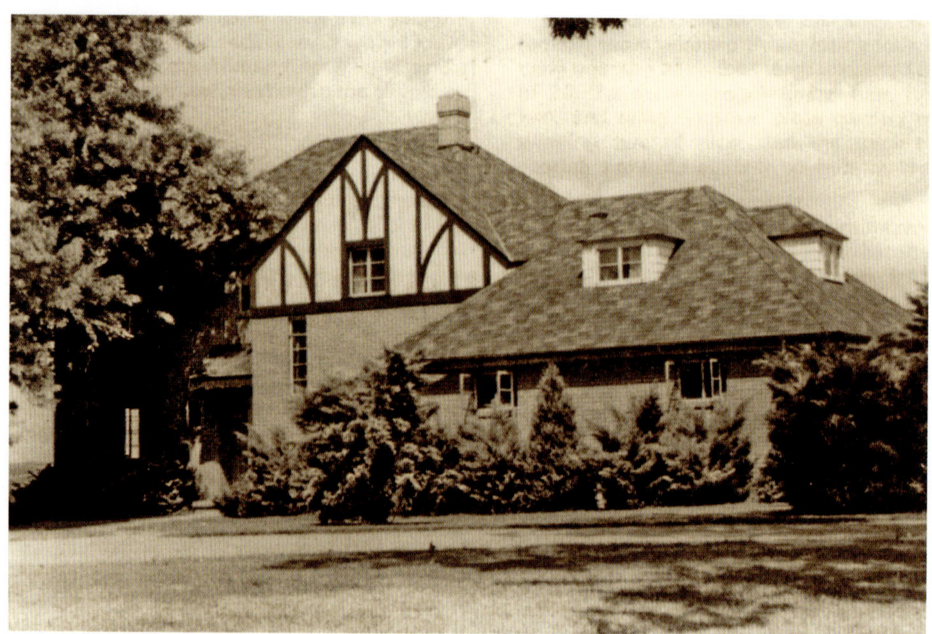

President's Manse: The residence for Westminster's presidents was completed and first occupied in January 1951. The photo above shows this home before it was remodeled and enlarged during President Remick's tenure from 1987-1997. The photo below shows the residence as it looks in 2014 and shows the additions and some of the remodeling. The residence is the personal home of the college president, as well as the site for various college-related functions hosted by the president. Some of these functions are faculty dinners, Trustees' events, the fall first-year-students picnic, and "Dinner with the Dormans" held by current President and Mrs. Dorman for students.

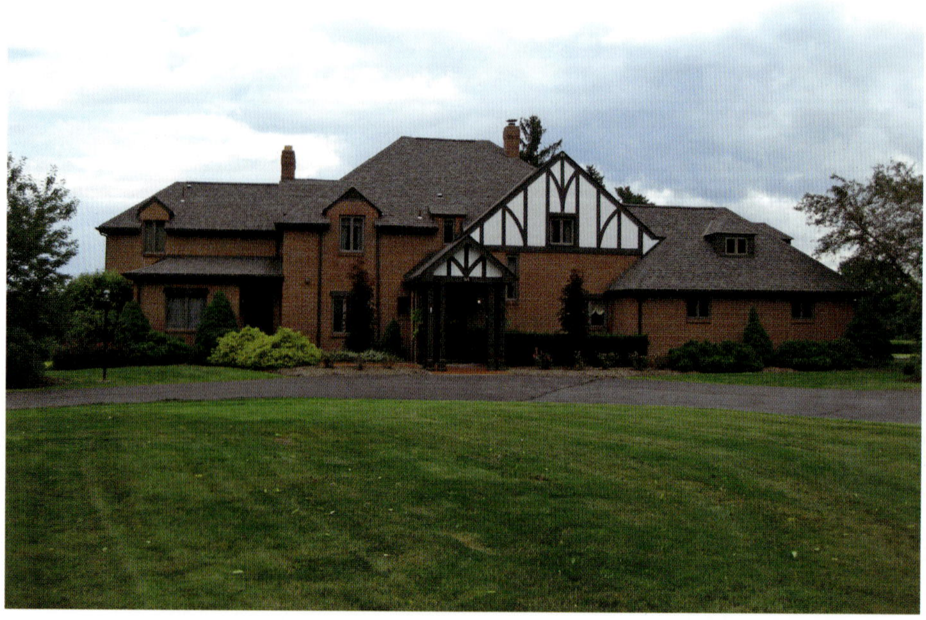

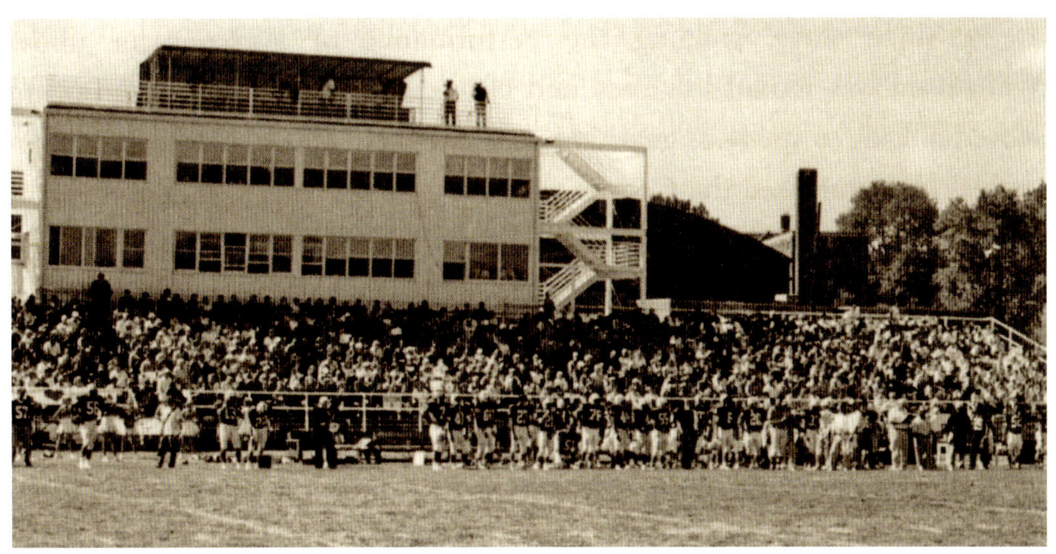

BURRY STADIUM: The home of Titan football since 1950-51. The stadium underwent renovations in 1997 and was dedicated at that time to the former Westminster football coach and athletic director Harold Burry, who had been posthumously inducted into the College Football Hall of Fame in 1996. In 2001, the stadium was again renovated with a new two-story press box, lighting, an all-weather track, refurbished bleachers, and a new artificial-turf playing surface. The photo above shows the Burry Stadium in 2001. The photo below shows the Burry Stadium in 2014.

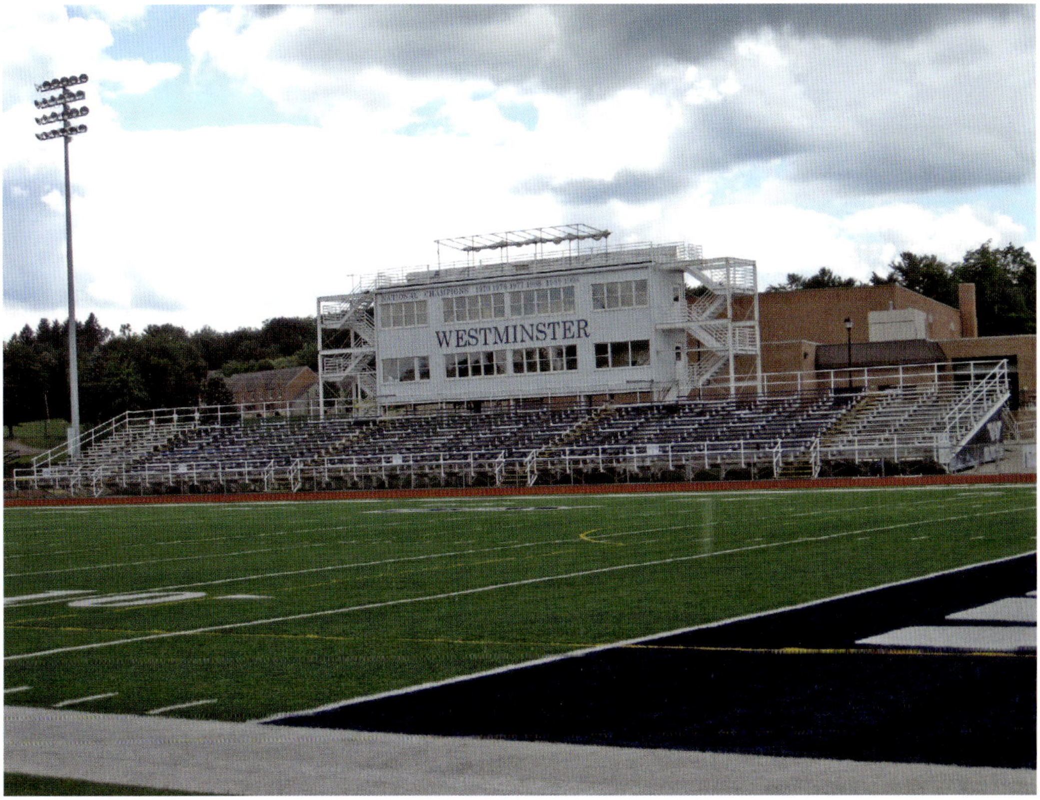

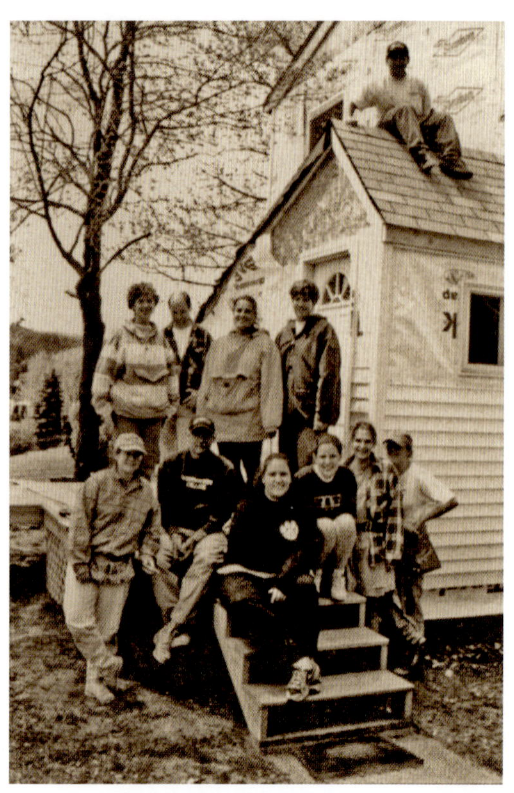

HABITAT FOR HUMANITY: A part of Westminster since 1989. The photo, left, shows some of the college's sixty-five student volunteers in Biloxi, Mississippi during spring break. Here, the students help build houses for those displaced by Hurricane Katrina. The photo below shows student volunteers in 2013. College Chaplain Reverend James Mohr is the campus advisor for the students and their Habitat projects.

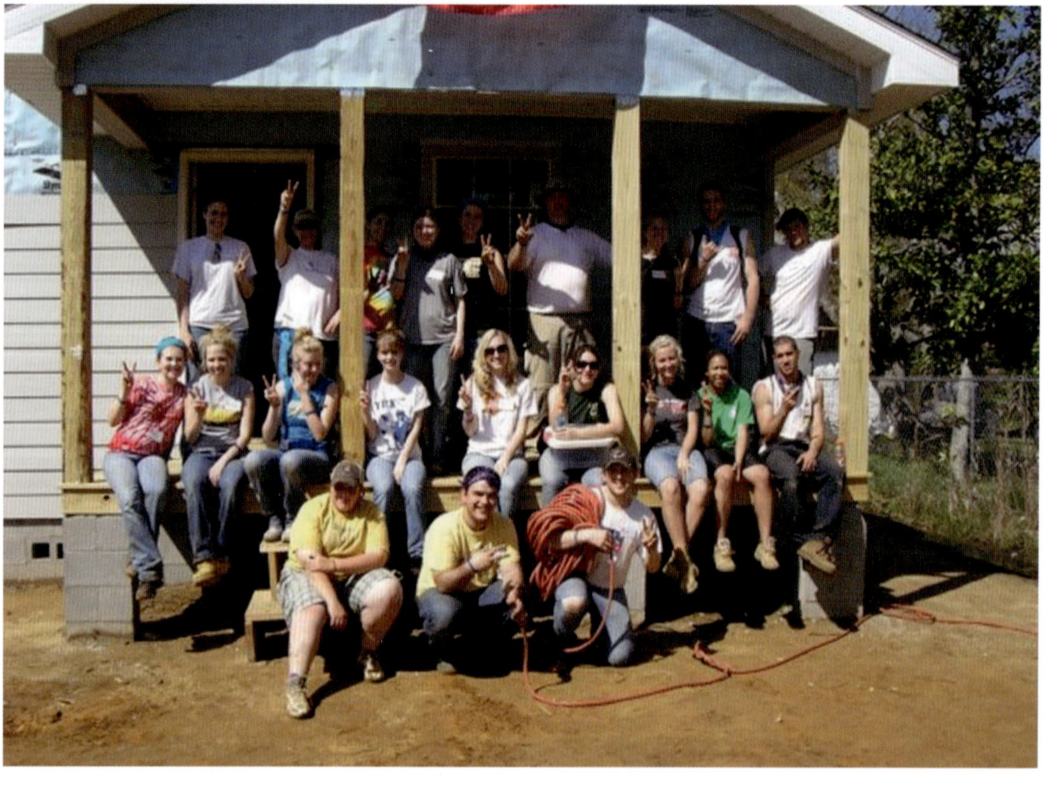

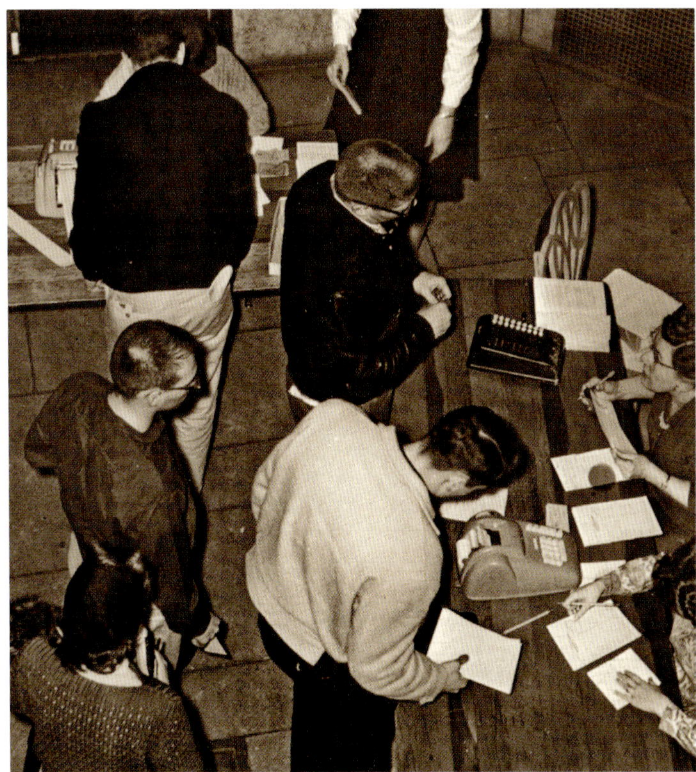

STUDENTS REGISTER FOR CLASSES: The 1964 photo, above, shows the registration lines used for so many years at Westminster when students signed up for classes. The photo below shows one of the computers in the library, which is how students register in 2014. No more waiting in registration lines. Students can use any computer to register for classes as everything has been made available online.

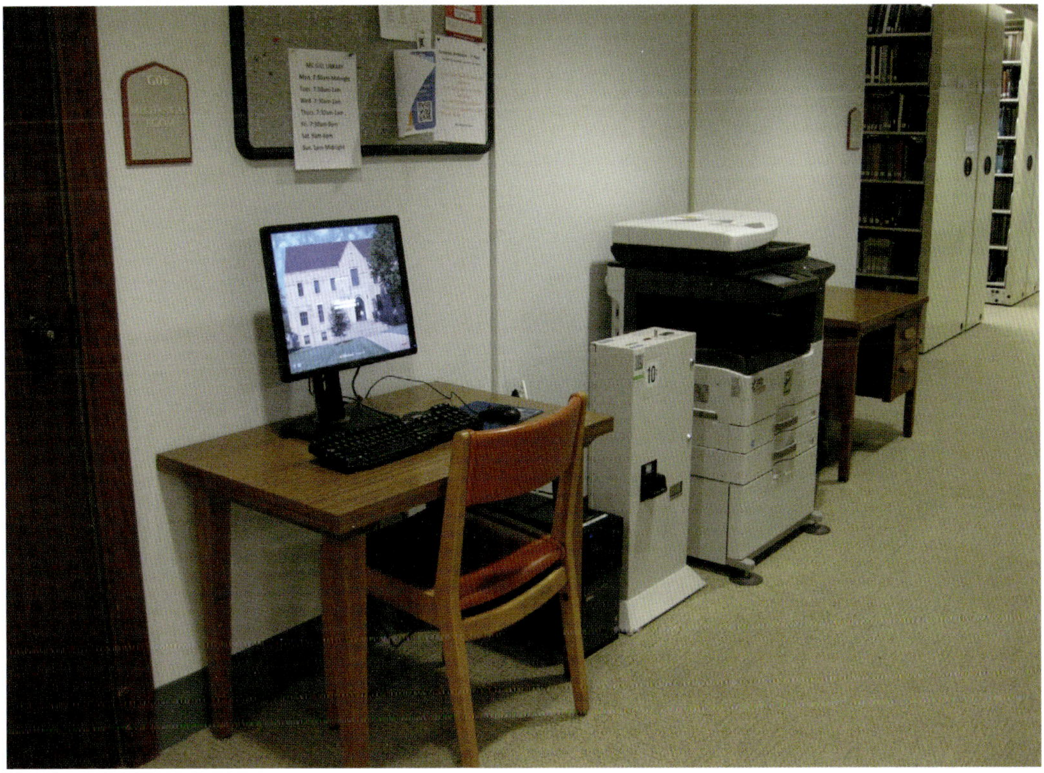

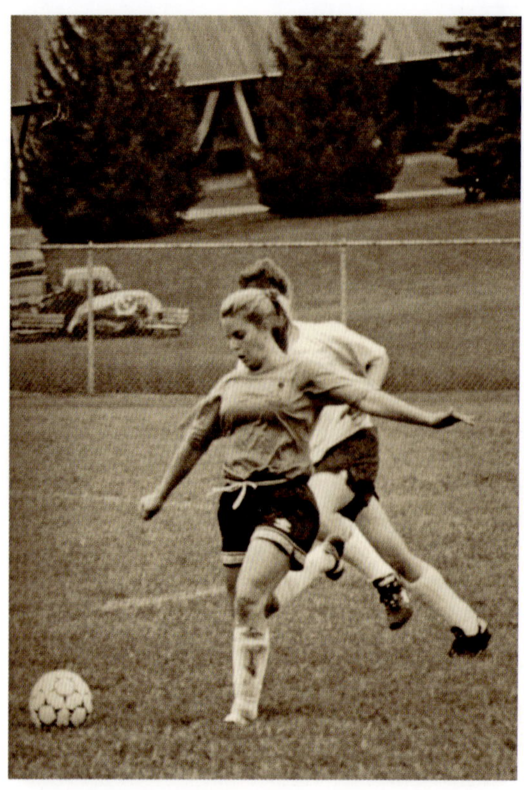

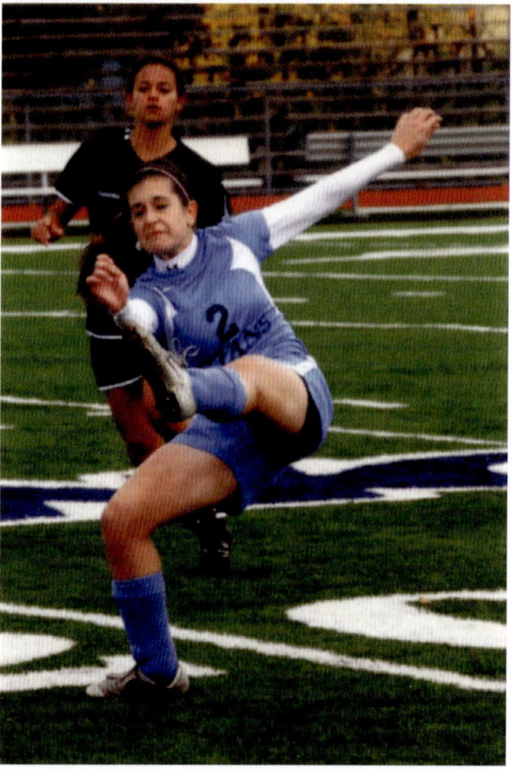

WOMEN'S SOCCER: Action shots from the 1994 team, left, and the 2011 team, below, show why the Westminster women's soccer teams have a thirteen-year winning record average of 65.9%. They have made five NCAA Division III Tournament appearances: 2002, 2003, 2004, 2005, and 2007, in addition to PAC league championships in 2002, 2003, 2004, 2006 and 2007. Go Titans!

MCGILL LIBRARY: Facing the quad in the center of campus, here's how it looked in 1939. The library was named after a Westminster graduate, Ralph McGill, who lost his life while serving as a missionary in Egypt. The size of the library was almost doubled in 1966 by a large addition onto the north end of the library. The photo below shows this addition to the right of the library entrance. The construction in the bottom photo is the replacement of the front entrance steps. The library was rededicated in 2008, following a $6.2 million renovation.

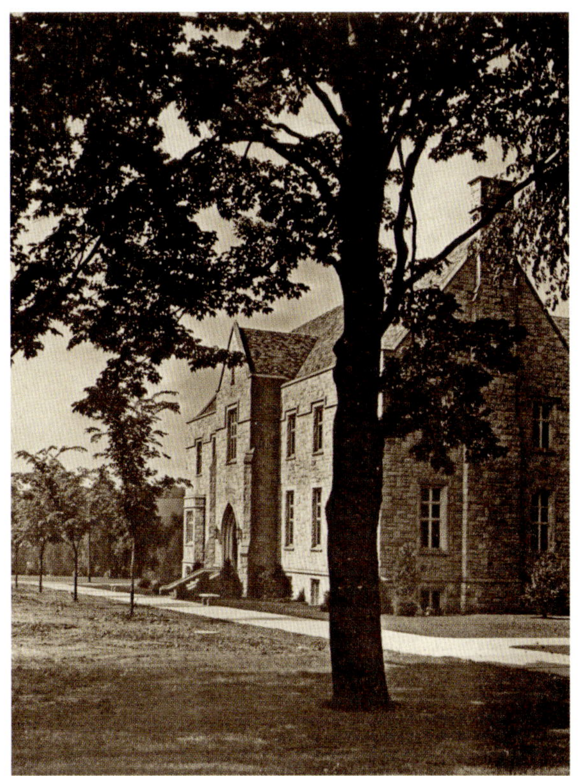

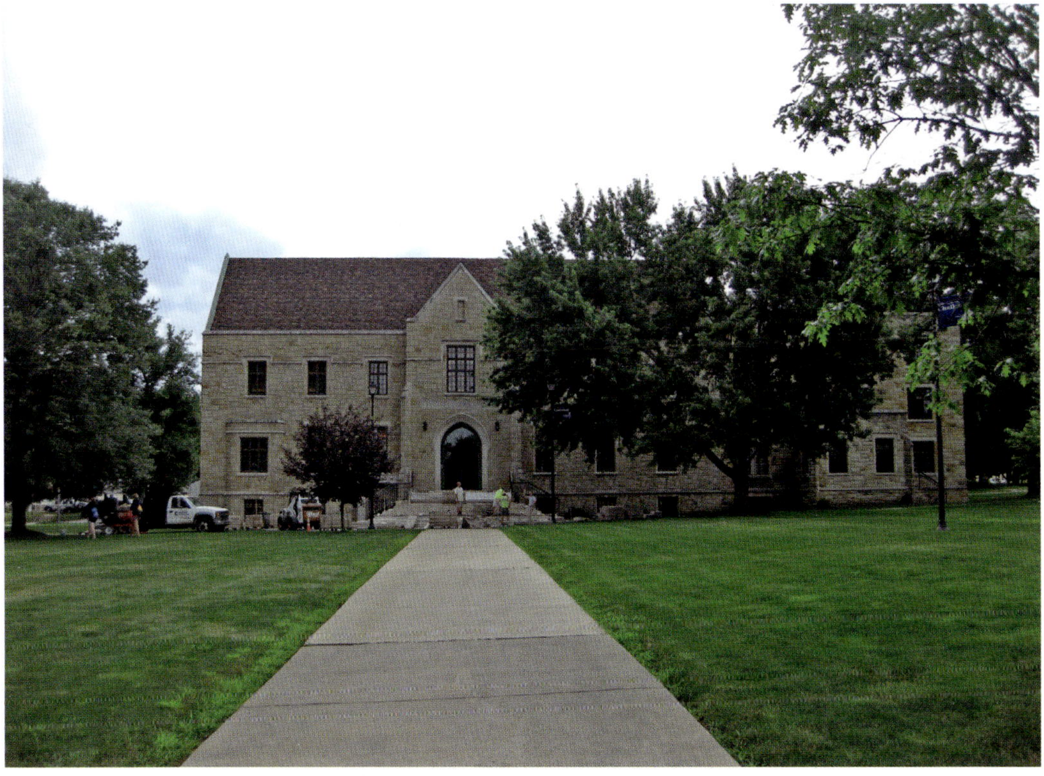

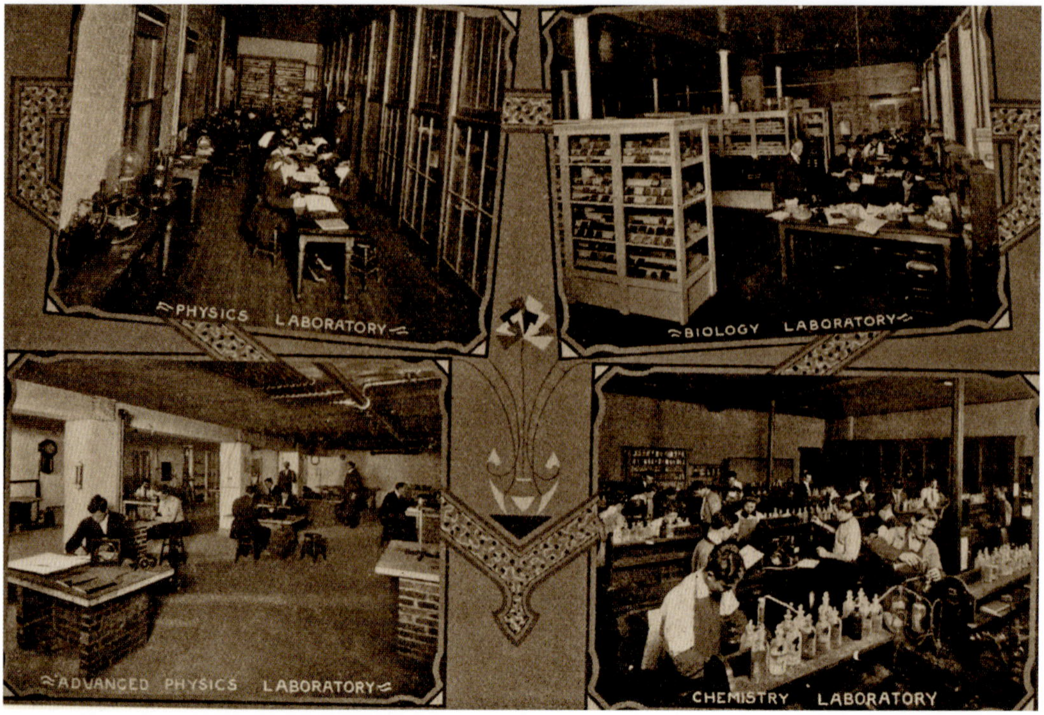

PHYSICS LABORATORY
BIOLOGY LABORATORY
ADVANCED PHYSICS LABORATORY
CHEMISTRY LABORATORY

SCIENCE LABS: The photo above shows Westminster science labs in 1913. The photo below shows a new science chemistry lab in the Hoyt Science Center in 2014. Westminster is proud of its state-of-the-art science offerings such as the acquisition in 2014 of 50 mm integrating sphere so students can perform solid-state spectroscopy.

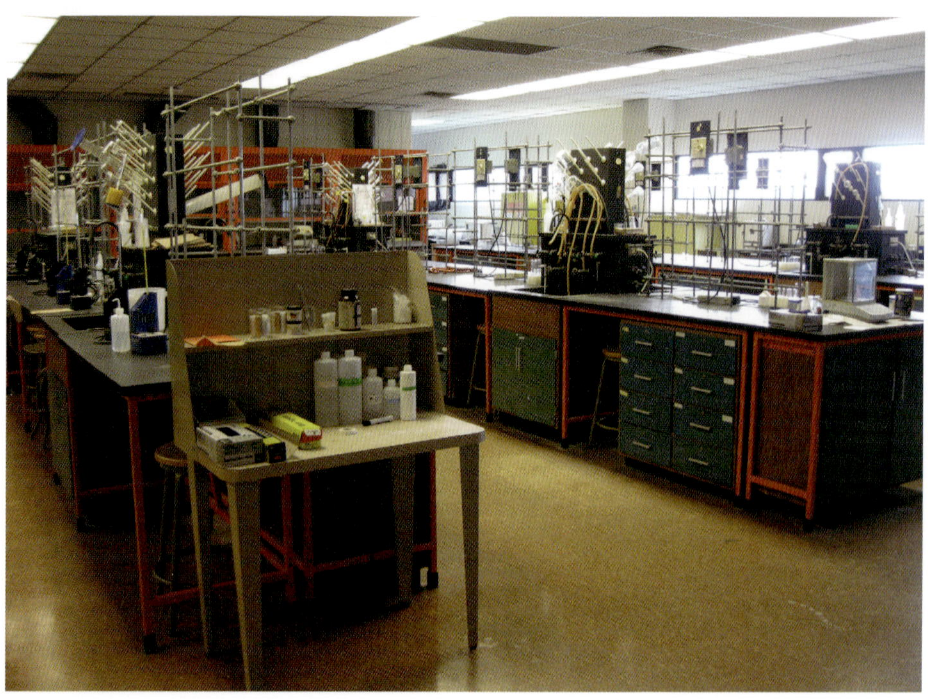

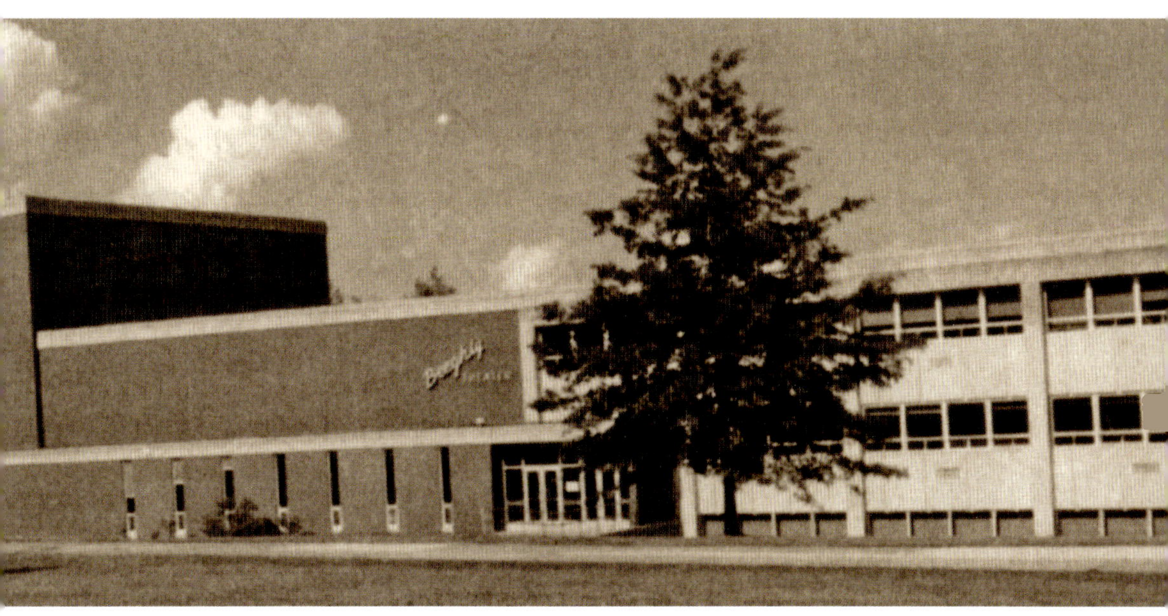

PATTERSON HALL: The hall was named after one of Westminster's presidents. It was remodeled and re-dedicated in 2012 after a $5 million update. This building was part of a series of buildings constructed at this site in the mid-1960s as the Arts and Sciences building. First, Orr Auditorium was built, then Patterson Hall was built onto the northern end of Orr, then Beeghly Theatre was built. In 2014, this complex – Orr Auditorium, Patterson Hall and Beeghly Theater – look like they were built all at one time, as one big long complex. The photo of Patterson, above, is from the late 1960s shortly after it was built. The photo of Patterson Hall, below, is from 2014.

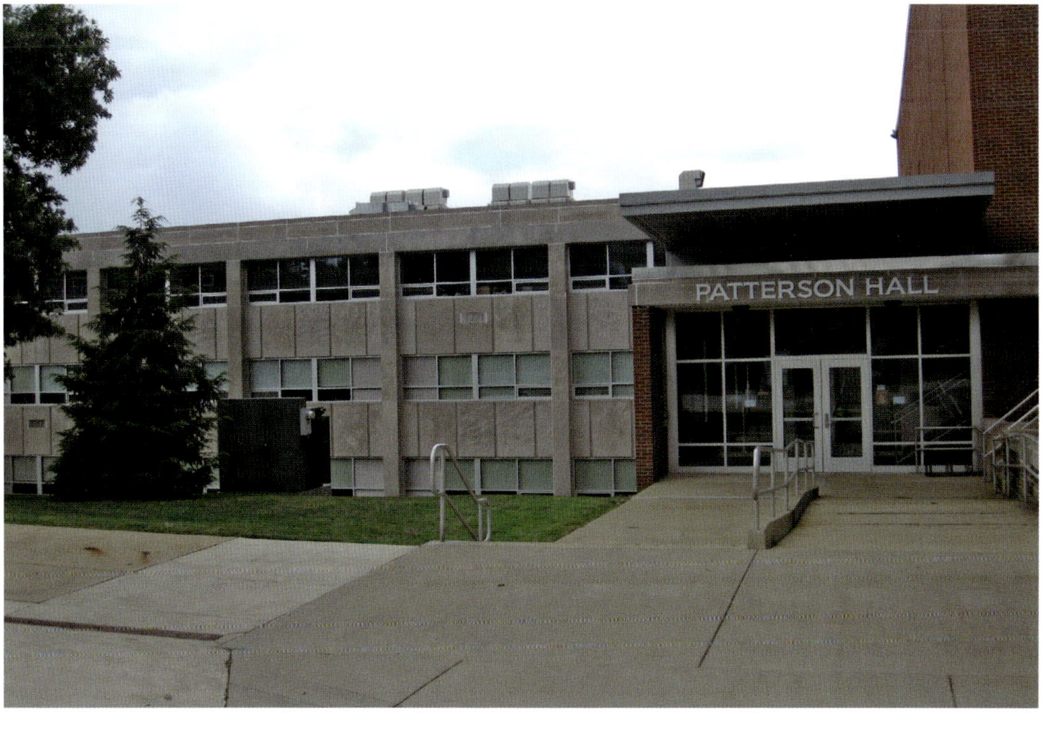

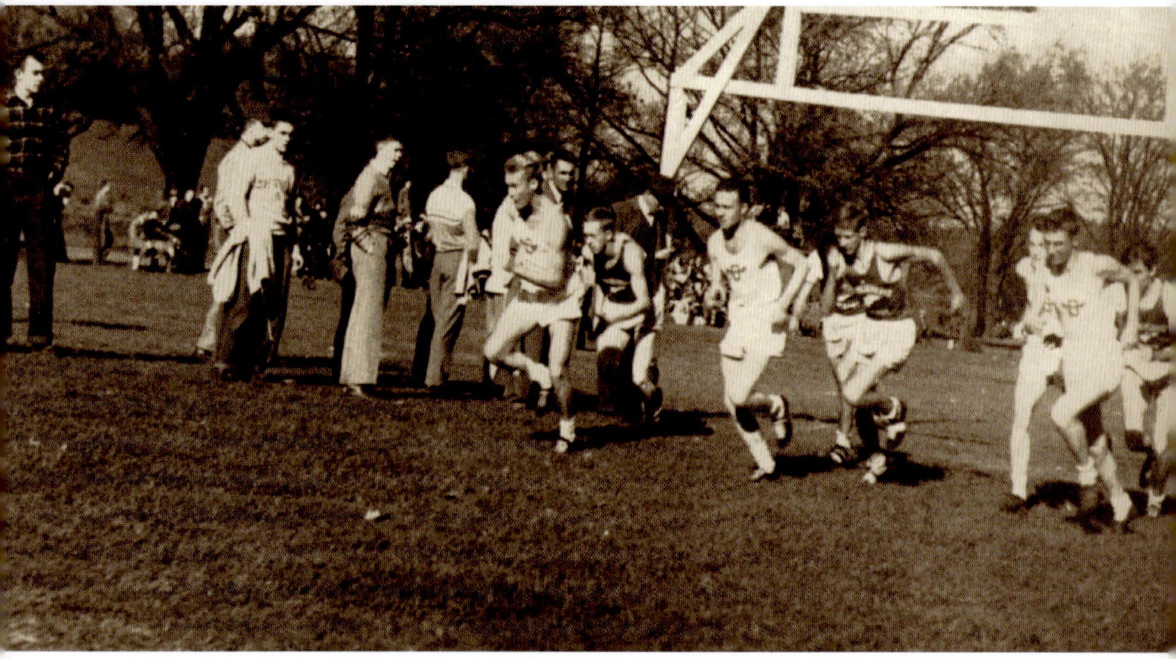

MEN'S CROSS COUNTRY: The 1951 men's team starts out at the football field on their run. The 2011 team, below, was one of 125 teams in the nation that was named a 2010 Division III All-Academic Association Team. To qualify for this honor, the team had a cumulative team grade-point average of 3.0 or better and had at least five runners finish in their respective NCAA regional championship.

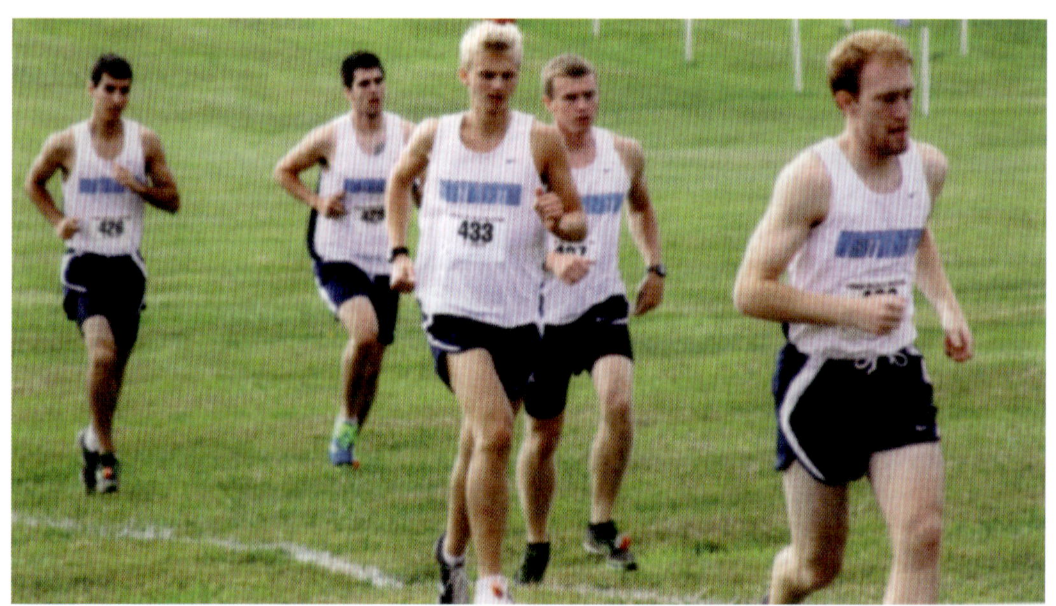

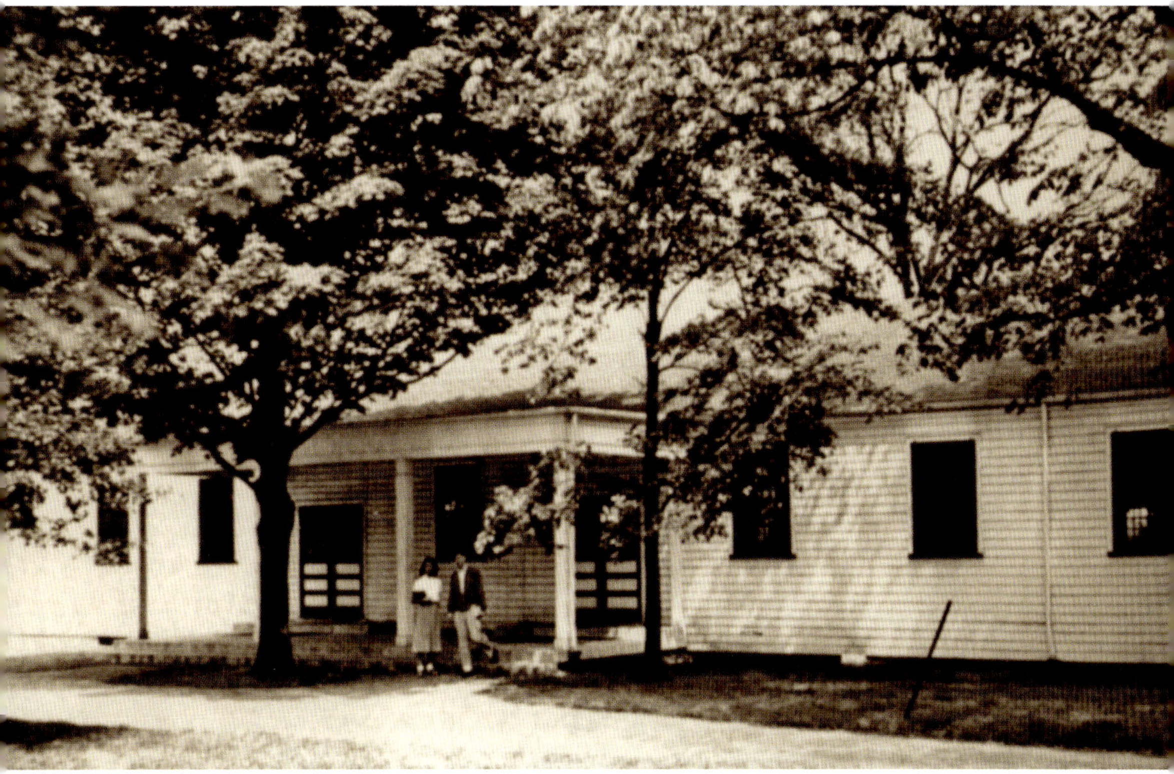

Student Union Building: The photo above is Westminster's first student union building, originally called the Titan Union Building, but affectionately dubbed by the students with the acronym the "TUB". It was actually an old army surplus building that served the college as a student center until the Walton-Mayne Student Union building opened in 1958. The students called this building the "TUB" too. The new McKelvey Campus Center was built in 2003 at a cost of $13 million. The food service area in this new building is affectionately still called the "TUB," carrying on an old Westminster tradition. The photo below shows the McKelvey Campus Center entrance in 2014.

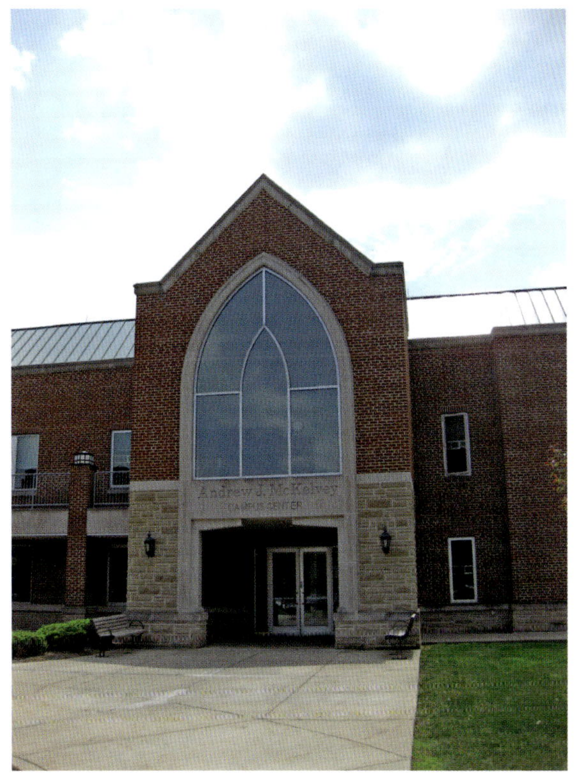

ACKNOWLEDGEMENTS

First and foremost, thanks to my wife, Joan, for her never ending encouragement from the first moment I told her about doing this book to the very day we sent it off to the publisher.

To Leigh Kelley, my granddaughter and research assistant on this project. Leigh spent many hours in the college library's archives going through old records and old photos. She also took many of the new photos and even typed captions for the photos.

President Richard Dorman for approving this endeavor, saying he thought many people associated with the college would enjoy seeing photos of the college: past and present.

Vice President Jane Wood for her support, citing such a book would bring back many fond memories for those associated with the college over the years.

Erin Smith, Associate Dean for library services and instructional technology for making accessible the college's archives of old records and old photographs.

Debbie Zorn Becherer and Pattie Zorn Kelley, my daughters, for their help in proof reading and working with photographs.

Alan Sutton of Fonthill Media for his encouragement that archival images and photographic captions would help present the distinctive story of Westminster College.

Heather Martino, also of Fonthill Media, for all her assistance and answering all my questions on so many occasions.

Last, but not least, to Gene Merdich of TPI Photography Lab for all the work and assistance with the photos, old and new.

AUTHOR

Dr. Robert Zorn is a graduate of Westminster College. He serves the college as Director of the Graduate School in 2014. Before that, he was a department coordinator in the Graduate School and was an adjunct faculty member for many years in the graduate school, while concurrently holding various administrative posts in area public schools.

Dr. Zorn's grandson, Tyler Kelley, is a 2010 graduate of Westminster. Grandson, Sam Becherer, is a 2012 graduate of Westminster. Grandson, Nathan Kelley, is the Resident Director of the Eichenhauer Dorm on campus in 2014. Granddaughter, Leigh Kelley, was his research assistant on this book. And granddaughter, Katie Becherer, is a junior at Westminster in 2014. All ties that bind people and families to Westminster College.

At the author's request, all royalties from the sale of this book go directly to the Westminster College Alumni Association.